RECOMMENDED DIAGRAMMING
STANDARDS FOR ANALYSTS
AND PROGRAMMERS

A   *James Martin*   **BOOK**

RECOMMENDED STANDARDS AND

A Basis

DIAGRAMMING FOR ANALYSTS PROGRAMMERS

for Automation

JAMES MARTIN

PRENTICE-HALL, INC. Englewood Cliffs, New Jersey 07632

Library of Congress Cataloging-in-Publication Data

MARTIN, JAMES (date)
   Recommended diagramming standards for analysts
and programmers.

   Includes bibliographies and index.
   1. System analysis.   2. Electronic digital
computers—Programming.   3. Flow charts.   I. Title.
T57.6.M3485   1987   004.2'1   85–16917
ISBN   0-13-767377-9

Editorial/production supervision: *Kathryn Gollin Marshak*
Jacket design: *Photo Plus Art*
Manufacturing buyer: *Gordon Osbourne*

Recommended Diagramming Standards for Analysts and Programmers:
A Basis for Automation
James Martin

Printed in the United States of America

10   9   8   7   6   5   4   3   2   1

ISBN 0-13-767377-9   025

PRENTICE-HALL INTERNATIONAL (UK) LIMITED, *London*
PRENTICE-HALL OF AUSTRALIA PTY. LIMITED, *Sydney*
PRENTICE-HALL CANADA INC., *Toronto*
PRENTICE-HALL HISPANOAMERICANA, S.A., *Mexico*
PRENTICE-HALL OF INDIA PRIVATE LIMITED, *New Delhi*
PRENTICE-HALL OF JAPAN, INC., *Tokyo*
PRENTICE-HALL OF SOUTHEAST ASIA PTE. LTD., *Singapore*
EDITORA PRENTICE-HALL DO BRASIL, LTDA., *Rio de Janeiro*

TO CORINTHIA

CONTENTS

4   Three Species of Decomposition   61

5   A Consistent Diagramming Notation   77

6   Action Diagrams   111

7   Decomposition Diagrams   139

TABLE OF BOXES

PREFACE

This book was written when the world of the systems analyst and designer was changing from pencil-and-template techniques to diagrams created at a workstation screen. When a workstation is used, the computer should decipher the *meaning* of the diagrams. The computer should help the designer to think clearly and should give as much help as possible in automating the design process and the generation of program code.

The diagrams and their manipulation by computer are a form of *thought* processing. The analyst, designer, programmer, user, and executive need a family of diagram types that help them to think clearly. These diagram types should be as clear and simple as possible. Although there are many types of diagrams, a minimum number of icons should have to be learned, and their meanings should be as obvious as possible.

The diagrams must be complete enough and rigorous enough to serve as a basis for code generation and for automatic conversion of one type of diagram into another. The diagrams of the early "structured revolution" are not good enough for this. This book describes an enhancement of such diagrams, adjusted to use a common family of icons.

The diagrams become the documentation for systems (along with a computerized encyclopedia that files the meaning of the diagrams and additional information collected when they were drawn). When changes are made to systems, the diagrams will be changed on the screen and the code regenerated. The design documentation does not slip out of date as changes are made.

The diagrams for designing systems are a language of communication. Design automation enforces precision in this language. As with other languages, it is necessary that *standards* apply to it so that diverse parties can communicate. It is vital today to prevent every researcher and developer from inventing their own form of diagramming. In Japan recently the author found multiple incompatible diagramming techniques, none of them as effective as those in this book. Incompatible diagramming is a barrier to communication.

Above all, the diagrams need to be standardized throughout the corporation so that all persons involved with computers have a common powerful language and can discuss one another's plans, specifications, designs, and programs.

ACKNOWLEDGMENTS   The genesis of this report was a monumental study of the computer industry's various structured techniques, carried out by myself and Dr. Carma McClure. This revealed that many of the diagramming techniques used were deficient in what they could draw. Major improvements in diagramming techniques are clearly needed if the computer industry is to achieve full computer-aided design of systems.

Meanwhile, similar conclusions had been reached by the leading technical executives—Ian Palmer, Al Hershey, and Ken Winter—in two companies of which I am chairman, James Martin Associates and KnowledgeWare Inc.

The recommendations in this volume incorporate the ideas of McClure, Palmer, and Hershey, all three of whom have spent arduous years with clients applying structured techniques and information engineering techniques. The recommendations have been refined repeatedly both in the field and in the building of tools for computer-aided systems analysis and design.

The author would like to thank these persons and the many computer professionals in the two companies mentioned who have discussed the use of the techniques and contributed to their evolution.

Tool building using the recommended standards took place at Arthur Young, KnowledgeWare Inc., Texas Instruments, InTech, Cortex, James Martin Associates, and elsewhere. Diagrams from these organizations appear in the book, and I am grateful for permission to publish them.

James Martin

DIAGRAMMING STANDARDS: THE BASIS FOR AUTOMATION

The chart on the next two pages summarizes the commonly used icons. They are used in many different types of diagrams, including entity-relationship diagrams, decomposition diagrams, dependency diagrams, data flow diagrams, decision trees, state transition diagrams, dialog design diagrams, data analysis diagrams, and action diagrams.

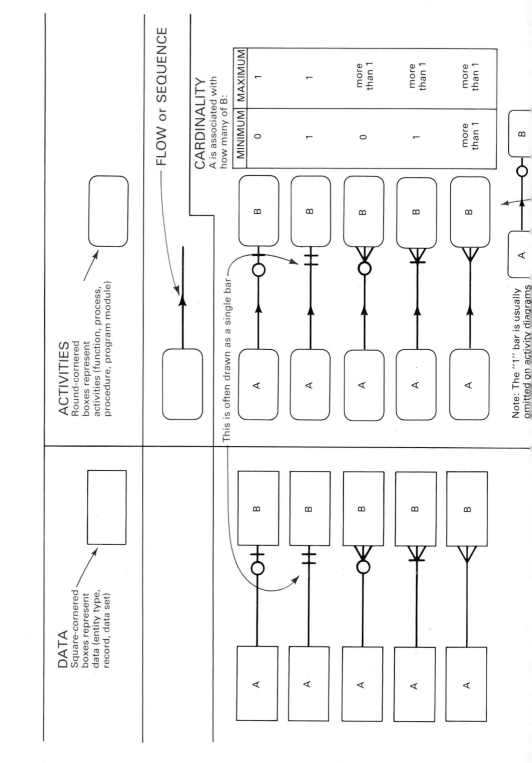

DATA
Square-cornered boxes represent data (entity type, record, data set)

ACTIVITIES
Round-cornered boxes represent activities (function, process, procedure, program module)

FLOW or SEQUENCE

This is often drawn as a single bar

CARDINALITY
A is associated with how many of B:

	MINIMUM	MAXIMUM
	0	1
	1	1
	0	more than 1
	1	more than 1
	more than 1	more than 1

Note: The "1" bar is usually omitted on activity diagrams

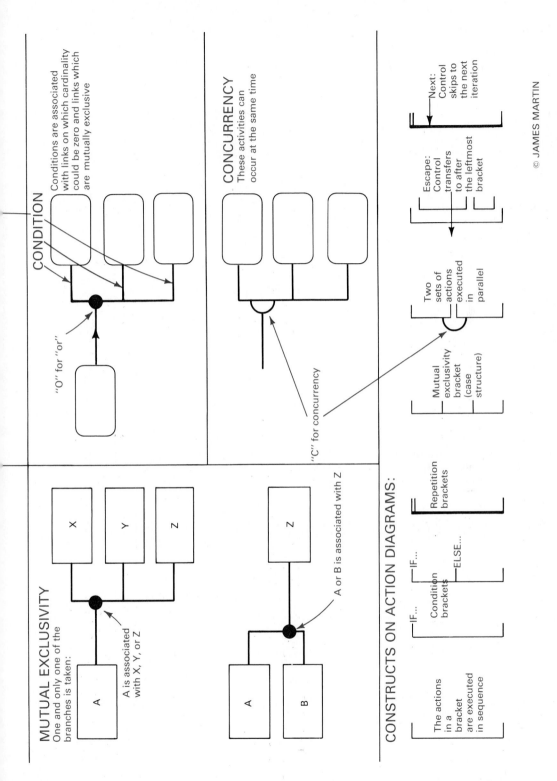

MUTUAL EXCLUSIVITY
One and only one of the branches is taken:

A is associated with X, Y, or Z

A or B is associated with Z

CONDITION

Conditions are associated with links on which cardinality could be zero and links which are mutually exclusive

"O" for "or"

CONCURRENCY
These activities can occur at the same time

"C" for concurrency

CONSTRUCTS ON ACTION DIAGRAMS:

The actions in a bracket are executed in sequence

IF...
IF...
Condition brackets
ELSE...

Repetition brackets

Mutual exclusivity bracket (case structure)

Two sets of actions executed in parallel

Escape: Control transfers to after the leftmost bracket

Next: Control skips to the next iteration

© JAMES MARTIN

xvii

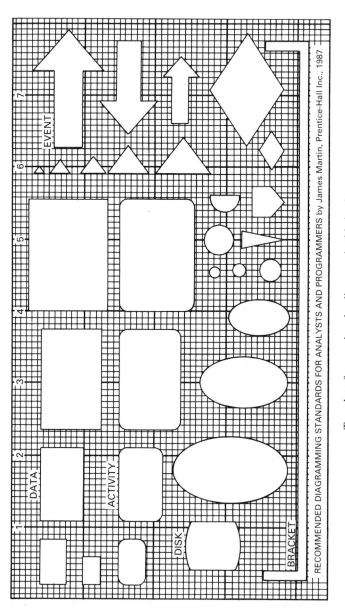

RECOMMENDED DIAGRAMMING STANDARDS FOR ANALYSTS AND PROGRAMMERS by James Martin, Prentice-Hall Inc., 1987

Template for creating the diagrams in this book.

RECOMMENDED DIAGRAMMING
STANDARDS FOR ANALYSTS
AND PROGRAMMERS

1 DIAGRAMS AND CLEAR THINKING

A FORM OF LANGUAGE
Good, clear diagrams play an essential part in designing complex systems and developing programs.

Philosophers have often described how what we are capable of thinking depends on the language we use for thinking. When humankind used only Roman numerals, ordinary people could not multiply or divide. That capability spread when Arabic numbers become widely used. The diagrams we draw of complex processes are a form of language. With computers we may want to create processes more complex than those we would perform manually. Appropriate diagrams help us to visualize and invent those processes.

If only one person is developing a system design or program, the diagrams that person uses are an aid to clear thinking. A poor choice of diagramming technique can inhibit thinking. A good choice can speed up work and improve the quality of the results.

When several people work on a system or program, the diagrams are an essential communication tool. A formal diagramming technique is needed to enable the developers to interchange ideas and to make their separate components fit together with precision.

When systems are modified, clear diagrams are an essential aid to maintenance. They make it possible for a new team to understand how the programs work and to design changes. When a change is made, it often affects other parts of the program. Clear diagrams of the program structure enable maintenance programmers to understand the consequential effects of changes they make. When debugging, clear diagrams are again a highly valuable tool for understanding how the programs ought to work and for tracking down what might be wrong.

Diagramming, then, is a language essential both for clear thinking and for human communication. An enterprise needs standards for data processing diagrams, just as it has standards for engineering drawings.

THE CASA/CAP REVOLUTION

Today, there is a new and very important reason for diagramming standards' being well thought out. The job of systems analysts and systems designers is undergoing revolutionary change. It is evolving from a pencil-and-paper activity to an activity of computer-aided design. This change will improve enormously the productivity of systems builders and increase the quality of the systems they build.

Architects, engineers, and circuit designers have tools with which they can draw and manipulate diagrams on a computer screen. It is perhaps surprising that so many systems analysts and programmers still draw diagrams by hand. We have CAI, CAD, and CAM (computer-aided instruction, computer-aided design, and computer-aided manufacturing). We need CASA and CAP (computer-aided systems analysis and computer-aided programming) of great power.

Interactive diagramming on a computer screen has major advantages. It speeds up the process greatly. It enforces standards. The computer may apply many checks to what is being created. It can automate the documentation process. The computer enforces discipline and permits types of cross-checking, calculation, and validity checks that humans often do not apply. The large three-ring binders of specifications that have been typical are full of errors and inconsistencies. Interactive graphics design with computers can eliminate much of the sloppiness and replace volumes of text with powerful, computable, symbolic design.

Data processing installations everywhere should be making themselves ready for the CASA/CAP revolution.

Some diagramming techniques are more appropriate for automation than others. Automation of diagramming should lead to *automated checking of specifications* and *automatic generation of program code*. Many of the diagramming techniques of the past are not a sound basis for computerized design. They are too casual and cannot represent some of the necessary constructs.

BETTER THAN A THOUSAND WORDS

Given appropriate diagramming techniques, it is much easier to describe complex activities and procedures in diagrams than in text. A picture can be much better than a thousand words because it is concise, precise, and clear. It does not allow the sloppiness and woolly thinking that are common in text specifications.

You might glance ahead to Fig. 14.3, for example. The information conveyed in this decision tree would be lengthy and clumsy to express in text. Indeed, all detailed diagrams in the text convey information with greater brevity and precision than text could.

Mathematics is the preeminent language of precision. However, it would be difficult to describe a large road map mathematically. If we succeeded in doing so, the road map would still be more useful than the mathematics to most people. Data processing is complex and needs road maps. We need to be able to follow the lines, examine the junctions, and read the words on the diagrams.

Some diagrams, however, have a mathematical basis. With mathematics, we may state axioms that the diagrams must obey. A workstation may beep at a designer whenever one of the axioms is violated. The mathematically based structure that emerges may be cross-checked in various ways and may be the basis of automatic generation of code.

THE NEED FOR FORMALITY

Architects, surveyors, and designers of machine parts have *formal* techniques for diagramming that they *must* follow. Systems analysts and program designers have an even greater need for clear diagrams because their activities are more complex and the work of many people must interlock in intricate ways. There tends, however, to be less formality in programming as yet, perhaps because it is a young discipline full of brilliant people who want to make up their own rules.

One of the reasons why building and maintaining software systems is so expensive and error-prone is the difficulty we have in communicating our ideas clearly to one another. Whether reading a functional specification, a program design, or a program listing, we often experience difficulty in understanding precisely what its author is telling us. Whenever we must rely on our own interpretation of the meaning, the chance of a misunderstanding leading to program errors is very great.

The larger the team, the greater the need for precision in diagramming. It is difficult or impossible for members of a large team to understand in detail the work of the others. Instead, each team member should be familiar with an overview of the system and see where his component fits into it. He should be able to develop his component with as little ongoing interchange with the rest of the team as possible. He has clear, precisely defined and diagrammed interfaces with the work of the others. When one programmer changes his design, it should not affect the designs of the other programmers, unless this is unavoidable. The interfaces between the work of different programmers need to be unchanging. To achieve this needs high-precision techniques for designing the overall structure of the system.

CHANGING METHODS

Diagramming techniques in computing are still evolving. This is necessary because when we examine techniques in common use today, many of them have *serious* deficiencies. Flowcharts are falling out of use because they do not give a structured view of a program. Some of the early structured diagramming techniques need replacing because they fail to represent some important ideas. Indeed, one of the remarkable deficiencies of the early structured techniques is their use of diagrams that cannot represent many of the important constructs. We are inventing more rigorous methods for creating better specifications. Vast improvements are needed and are clearly possible in the specification process. These improvements bring new diagramming methods.

One of the problems with computing is that it is so easy to make a mess. Very tidy thinking is needed about the complex logic, or a rat's nest results. Today's structured techniques are an improvement over earlier techniques. However, we can still make a mess with them. Most specifications for complex systems are full of ambiguities, inconsistencies, and omissions. More precise, mathematically based techniques are evolving so that we can use the computer to help create specifications without these problems. As better, more automated techniques evolve, they need appropriate diagramming methods.

Just as advocates of different structured techniques tend to defend their methods emotionally, so advocates of diagramming methods put up passionate defenses even when a different technique has superior qualities.

Sometimes the advocates or owners of a particular diagramming technique defend it more like pagan priests defending a religion than like computer scientists seeking to advance their methods. It is very necessary to look objectively at the changes needed for full *automation* and *integration* of diagramming techniques and to speak openly about the defects of earlier techniques.

Many of the diagramming techniques in common use are old and obsolete. The IBM diagramming template, which most analysts use, is two decades old. It contains symbols for ''magnetic drum,'' ''punched tape,'' and ''transmittal tape.'' It was created before data-base systems, visual display units, or structured techniques were in use.

Most of the courses for systems analysts and programmers are obsolete. The courses took much time to develop, so professors and seminar firms keep them in use. They milk the old material for as long as it can generate revenue.

In doing the research for this book, it became clear that many organizations had not made a good choice of diagramming techniques. The techniques they taught their analysts were difficult in various ways, and this did great harm to their efforts to use computers as effectively as possible. After analyzing the capabilities of the various methods of the 1970s, some stand out more for what they *cannot* do than for what they can do. Some of the most publicized and popular techniques were poor in their capabilities.

We need an integrated set of diagramming standards with which we can express all the constructs necessary for the automation of system design and programming. The old techniques *must* give way to techniques that can draw all the concepts we need in an integrated fashion appropriate for computer-aided design and code generation.

STRUCTURED TECHNIQUES

The introduction of structured techniques into computing was a major step forward, referred to by its advocates as the "structured revolution." The early structured techniques were pencil-and-paper methods. Today these techniques need automation. Designs should be created with the aid of a computer. The design should be of such a form that it leads to automated code generation. The *true* structured revolution is the one that makes the programmer unnecessary through the use of code generators working from structured designs.

Structured techniques need structured diagramming. We must be able to draw all the desirable constructs in a way that makes their meaning clear and obvious.

Unfortunately, most of the diagramming techniques of the early structured methods are not able to represent some of the major constructs that are needed [1]. A major improvement is needed in the completeness and precision of the diagrams used for structured design if these diagrams are to act as a basis for code generation.

Most structured diagramming techniques support a top-down structured development approach. They can describe a system or program at varying degrees of detail during each step of the decomposition process. They clarify the steps and the results of the decomposition process by providing a standardized way of describing procedural logic and data structures. Structured diagramming techniques help developers deal with the large volume of detail generated during the program development process.

It is generally desirable that the diagrams act as a basis for automatic code generation.

END-USER INVOLVEMENT

Particularly important in computing today is the involvement of end users. We want them to communicate well with systems analysts and to understand the diagrams drawn so that they can think about them and be involved in discussions about them.

Increasingly, some end users are likely to create their own applications with user-friendly fourth-generation languages. Where they do not build the application themselves, we would like them to sketch their needs and work hand in hand with an analyst, perhaps from an information center, who builds the application for them. User-driven computing is a vitally important trend for enabling users to get their problems solved with computers [2].

For these reasons, diagramming techniques should be user-friendly. They should be designed to encourage user understanding, participation, and sketching. Many DP diagramming techniques have been designed for DP professionals only. To be user-friendly, a diagram should be as obvious in meaning as possible. It should avoid symbols and mnemonics that the user may not understand.

PROGRAM DOCUMENTATION TOOLS

Structured diagramming techniques are very important as program documentation tools. They are used to define the program specifications and to represent the program design. They provide the blueprint for implementing the design into program code. They describe the program organization structure and its internal workings. The programmer translates them into actual programming-language instructions during the coding phase.

Diagrams can give both high-level and detailed descriptions of a program. For example, HIPO diagrams and structure charts have been used to give a high-level overview of a program. They can be used to explain in general terms what major functions the program performs and what data and components make up the program. On the other hand, pseudocode and Nassi-Shneiderman charts have been used to give an instruction-level view of a program. They show where each program variable is initialized, tested, or referenced in the program code. Today it is desirable that we have one drawing technique that accomplishes *both* the overview diagramming *and* the diagramming of detailed internals. The overview diagram should be successively decomposed into the code structure. Action diagrams accomplish this.

A high-level or a detailed view of a program is important, depending on the user's purpose. If he is searching for a bug, detailed documentation may guide him to the exact location of the error. If he wants to determine in which of several programs a certain function is performed, high-level documentation may be the most helpful.

However, to use different and incompatible techniques for high-level design and low-level design is generally undesirable. It dates back to an era when the program architect was a separate person from the detail coder. Today it is desirable that the high-level design be steadily decomposed into low-level design using the same diagramming technique. This decomposition should be done by one person, preferably at a computer screen. As fourth-generation languages become more popular, the era of the separate coder will go. We need one diagramming technique that enables a person to sketch an overview of a program and decompose it into detailed logic. Action diagrams give this ability.

Data-base design has become very important and has spawned its own collection of diagramming techniques. The systems analysis process and the programming process need to be linked into the data-base design. In Chapters 12 and 13 we will see an integration of these. A data structure diagram is developed (often by a data administrator). A data navigation diagram is drawn on top of this. The data navigation diagram is converted (automatically) into an action diagram, which is edited to produce executable code.

UTILITY OF DOCUMENTATION

Diagramming techniques produce both internal and external program documentation. *Internal documentation* is embedded in the program source code. *External documentation* is separate from the source code.

External program documentation, such as data flow diagrams and pseudocode, has often been discarded once the program is developed. It is considered unnecessary and too expensive to keep up-to-date during the remainder of the system life cycle. If a program is well structured and properly documented internally, external program documentation becomes ignored.

Maintenance programmers mistrust most external documentation because they know that in practice it is seldom updated. Even the external documentation for a newly released system is unlikely to describe a program accurately.

Documentation can be trusted to be accurate in two cases. First, when information about a program is automatically *generated from the code* (cross-reference listings, automatically generated structure charts, flowcharts, etc.). Keeping all the program documentation within or generated from the source code will make it more accessible and more accurate. Second, when the documentation is in the form of computerized diagrams or representations and the program is automatically *generated from these diagrams*. In one of these two ways (preferably the latter), the code and the diagrams are automatically linked, and the diagrams *are* the documentation used for maintenance.

We should distinguish between different types of external documentation:

1. High-level structure vs. detailed logic
2. Procedural structure vs. data structure

High-level documentation will change very little, can be easily updated, and is a valuable source of information about a program throughout its life. Data flow diagrams, data models, data navigation diagrams, and action diagrams are valuable introductions to understanding a complex program.

The subject of data administration is particularly important. A data administrator is the custodian of an organization's data dictionary and data structures. He is responsible for maintaining and creating a model of data that will be used on many different projects. This central representation of data is a basic foundation stone of multiple programs. Having separate programs employ views of data extracted from a common data model ensures that data can be exchanged among these programs and that data can be extracted from a common data base for management reporting and decision-support purposes. A clear diagramming technique is needed to represent the data models and views of data that are extracted from it.

The programmer must often navigate through a complex data base. Data navigation diagrams, described in Chapter 13, give a diagramming technique for this, linked to the data model and to action diagrams, which represent program structures that use the model.

If the data model is properly designed, the data structures should not usually change in disruptive ways throughout the system life. A canonical data model can be largely independent of individual applications of the data and also the software or hardware mechanisms that are employed in representing and using the data [3]. The data model and the data dictionary are valuable tools to aid program understanding. There may be many data navigation diagrams associated with one data model.

BATTLE WITH COMPLEXITY

Much of the future of computing is a battle with complexity. To push frontiers forward, we have to learn how to build more complex systems. We cannot do this without harnessing the power of the computer itself.

The battle with complexity became more urgent in the world of hardware than the world of software. Designers of the most complex chips and wafers could not succeed without highly sophisticated computer graphics tools. The 3-inch-square ceramic modules that hold chips in today's mainframes contain over a mile of wiring.

While designers of hardware logic have taken their computer-aided tools very seriously, most analysts and programmers have not. Analysts and programmers often regard themselves as artists needing pencil-and-paper tools. We tolerate errors in their work to a much greater extent than we would in the work of hardware designers.

It is necessary that computer-aided design (CAD) and computer-aided thinking (CAT) be employed as much by software and application designers as by hardware and chip designers.

CHANGING SYSTEMS

Data processing systems are not static. Like a living organism, they are modified and evolve with time. We grow parts of them and prune other parts. We need to make constant adjustments.

This process of changing systems, however, has been very difficult with traditional methods. Changes tend to have unforeseen consequences. A change made in one part of a system causes errors in other parts. Often the documentation is such that these consequential errors are neither foreseen nor detected until the system causes problems.

One of the most desirable features of computer-aided methodologies is that they should make systems easy to change.

On-line diagrams make clear the structure of the data, procedures, and activities and make them easy to modify. When a modification is made, they automatically reveal where this has effects and show what else has to be changed as a consequence of the modification.

FUNCTIONS OF STRUCTURED DIAGRAMS

Good diagramming techniques, then, have the following important functions:

- An aid to clear thinking
- Precise communication between members of the development team
- Linkage to automatic generation of code
- Standard interfaces between modules
- Systems documentation
- Enforcement of good structuring
- An aid to debugging
- An aid to changing systems (maintenance)
- Fast development (with computer-aided diagramming)
- Enforcing rigor in specifications (when linked to computerized specification tools)
- Automated checking (with computer-aided tools)
- Linkage to data administration tools
- Enabling end users to review the design
- Encouraging end users to sketch their needs clearly

A function that is achieved on only a few systems today ought to be emphasized and will become extremely important. The diagram, drawn on a computer screen, is decomposed into finer detail until executable program code can be generated from it *automatically*. Conventional programming then disappears.

REFERENCES

1. J. Martin and C. McClure, *Structured Techniques for Computing*. Englewood Cliffs, N.J.: Prentice-Hall, 1985.

2. J. Martin, *Application Development Without Programmers*. Englewood Cliffs, N.J.: Prentice-Hall, 1982.

3. J. Martin, *Managing the Data Base Environment*. Englewood Cliffs, N.J.: Prentice-Hall, 1983.

4. J. Martin, *System Design from Provably Correct Constructs*. Englewood Cliffs, N.J.: Prentice-Hall, 1985.

2 TYPES OF DIAGRAMS NEEDED

A systems analyst, like a carpenter, needs a number of different tools at his workbench. The tools that this book describes are among his most important: diagramming techniques that enable him to think clearly about complex system design.

Many systems analysts in the past have drawn one or perhaps two types of diagrams. In early training courses, flowcharts were the only type of diagramming taught. More recently, many analysts have learned only data flow diagrams and structure charts—both limited in what they can draw. We believe that a well-trained analyst should be comfortable in the use of the following techniques (or their equivalent):

- Decomposition diagrams
- Dependency diagrams
- Data flow diagrams
- Action diagrams (a replacement for structure charts)
- Data analysis diagrams
- Data structure diagrams
- Entity-relationship diagrams
- Data navigation diagrams
- Decision trees and tables
- State transition diagrams
- Dialog design diagrams

This list does not include diagrams of machine configurations, data networks, or other representations of hardware.

The list is not as formidable as it might appear. There are similarities among the diagrams, and they can use a common, simple set of icons.

THE DP PYRAMID

Analysis and design for computing can be thought of as having a pyramid structure, as shown in Fig. 2.1. At the top is the strategic planning (which is too often not done). Next is the layer of architecture or general analysis. For complex system software, this relates to the overall architecture, the understanding of the data needed, and the mapping out of processes and how they are dependent on one another. In business systems, it relates to the analysis of what data are needed to run the enterprise, what processes occur, and how these processes are dependent on one another.

The third layer is the design of systems, showing the procedures needed to accomplish various processes and how data pass among these procedures. Level 2 was concerned with *what* needed to be done but not, in detail, *how*. Level 3 is concerned with *how* the work is accomplished.

Level 3 describes the procedures in user terms not yet concerned with the implementation detail except for user input and output. Level 4 is concerned with the data sets, data-base management systems, program structures, technical design, and in general the implementation detail.

Different approaches to computing give different labels to these four lay-

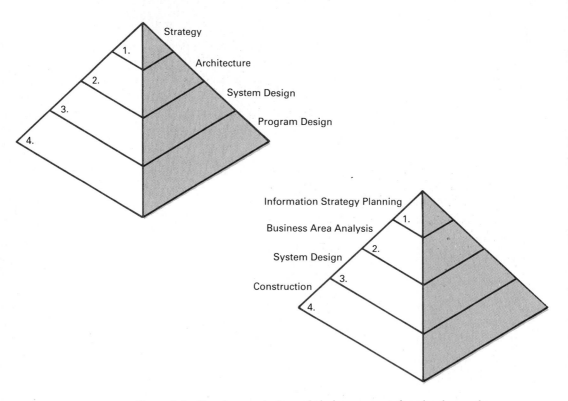

Figure 2.1 Planning, analysis, and design occur at four levels, as shown here. The different levels need different diagrams.

ers. The labels on the bottom pyramid of Fig. 2.1 are appropriate for the stages of building up business data processing.

DATA AND PROCESSING

The analysis and design of data processing systems can be divided into two parts: the *data* and the *processing*. The methodologies that are often the most effective analyze and design the data first, then build processing that employs these data.

The left side of the pyramids of Fig. 2.1 relates to data; the right side relates to processing.

A fundamental step in the creation of data processing facilities for a corporation is the development of a data model that represents the data in the corporation in a stable, well-defined, clearly structured fashion. The term *data model* in this context implies that the data are represented in a fashion that is independent of technology. This is important for stable design because the technology is likely to change rapidly. This technology-independent representation of the corporate data is a foundation stone on which much else will be built. It is represented by the second layer of the pyramid on the left:

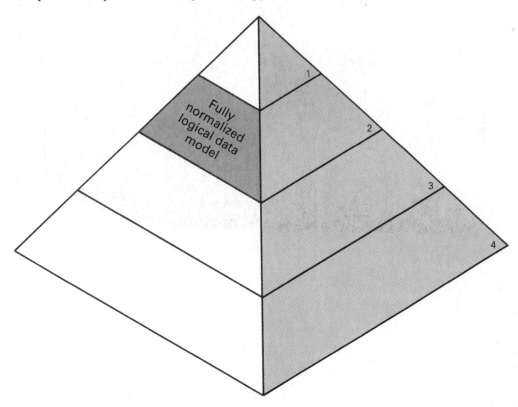

Above that is the strategic planning of data in an enterprise. Below it, at level 3, is the design of records or data-base structures that are used by specific procedures. These may be the *schemas* of a CODASYL data base, for example. At the bottom level are the views of data seen by the program and the storage structures, for example the physical placement of data sets.

These four levels of representation of data are shown on the left side of the pyramid in Fig. 2.2.

Activities

The right side of the pyramid shows the following activities:

- At level 1, the high-level, strategic overview of the functions in an enterprise
- At level 2, the processes necessary to run the business and how they are related, or the processes that constitute an overall architecture of a system
- At level 3, the procedures that are designed to support the business processes
- At level 4, the modules that constitute the programs

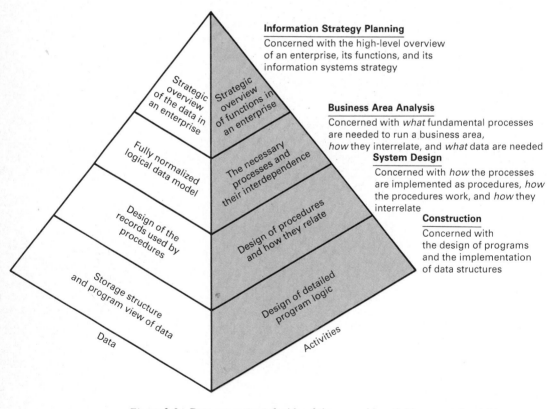

Figure 2.2   Data are at the left side of the pyramid; activities are at the right.

Figure 2.2 shows these activities.

At each level there are modules of activity to which our diagrams relate. At the highest level we refer to these as *business functions*—the high-level functions necessary to run an enterprise.

At level 2 we refer to the modules of activity as *processes*. The analysis at this level is concerned with what processes must be carried out and how these processes are dependent on one another. We are not, at this level, concerned with *how* the processes are implemented.

At level 3 we refer to the modules as *procedures*. Whereas a process is merely concerned with *what* is done, a procedure is concerned with *how* it is done. At level 3 a design is created showing what procedures will be used, how they work, and how they interrelate.

Level 4 is concerned with program design, and we refer to the modules of activity as *program modules*.

Activity is thus a general term that is subdivided into four more precise terms:

- business function
- process
- procedure
- program module

In the diagrams in this book, activities are drawn as round-cornered boxes; data are drawn as square-cornered boxes:

A variety of types of diagrams employ these activity and data objects and interlink them to show different aspects of analysis or design.

Figure 2.3 shows the activity objects at the four levels of the pyramid and the data objects that correspond to them.

TECHNIQUES FOR THE EIGHT AREAS   Figure 2.4 shows where the various diagramming techniques discussed in this book fit into the pyramid. The techniques need to fit together, and they should, as far as possible, use a consistent notation. They need to be integrated in one computerized workbench.

Figure 2.5 shows a minimal shortlist of the techniques and how they inter-

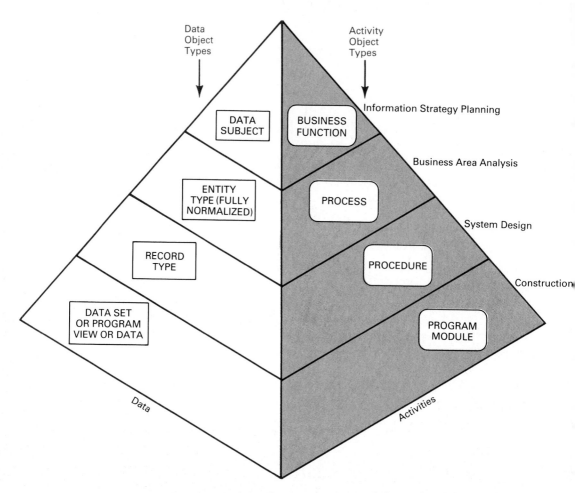

Figure 2.3 Many of the diagrams for system design and analysis contain blocks that represent data and blocks that represent activities. The data blocks are drawn with square corners. The activity blocks are drawn with round corners.

link. Automatic or computer-aided conversion is shown by the red arrows. From the action diagram and data structure diagram, executable code should be generated.

Code generators require specifications of screens and reports that are used. Certain fourth-generation languages contain excellent screen pointers and report specifiers. Figure 2.6 indicates how these, combined with diagramming techniques, can create a graphically oriented application generator.

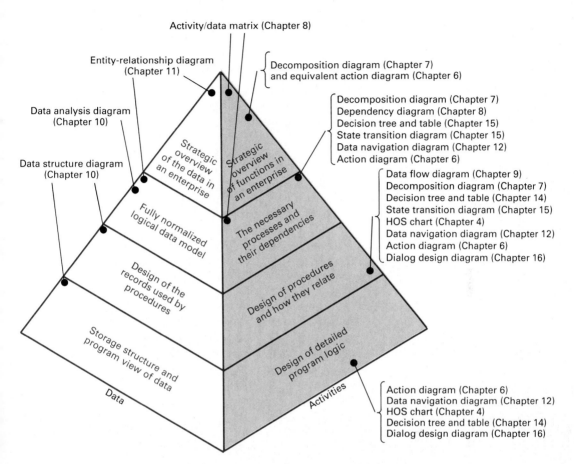

Figure 2.4   The areas in which the different diagramming techniques are applicable.

DIAGRAM TYPES: SUMMARY

The following paragraphs summarize briefly the various techniques.

1. *Action diagrams* (Chapter 6). A simple technique for drawing high-level decomposition diagrams, overview program structures, and detailed program control structures (condition, case, DO WHILE, and DO UNTIL constructs). Most diagramming techniques cannot draw both the overview structure of programs and the detailed control structures; action diagrams can. (Examples: Figs. 6.6, 6.7, 6.10, 6.12.)

2. *Decomposition diagrams* (Chapter 7). High-level activities are decomposed into lower-level activities showing more detail. This top-down structuring makes complex organizations or processes easier to comprehend. Decomposi-

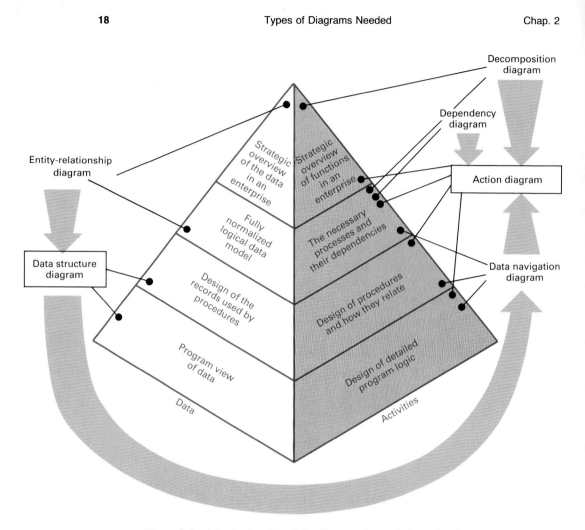

Figure 2.5   A basic shortlist of the diagramming techniques in Fig. 2.4. The red arrows indicate automatic or computer-aided conversion. Executable code should be generated from the action diagram and the data structure diagram.

tion diagrams are a basic tool for structured analysis and design. Most decomposition diagrams are simple tree structures. It is useful to add other notation in some cases to show sequence, one-to-many decomposition, optionality, and conditions. (Example: Fig. 7.3.)

   3. *Dependency diagrams* (Chapter 8). A dependency diagram has blocks showing activities and arrows between blocks showing that one activity is dependent on another. It is used, for example, for analyzing the processes that are needed in a business area. (Example: Fig. 8.3.)

   4. *Data flow diagrams* (Chapter 9). A data flow diagram shows procedures and flows of data among procedures. It is a high-level design tool for

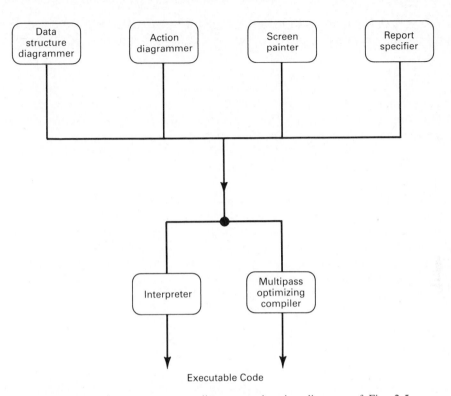

Figure 2.6 The data structure diagrams and action diagrams of Fig. 2.5 should be used to generate executable code.

mapping out the procedures required to automate a given area. (Example: Fig. 9.1.)

5. *Data analysis diagrams* (Chapter 10). Diagrams for analyzing data, showing fields and dependencies among fields. They are the input to the normalization process. They can show derived fields. (Example: Fig. 10.6.)

6. *Data structure diagrams* (Chapter 10). Diagrams designed to show detailed data structures used in data-base or file systems. (Example: Fig. 10.8.)

7. *Entity-relationship diagrams* (Chapter 11). Diagrams that draw entity types and relationships among entity types (an entity is anything we store data about). Entity-relationship diagrams are the basis of high-level data models. Data structure diagrams show details of attributes in specific data bases, or files. (Example: Fig. 11.2.)

8. *Data navigation diagrams* (Chapter 12 and 13). Diagrams showing the access paths through a data model or data-base structure that are used by a process or procedure. A first step in charting procedures that use data bases or multiple files. Appropriately drawn data navigation diagrams can be automatically converted to action diagrams. (Example: Fig. 12.2.)

9. *Decision trees and tables* (Chapter 14). A technique for drawing logic that involves multiple choices or complex sets of conditions. (Example: Fig. 14.2.)

10. *State transition diagrams* (Chapter 15). A technique for drawing complex logic that involves many possible transitions among states. Based on finite-state machine notation, neither decision trees nor state transition diagrams are useful with every type of system or program; both relate to situations with certain types of complex logic. (Example: Fig. 15.7.)

11. *HOS Charts* (Chapter 4). A controlled form of functional decomposition diagram (a tree structure) in which the data types that are the input and output of each block are shown and each decomposition is of a precise type defined with mathematical axioms. This is the basis of the HOS (Higher Order Software) methodology with which specifications can be created for complex systems that are proven to have no inconsistencies or internal bugs. Bug-free code can be generated from these specifications. (Example: Fig. 4.10.)

12. *Dialog design diagrams* (Chapter 16). Diagrams showing the structure of dialogs in terms of the screens used and operator actions that cause transitions from one screen to another. (Example: Fig. 16.1.)

STRUCTURED TECHNIQUES

Many of the diagramming techniques used today relate to methodologies for structured analysis, design, and programming. Any data processing organization ought to be using structured techniques today. It is simply bad management not to. A choice has to be made about *which* structured methodology to make an installation standard.

It is important to understand that structured techniques are themselves changing. Many of the techniques introduced in the 1970s were deficient in serious ways and need to be supplanted with methodologies that are

- More complete
- Faster to use
- Based on sound data administration
- Suitable for fourth-generation languages and application generators
- Enhance end-user communication
- Apply thorough verification techniques
- Solve the severe problems of maintenance
- Are, above all, suitable for computer-aided design with interactive graphics

The objectives are to speed up the work of the analyst as much as possible, automate the creation of programs, improve the quality of systems, and make systems easy to change.

Figure 2.7 shows the evolution of structured techniques.

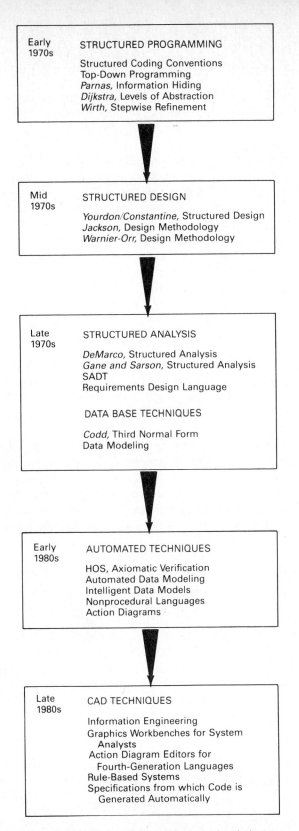

Figure 2.7 The evolution of structured techniques.

COMPUTER-AIDED DESIGN

The work of hardware logic designers is done today almost entirely with interactive computer graphics. Eventually, every systems analyst will be expected to use computer graphics tools also.

Some diagramming techniques in common use are of little value for computerized design. They are insufficiently precise or complete. Thorough automated validation cannot be applied to them. Their deficiencies have to be patched with techniques like writing structured English or pseudocode. They do not form a basis for automatic code generation.

An analyst needs a family of tools like those listed at the start of this chapter. With many of today's methodologies, the tool kit is incomplete and the separate tools are incompatible. The analyst and designer use human intelligence to bridge the gaps between incompatible diagramming techniques. To benefit fully from computer-aided design, a complete and integrated set of diagramming conventions is needed.

USE OF AN ENCYCLOPEDIA

It is the meaning of a diagram rather than the graphic image that is valuable. When using computer graphics, the meaning should be encoded and filed. One or more types of diagram may be generated from this representation of meaning.

The facility that stores the meaning of the diagrams is referred to as an *encyclopedia*. From the information in the encyclopedia, diagrams can be quickly generated. The encyclopedia may be large, storing information about an entire business area or the results of enterprisewide strategic planning or modeling. By using the encyclopedia, one type of diagram may be converted into another or used as a component of another.

The encyclopedia often stores information that is not shown graphically on the diagram. Some of this information may be collected from the analyst or designer when he builds the diagram at the screen. It is desirable that the user of a graphic workstation be able to display the more detailed information. He may do that by pointing to an icon and using the SHOW command. The icon may expand into a window that contains the details either in text or table form or in the form of another diagram.

Figure 2.8 illustrates the encyclopedia concept.

An encyclopedia representing the meaning of the diagrams, and the detail associated with them, needs to grow from the high-level planning activities down to the detail necessary for code generation. Representations of the business processes and data models are maintained to help integrate the procedures and speed up the building of computer applications.

COMPUTER GRAPHICS TOOLS

Computer graphics tools for analysts and system builders are destined to play a very important role.

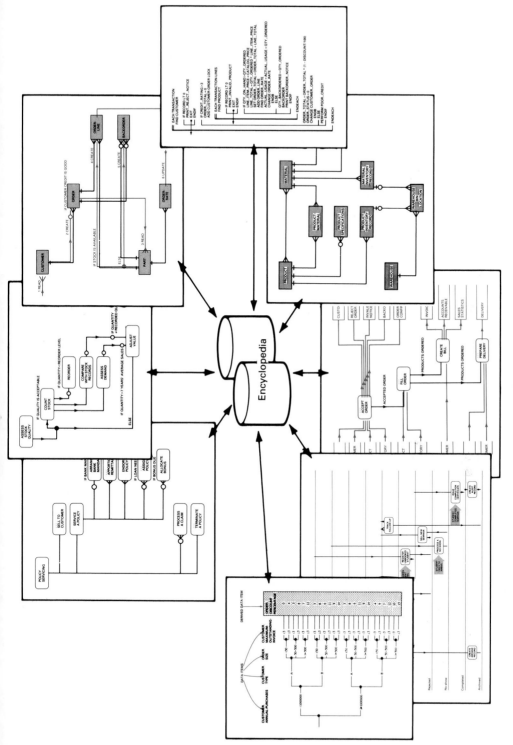

Figure 2.8 The meaning of the diagrams is stored in an encyclopedia. Using the encyclopedia, diagrams may be generated or one type of diagram may be converted into another. The encyclopedia often contains more detail than are displayed on a diagram. The additional detail may be displayed by pointing to an icon and using the SHOW command.

They vary greatly in their capabilities and value. We can categorize computer graphics tools as follows. The first two categories are general-purpose tools that can be used with various design methodologies. The other categories in this list relate to tools for specific methodologies.

1. *General-purpose drawing tool.* A tool with which static drawings of any type can be created. (Example: MACDRAW and MACPAINT, from Apple, Inc.)

2. *Tool for using dynamic drawings.* A *static drawing* is one without any built-in mechanisms. If one part of the drawing is changed or moved, it has no effect on any other part except perhaps to hide it or uncover it. A *dynamic drawing* is one with defined linkages between components or relationships between icons. When part of the drawing is changed or moved, other changes of related meaning may occur *automatically*. A common example is that blocks on the drawing are connected by links (as with most of the diagrams in this book), and when one block is moved, the links automatically move with it such that they retain their logical meaning. Defined logical relationships among other elements of the drawing may also be automatically preserved. If the designer attempts to change the drawing in a way that makes it illogical or violates an integrity constraint, he will be automatically warned. The designer can build and manipulate dynamic drawings on a screen faster than static drawings. (Example: EXCELERATOR, from Index Technology, Inc.)

3. *Tools for existing methodologies.* Several graphics tools have been built for implementing the methodologies that evolved in the 1970s—data flow diagrams, structure charts, Jackson diagrams, etc. They provide the icons with which these diagrams can be created and modified quickly on the screen. Some of these tools employ menus, fill-in-the-blank panels, or dialogs for helping to create the diagrams, consider the integrity constraints, and generally do sound design. (Example: STRADIS/DRAW, from MCAUTO, which produces graphic support for Gane and Sarson's methodology using data flow diagrams and structure charts.)

4. *Methodologies designed to harness computer power.* There can be a world of difference between computerized versions of *hand* methodologies and new methodologies designed to take advantage of the computer. The computer can employ large, precise libraries and can execute algorithms far too complex to be reasonable as manual methods. Computer graphics thus challenges us to redesign our methodologies.

Using a computer we can access large data models, automate the normalization and synthesis of these data models, extract and edit portions of the data models, create navigation paths through the data, generate screens, reports, and dialogs, generate and edit action diagrams, and apply mathematical axioms for enforcing correctness. We can automatically convert one type of diagram into another. High-level constructs can be automatically expanded into detail. (Example: USE.IT, from Higher Order Software, Inc., which uses mathematical axioms to check the correctness of graphically built specifications and ensure that they are internally bug-free—a powerful technique that would be much too tedious to do by hand.)

5. *Graphic designs that generate executable code.* Sufficient detail can be added to graphics diagrams to permit code generation. Several application generators use graphics to generate part but not all of an application's code; for example, reports, screens, dialogs, and data-base structures are generated from graphics. The program structure and logic can also be generated from dependency diagrams, data navigation diagrams, HOS charts, or action diagrams.

The graphics tools may be linked directly to an interpreter or optimizing compiler or may create code in a fourth-generation language that has its own interpreter or compiler.

6. *An integrated family of consistent tools.* It is desirable that the future system designer employ an integrated set of tools with which to represent different aspects of system design. A consistent graphics notation is needed throughout this tool kit. The tool kit should be designed for automatic code generation.

The tools should all run on the same computer, with automatic conversion from one type of representation to another.

A DIAGRAMMATIC BASIS FOR AUTOMATION

To achieve CAD/CAM–like automation of system building, a consistent diagramming notation is needed for the various tools that represent different aspects of thinking about systems. The integrated set of diagramming conventions that form a good basis for automation is summarized in Chapter 5.

3 FORMS OF STRUCTURED DIAGRAMS

The form or style of a diagram has a major effect on its usefulness. Complex charts can be drawn with a variety of techniques.

Humans like to draw artistic charts with curvy arrows sweeping gracefully from one block to another. We position the blocks as our fancy takes us. Such charts may look nice, but they cannot be easily maintained by computer. To enlist the computer's help in drawing and modifying our diagrams, the diagrams have to be reasonably disciplined.

Undisciplined diagramming becomes a mess when the diagrams grow in complexity (Fig. 3.1). Many diagrams that look nice in textbooks grow out of control in the real world, where they have hundreds of blocks instead of ten. It is necessary to select forms of diagramming that can handle complexity.

**FORMS OF
TREE STRUCTURE**
A construct that appears in many places in structured design is the hierarchy or tree structure. There are various ways to draw a tree structure. You should be familiar with them and understand that they are equivalent.

A tree structure is used to indicate that an overall facility, such as CORPORATION, includes lower-level facilities, such as SALES DIVISION, MANUFACTURING DIVISION, and PLANNING DIVISION. One of these, such as MANUFACTURING DIVISION, includes still lower-level facilities, such as PURCHASING, PRODUCTION, and WAREHOUSE. We could draw this inclusion property as in Fig. 3.2.

Figure 3.2 makes it clear what includes what but would be clumsy to draw if there were many levels in the hierarchy. We can make it smaller by drawing it as subdivided rectangles, as in Fig. 3.3. This is neat and indicates clearly what includes what. A concern with Fig. 3.3 is that the writing of the lowest

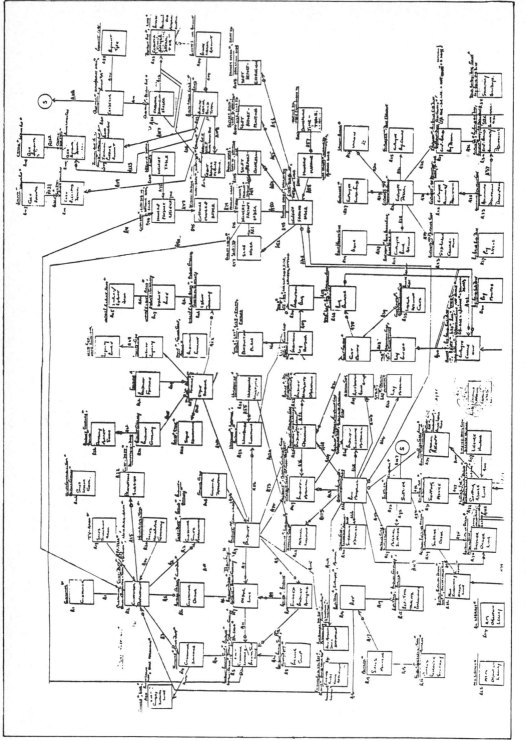

Figure 3.1 A portion of a complex hand-drawn diagram. Such diagrams encourage errors and inhibit change. Modifying them is much too time-consuming. They need to be replaced with diagramming at a computer screen.

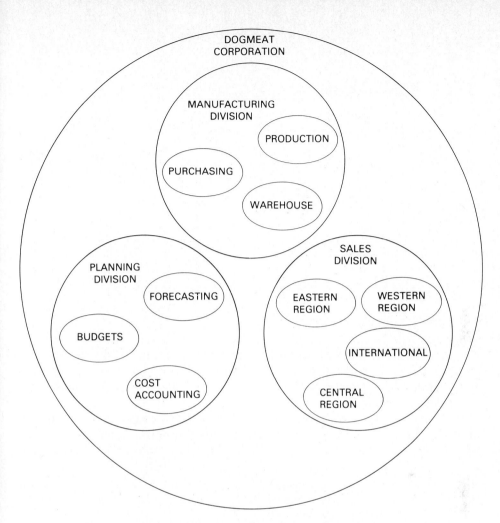

Figure 3.2   A tree structure showing what facilities include other facilities.

level is sideways. A normal printer cannot print sideways letters. It could print letters in a column:

```
P
U
R
C
H
A
S
I
N
G
```

But this becomes tedious to read.

DOGMEAT CORPORATION									
MANUFACTURING DIVISION			PLANNING DIVISION			SALES DIVISION			
PURCHASING	PRODUCTION	WAREHOUSE	BUDGETS	FORECASTING	COST ACCOUNTING	EASTERN REGION	WESTERN REGION	CENTRAL REGION	INTERNATIONAL

Figure 3.3   A box representation of a tree structure.

A more usual way to draw a tree structure is like Fig. 3.4. This form of diagram is used by many analysts and programmers. It is the basis of structure charts showing hierarchical structure in programs. It is also used to draw hierarchical data structures.

It looks good in textbooks because there it has a relatively small number of blocks. In real life there can be a large number of blocks at the lower levels, and the diagram will not fit on the width of a page. Drawing it might require

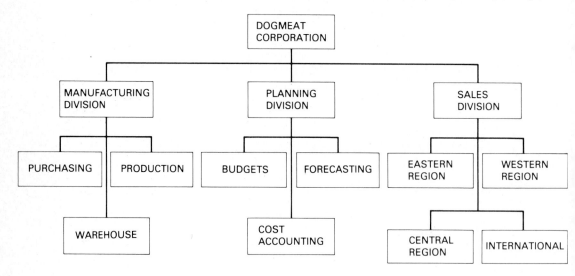

Figure 3.4   A common way of drawing the tree structure of Figs. 3.2 and 3.3.

paper 6 feet wide, and that is exactly what analysts, programmers, and data administrators use. They know that their work looks more impressive if it occupies a wall rather than resides in a binder. It is still more impressive if they draw it in various colors.

INHIBITION OF CHANGE

The problem with wall charts and hand-drawn works of art is that they are difficult to change. They inhibit change. In the design and analysis process there ought to be much change. The more a design can be discussed and modified in its early stages, the more the end result is likely to be satisfactory.

The best way to make a design easy to change is to draw it with a computer, on a screen, with software that makes it simple to modify. Automation of structured analysis, design, and programming using a workstation that draws graphics is generally desirable. We will need a printout of the diagrams created with a computer.

With a Calcomp plotter we can produce a 6-foot wall chart, in color, that is sure to impress our colleagues. Such plotters, however, are not freely available to every analyst and programmer. We would like to obtain a printout from our terminal or personal computer. This machine cannot produce wide wall charts unless we are prepared to stick many pieces of paper together with tape. In any case, wall charts are difficult to send to other people or to take home.

LEFT-TO-RIGHT TREES

We can solve the problem by turning the tree on its side. Figure 3.5 redraws the tree of Fig. 3.4. Now if there are many, many items at level 3, it spreads out vertically rather than horizontally and can be printed with a cheap printer.

Tree structures are used for drawing organization charts for people. Here the tree may not be turned on its side because the person who runs the show wants to see his name at the *top* of the tree. With program or data structures, there are no such ego problems, so left-to-right trees are fine.

A tree can be drawn with brackets, as in Fig. 3.6. The left bracket implies that DOGMEAT CORPORATION *includes* MANUFACTURING DIVISION, PLANNING DIVISION, and SALES DIVISION, and so on.

Suppose there are many levels in the tree. A many-level tree drawn like Fig. 3.4 or Fig. 3.6 would again spill off the right-hand edge of the page. To solve this, we can have a more compact version of a left-to-right tree, as shown in Fig. 3.7.

Incidentally, Fig. 3.7 solves the ego problem. The great leader can again be at the top of the tree.

The analyst has quite a number of lines to draw in Fig. 3.7. We would like him to have a small number of lines to draw so that he can make sketches quickly. Figure 3.8 shows a variant of Fig. 3.7 drawn with square brackets.

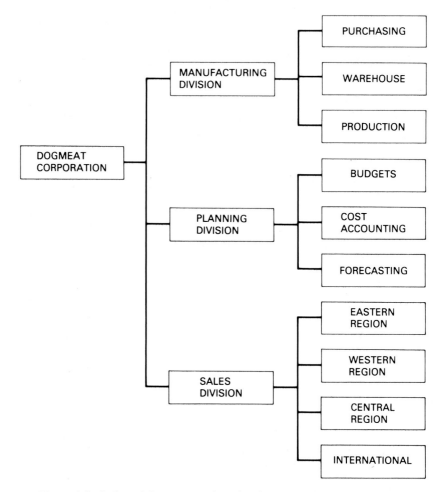

Figure 3.5 Left-to-right trees can be printed on normal-width paper, even when they have many items at one level.

This makes the hierarchical structure clear with a small number of lines. Each line of text in Fig. 3.8 could occupy much of the page. It could be a paragraph if so desired.

SEQUENCE OF OPERATIONS

Structure charts are drawn like Fig. 3.4. As commonly used, they do not show *sequence*. In much structured design, it is necessary to show sequence— of data items, of program modules, of instructions. If blocks are clustered— more clustered than at the bottom right of Fig. 3.4—their sequence may not be clear unless precise sequencing rules are used. To hide the sequence of opera-

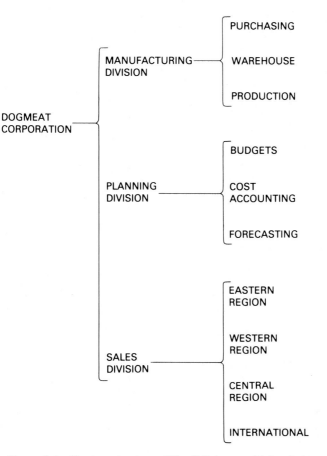

Figure 3.6   The tree structure of Fig. 3.5 drawn with brackets.

tions further, structure charts are often drawn with a common subroutine having links to two or more parents. In Figs. 3.5 through 3.8 the sequence is clear. The items are implemented in a top-to-bottom sequence.

Figure 3.8 is much closer than the other diagrams to structured program code. If we remove the lines and boxes, it looks like Fig. 3.9.

We must eventually convert our diagrams into code. This conversion should change the format as little as possible to minimize the likelihood of making mistakes and to make checking simple.

MESH-STRUCTURED DIAGRAMS

It is easier to make a mess with mesh-structured diagrams than with tree structures. Figure 3.10 shows a mesh structure, often called a network structure.

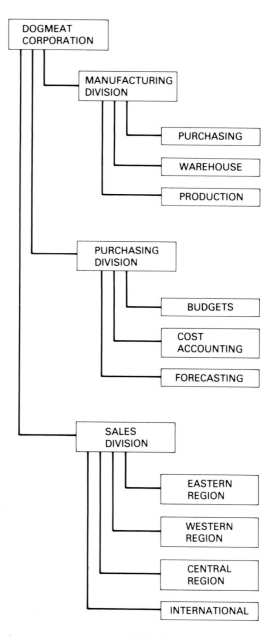

Figure 3.7 A more compact version of Fig. 3.5. With this form, many levels could be included on one page.

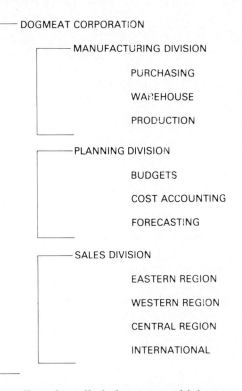

DOGMEAT CORPORATION

MANUFACTURING DIVISION

PURCHASING

WAREHOUSE

PRODUCTION

PLANNING DIVISION

BUDGETS

COST ACCOUNTING

FORECASTING

SALES DIVISION

EASTERN REGION

WESTERN REGION

CENTRAL REGION

INTERNATIONAL

Figure 3.8 Square brackets enable us to draw Fig. 3.7 with a small number of lines.

In a tree structure, there is one overall node called the *root,* which we draw at the top in diagrams like Figs. 3.3, 3.4, 3.7, and 3.8 and at the left in diagrams like Figs. 3.5 through 3.8. This node has *children,* drawn below or to the right of their parent. They in turn have children, and so on until the lowest or most detailed node is reached. This terminal node is called a *leaf.*

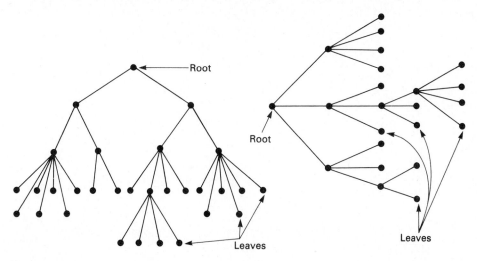

DOGMEAT CORPORATION

        MANUFACTURING DIVISION
            PURCHASING
            WAREHOUSE
            PRODUCTION
        PLANNING DIVISION
            BUDGETS
            COST ACCOUNTING
            FORECASTING
        SALES DIVISION
            EASTERN REGION
            WESTERN REGION
            CENTRAL REGION
            INTERNATIONAL

Figure 3.9 Figure 3.6 drawn without lines or boxes has a structure-like program code.

In a mesh structure, there is no such neat ordering. A node may have numerous parents. Anything can point to anything. Chaos rules.

The objective of structured design is to prevent chaos from ruling—to impose neatness on what otherwise might be disorder. GO TO instructions in programs can go to *anywhere,* permitting the programmer to weave a tangled mess. So structured design bans GO TOs and decomposes programs hierarchically.

Program structures, file structures, and document structures can, and should, be decomposed hierarchically. Unfortunately, there are some types of structures that cannot be decomposed hierarchically. A diagram showing how

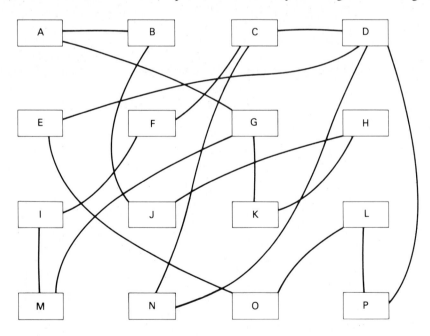

Figure 3.10 A mesh-structured (network-structured) diagram. This would become a mess if it had a large number of nodes.

data flows through an organization cannot be beaten into a tree-like shape. A chart showing the relationship between entity types in a data model is not tree-like.

Some structured methodologists almost refuse to accept the existence of anything that is not hierarchical. Because data models cannot be drawn with their hierarchical diagrams, they refuse to work with data models and will not heed the school of thought that regards data models as the foundation stone of modern DP methods.

COW CHARTS

Nevertheless, it is necessary to draw mesh-structured diagrams for some important aspects of design. Figure 3.10 has 16 blocks. Its spaghetti-like structure makes it difficult to work with. Real life is worse; often such charts have several hundred items. Such a chart may be cut up into pieces, but this does not clarify it unless done in a carefully structured way. The spaghetti-like pointers wander among the pages in a manner that is confusing and difficult to follow.

Some designers create hand-drawn charts that are too big to redraw quickly, and attempts to modify them create a rapidly worsening mess. The much modified chart is at last redrawn by hand and becomes regarded as a work of art, a triumphant achievement—but don't dare to modify it again!

I have been horrified by some of the charts that data administrators keep. There is no question that these charts inhibit progress and thwart improvement of the data structure. The data administrators will not dare to let end users propose changes to them. Sometimes these are called COW (''can of worms'') charts.

Most COW chart creators are impressed by their rococo masterpieces and pin them up on the wall.

NESTED CHARTS

To ease modification, certain types of charts can be nested. They are divided into modules that fit on normal-sized pages. In a tree structure, any of the blocks or brackets may be expanded in detail on another page. In a data flow diagram, any of the processes may be expanded on another page.

Figure 3.11 shows a data flow diagram. Many data flow diagrams in practice have much larger numbers of processes (drawn as circles in Fig. 3.11) and would require vast charts unless they were broken into nested pieces. Figure 3.12 shows Fig. 3.11 divided into two pieces.

The block labeled PROCESS 17 is expanded in a separate diagram, as shown. Blocks from this diagram—for example, PROCESS 17.3—could be shown in further detail on another page. This subdividing of data flow diagrams is called *layering*. The layered structure of data flow diagrams within data flow diagrams is itself a hierarchy, like Fig. 3.2, and is often drawn as a tree structure.

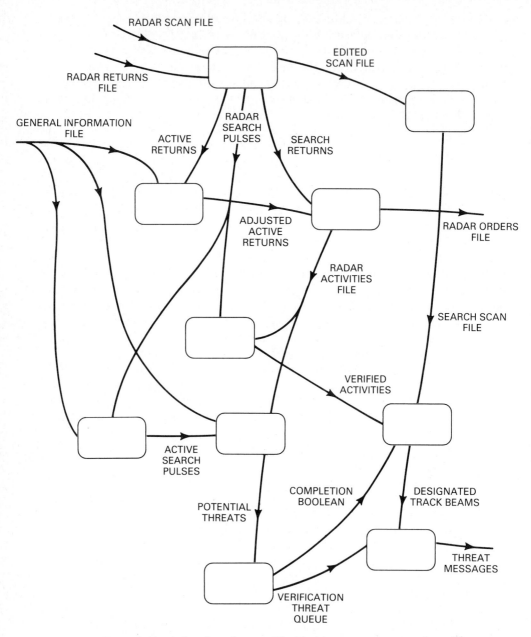

RADAR SCAN FILE

EDITED
SCAN FILE

RADAR RETURNS
FILE

GENERAL INFORMATION
FILE

RADAR
SEARCH
PULSES

ACTIVE
RETURNS

SEARCH
RETURNS

ADJUSTED
ACTIVE
RETURNS

RADAR ORDERS
FILE

RADAR
ACTIVITIES
FILE

SEARCH SCAN
FILE

VERIFIED
ACTIVITIES

ACTIVE
SEARCH
PULSES

COMPLETION
BOOLEAN

DESIGNATED
TRACK BEAMS

POTENTIAL
THREATS

THREAT
MESSAGES

VERIFICATION
THREAT
QUEUE

Figure 3.11 A data flow diagram. The blocks are computer procedures. The arrows are data. It is desirable to divide complex mesh structures into modules of less complexity. This diagram is divided (''layered'') in Fig. 3.12.

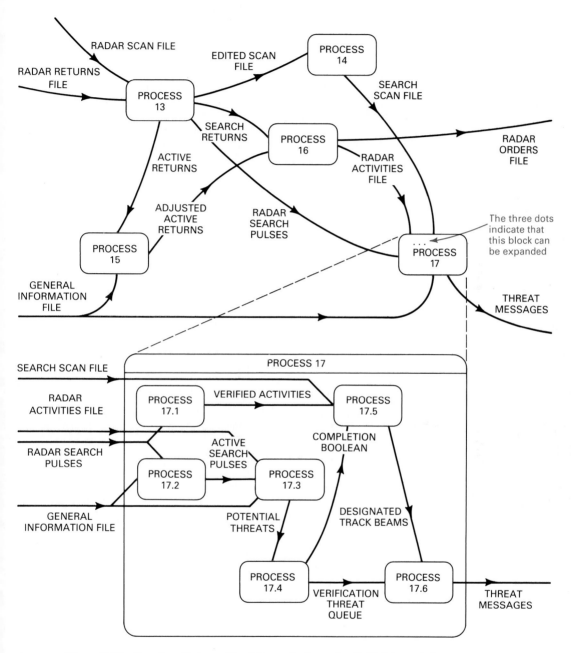

Figure 3.12 Complex diagrams like this can be layered—divided in nested modules. The bottom diagram shows details of PROCESS 17 in the upper diagram.

Most analysts draw free-form data flow diagrams with curvy lines like Fig. 3.11. Using a computer to draw the diagrams speeds up the process, and the software can perform some checking. Automated checking is very valuable in large projects with many data flow diagrams nested down to many layers. When the diagrams are computerized, they are easy to change, which is important because of the expense and difficulties of maintenance.

Some computerized data flow diagrams need large paper and plotting machines to print them. They can, like other diagrams, be designed to spread out vertically rather than horizontally so that they can be printed by personal computers or normal printers and can be put in three-ring binders rather than pinned on the wall.

Figure 3.13 shows a version of Fig. 3.12 designed for computer editing, layout, and routing of lines.

DATA-MODEL CHARTS

Whereas program structure diagrams and data flow diagrams can be modularized and nested, data models are more difficult to break into pieces. Figure 3.14 shows 16 entity types in a data model and the associations among them. A line with a bar means a one-with-one association, for example:

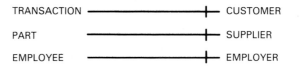

The line with a crow's foot means a one-with-many association, for example:

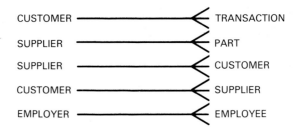

(We will expand on such cardinality symbols later.)

With this notation, a hierarchical structure of data is drawn with the crow's feet pointing down or to the right and the one-to-one bars pointing up or to the left, as shown in Fig. 3.15.

A tree structure like this works well for representing a file or a document. One can draw a purchase order or bank statement with a tree structure. However, it does not work by itself with data bases. The problem is apparent in Fig. 3.15. An order item is for a product. We would therefore like to draw a one-

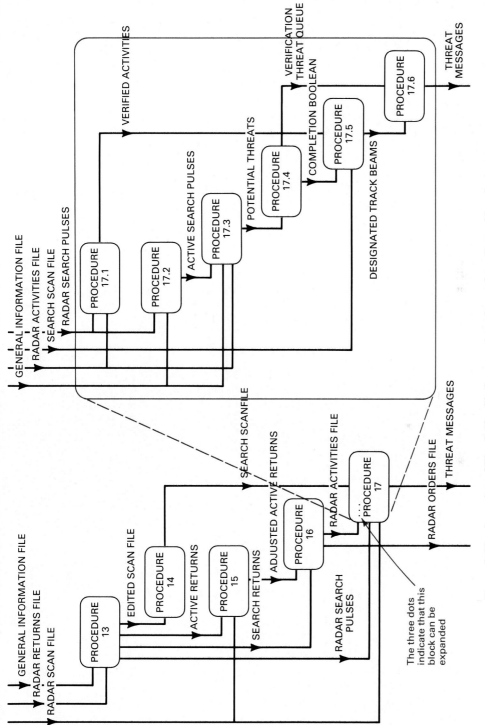

Figure 3.13 A version of Fig. 3.12 with the procedures boxes formally positioned. A computer can position the boxes and route the lines.

41

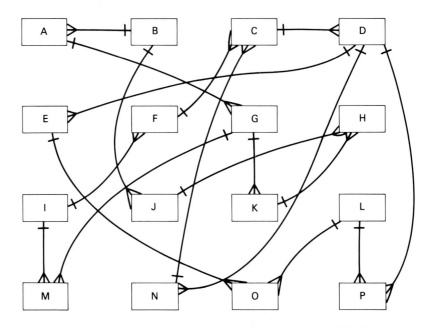

Figure 3.14   A data-model chart drawn in an unstructured fashion.

with-one link from ORDER ITEM to PRODUCT. We will do that, but then we no longer have a pure tree structure. Worse, a spare part *is* a product; it has a product number. We do not really want to regard it as a separate entity. Some PRODUCT records need to point to other PRODUCT records, indicating that the latter PRODUCT is a spare part for the former or that the former contains the latter. We can draw this by labeling two one-with-many links (or a many-with-many link) thus:

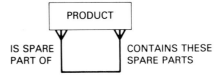

Figure 3.16 redraws the right-hand version of Fig. 3.15 to show these associations. Still more complications are introduced if we include customers in the diagram. (You might like to explore this.)

The data-base world, then, is full of constructs that cannot be drawn as pure tree structures. In drawing the associations among entity types, network structures like Fig. 3.14 grow up. A medium-sized corporation has many hundreds of entity types and needs to represent them in a data model. The data model cannot be nested simply like a data flow diagram, so how should we draw a king-sized version of Fig. 3.14? How can we make it clear and more structured?

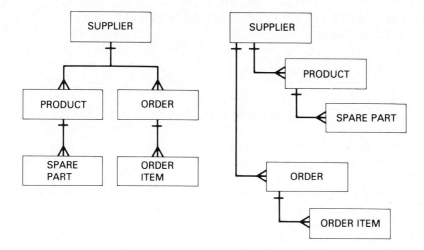

Figure 3.15   Hierarchical structures of data.

An important variant of the same question is: How can we structure it so that it can be drawn and manipulated by a computer?

ROOT NODES

We can describe certain nodes in a mesh-structured chart as *root* nodes. A tree has one root node. We draw it at the top or the left. A mesh structure has numerous root nodes. We can pull these also to the top or left. If we pull them to the top, we will end up

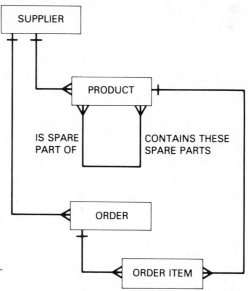

Figure 3.16   Figure 3.15 with associations between entities that are not hierarchical.

with a diagram that spreads out horizontally, which is difficult to print. So let us pull them to the left.

The root of a tree structure is the only node with no one-with-one links leaving it. This can be seen in Fig. 3.15. We can use the same rule for discovering the root nodes of a mesh structure. Figure 3.17 marks the root nodes of Fig. 3.14.

We could remove the root nodes and their links from Fig. 3.17 and again identify the roots in the remaining chart. We will call the original roots *depth 1* nodes, these second level roots *depth 2* nodes, and so on.

A *depth 2 node* can then be defined as a node that has a one-with-one link pointing to a depth 1 node. A *depth 3 node* can be defined as a node that has a one-with-one link pointing to a depth 2 node but no one-with-one link pointing to a depth 1 node. A *depth N node* $(N > 1)$ can be defined as a node with a one-with-one link pointing to a depth $(N - 1)$ node but no one-with-one link pointing to a lower depth node. Figure 3.18 shows the depth numbers of the nodes on the chart in Fig. 3.17.

The depth 1 nodes are then plotted on the left-hand side of the chart. The depth 2 nodes are offset by one offset distance. The depth N nodes are offset by $(N - 1)$ offset distances. The depth N node $(N > 1)$ is plotted underneath the depth $(N - 1)$ node to which it points. The nodes under one depth 1 node

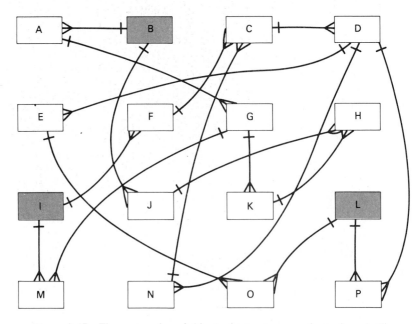

Figure 3.17   The root nodes of this mesh structure are shown in red. They are the nodes that have no one-with-one links to another node.

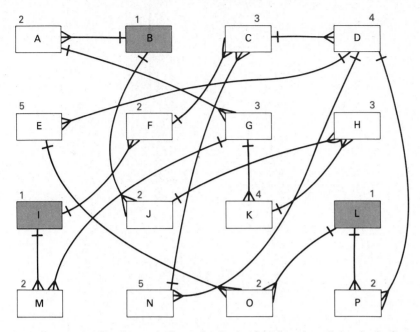

Figure 3.18 The figures indicate the depth of each node and are the basis for restructuring the diagram as shown in Figs. 3.19 and 3.20.

form a cluster. Arrows that span these clusters are drawn on the left of the chart, away from the clusters, as shown in Fig. 3.19, which redraws Fig. 3.14.

The redrawing of a chart such as Fig. 3.14 begins with the identification of the depth 1 nodes (no one-with-one links leaving them). Then the depth 2 nodes can be marked, then the depth 3 nodes, and so on until all the nodes have been given a depth number. The clusters under each root node are drawn, and the links spanning these clusters are added.

FIND THE TREES   Every mesh structure has little tree structures hidden in it. The process we have just performed might be called "find the trees." In Fig. 3.14, you cannot see the trees for the forest. We can extract the trees, draw them as in Fig. 3.20, and then complete the diagram by drawing the links that span the trees.

In some mesh structures, a choice of trees could be extracted. A level 2 node might have two level 1 parents, for example. We make a choice based on which is the most natural grouping or which is the most frequently traversed path. Usually the trees extracted from a mesh structure turn out to be items that belong together naturally. Drawing an entity chart, as in Fig. 3.20, clarifies these natural associations.

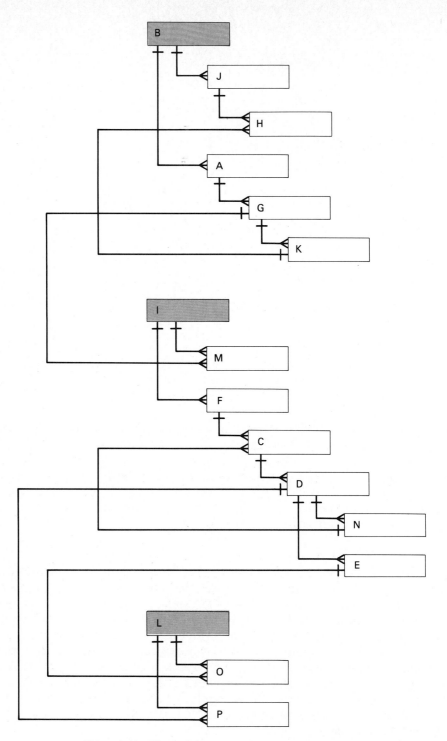

Figure 3.19 Figure 3.18 redrawn in a structured fashion.

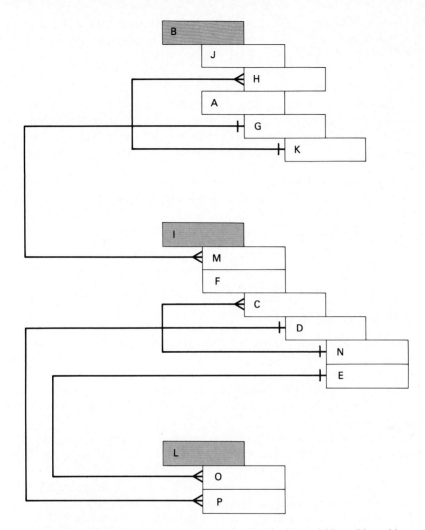

Figure 3.20   Figure 3.19 simplified by drawing its internal hierarchies without one-with-one links.

Fig. 3.20, like Figs. 3.8 and 3.13, is a well-structured version of a chart that was messier. It is designed for computerized drawing and modification and for an inexpensive desktop printer. Even though Fig. 3.20 looks relatively neat, an entity chart with hundreds of entities becomes complex, with too many lines to be easy to follow. Such a chart should be kept in a computer, and users should not normally see the whole chart. The computer presents them with a portion of the chart when they need it. Computerized extraction of subsets of large charts is extremely helpful.

LATERAL VERSUS HIERARCHICAL SUBDIVISION

In designing systems, we need to cope with diagrams that are too large and complex to be viewed at one time. The diagram has to be divided into pages or screens. This can be done in two ways, *laterally* and *hierarchically*.

In *lateral subdivision,* all pages show the same level. This is like a road atlas in which every page contains a map at 5 miles to the inch. On a computer screen, the user may pan across a large chart. (The movie director's words *pan* and *zoom* have come into our computer vocabulary.) The computer user may also skip among pages or "turn" pages.

Hierarchical subdivision is often more appropriate. A block on a high-level view can be expanded to show more detail. Figures 3.12 and 3.13 are illustrations of hierarchical subdivision. When a block is expanded into detail on a separate diagram, this diagram may show the shape of the parent and its title, as in Fig. 3.12.

EXPAND and CONTRACT

Using computer graphics, the analyst may point to a block and ask to see it in more detail. Conversely, the analyst may point to a group of blocks and shrink them to one block.

In Figs. 3.12 and 3.13, a block is exploded such that the resulting diagram is of the same form. We will refer to this as *expanding*. The converse process is called *contracting*.

The EXPAND and CONTRACT commands are very useful with graphics workstations. When a hierarchical diagram is used, the designer may point to a block and use the command CONTRACT. The lower blocks in the hierarchy disappear from the screen. The user may display them in their original form by pointing to the block in question and commanding EXPAND.

To tell the user that a block can be expanded, it should contain three dots in front of its text, as shown in Figs. 3.12 and 3.13. The three dots are placed there whenever other blocks are contracted into that block.

A hierarchical diagram (decomposition diagram, action diagram, decision tree) or a diagram containing subhierarchies (entity-relationship diagram, data analysis diagram, dialog design diagram) can be contracted by pointing to a parent block and saying CONTRACT. A mesh-structured diagram is more complex (dependency diagram, data flow diagram, state transition diagram). Here the user may point to several connected blocks and say CONTRACT.

Expanding is easy; the user points to any block containing three dots and orders EXPAND.

SHOW and HIDE

EXPAND refers to exploding a block into a diagram *of the same form*. It is also necessary to explode blocks into a different type of representation. For this command SHOW DETAIL is used. The converse command is HIDE DETAIL.

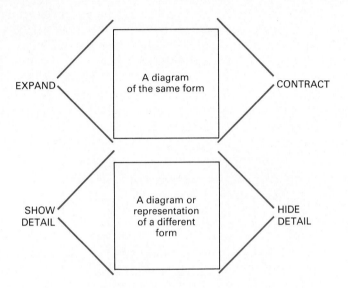

Here are some examples of SHOW DETAIL:

- Exploding a data box to show details of the data structure
- Exploding a relationship line between data boxes (entity types) to show details of the relationship
- Exploding a condition symbol to show details of the condition
- Exploding a derived data item to show the equation or procedure for deriving it

Figure 3.21 illustrates EXPAND; Fig. 3.22 illustrates SHOW DETAIL. These commands for exploding parts of diagrams are particularly effective on personal computers on which windowing mechanisms can enlarge a part of a diagram into a separate window.

OTHER WAYS TO MANIPULATE LARGE DIAGRAMS

Box 3.1 lists the techniques used for computer manipulation of large diagrams.

The term *zoom* refers to enlarging or shrinking

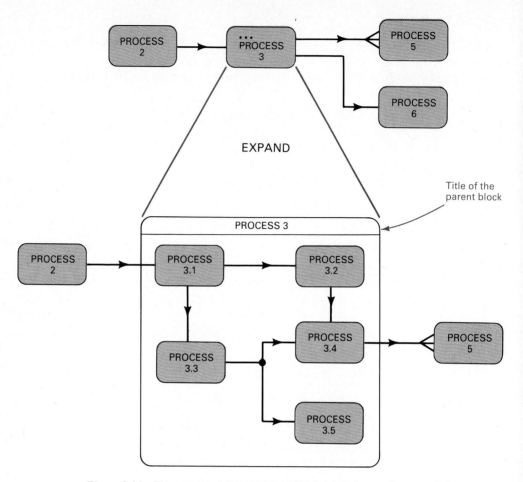

Figure 3.21 The command EXPAND explodes a box into a diagram *of the same type.* The converse command is CONTRACT.

a diagram within a window without otherwise changing the diagram, as with a zoom lens on a camera.

The term ZOOM AND CHANGE or ZOOM AND CLARIFY is abbreviated to ZOOC. When we zoom out of a complex diagram, the words often become too small to read. A zoom and clarify operation may retain certain words only and keep them large enough to read. For example, if we zoom out from a large tree structure, we may change the lettering so that only the higher-level nodes are labeled.

The terms NEST and DETAIL are used in Box 3.1, the first referring to expanding and contracting where the detailed diagram is *of the same form,* as in Fig. 3.13, and the latter referring to SHOW DETAIL and HIDE DETAIL where the detailed diagram is of a different form.

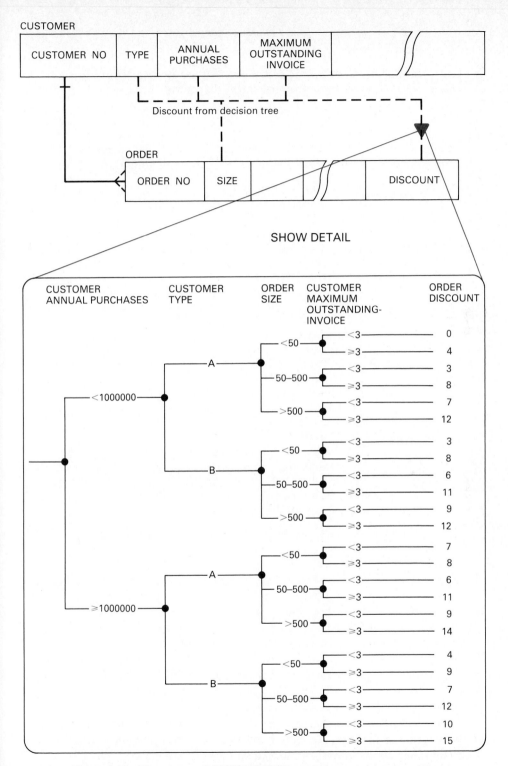

Figure 3.22 The command SHOW DETAIL explodes an icon *into a different form of representation*. Here the deviation of a field is shown as a decision tree. The converse command is HIDE DETAIL.

BOX 3.1   Commands and subcommands for computer manipulation of large diagrams

Large diagrams may be manipulated as follows. It is suggested that the command words be standardized on the diagramming tools.

- **Paging**   **LEFT, RIGHT, UP, DOWN, HOME, JUMP**
  Reveals a different page of a large diagram.

- **Scrolling** **SCROLL, CENTER**
  Moves across a diagram. Scrolling is best achieved with a mouse. If the user selects CENTER and points to a block, the diagram will be scrolled so that the block is at the center.

- **Zooming**   **ZOOM IN, ZOOM OUT, FULL ZOOM**
  Expands or shrinks the diagram without changing it. Full zoom shows the entire diagram shrunk to fit one screen.

- **Zoocing**   **ZOOC IN, ZOOC OUT, FULL ZOOC**
  Zooc stands for *zoom and change* or *zoom and clarify*. It expands or shrinks a diagram, like a zoom, but adjusts it for readability or clarification.

- **Nesting**   **EXPAND, CONTRACT**
  Changes to a more or less detailed diagram *of the same form*. For example, it may reveal blocks within blocks. Three dots will indicate that more detail is available.

- **Detailing** **SHOW, HIDE**
  Changes to a more or less detailed representation *of a different form*. Pointing to an icon and saying SHOW reveals detail about that icon that is in the encyclopedia. This may be shown in a separate window. It may be text, a table, or a different type of diagram.

COMPUTER MAGIC   Once we use a computer, all sorts of magic becomes possible in the manipulation of diagrams. A computer enables us to build big charts that it checks for consistency with a thoroughness far beyond that of most humans. We can see an overview—just the highest layer. We can drop down to detail, descending through numerous layers. The computer can add color to show items of different meaning. It can highlight whole areas of a chart. It can extend the brackets of Fig. 3.8 into boxes. It can show detailed program logic or code within any box we point to. It can explode portions of diagrams with several windows.

The diagramming technique may be designed so that humans draw relatively few lines when they do it by hand, but once the computer goes to work, it can dress up the diagrams to make them elegant and clear.

Some graphics software enables us to zoom in to a diagram. As we move the cursor to an item and zoom in, the diagram changes to show us more detail—and more, and more, until perhaps we reach the coding level. Similarly, we can zoom out to see the overview. In some cases, the diagram changes to another diagram of *similar* form; in other cases, it changes to a display of a *different* form. The user may point at objects and reveal their inner details.

Particularly important, a complex design can be represented by multiple types of diagrams. The information on these different diagrams can be linked and made consistent by the computer. A program or complex design cannot be fully represented by any one type of diagram. It needs multiple diagram types linked together.

The designer can duplicate and change procedures or code. He can cut and paste. He may assign different colors to different parts of his design to help him keep track of complex structures.

When we change an item on a computerized chart, we may have to change other items to keep the chart consistent. The software should point out all such consequential changes and insist that they be completed. In some cases, it can make the consequential changes automatically.

The graphic symbols can have logic associated with them so that when one change is made, consequential changes occur. If a box is moved, the lines and arrows connected to that box follow it. If a box or other symbol is connected illegally or in a way that raises questions, the designer is warned. The designer can quickly reorganize the diagram and have the computer reconnect it correctly.

The designer is provided with advice, menus, guidelines, or other design aids. These may appear automatically, or the designer may call them up when he wants them. When computer graphics are employed, the diagramming technique needs to be designed so that the computer can give the maximum help. It may guide the designer through a complex procedure. It may apply rules as in an expert system.

SYMBOLS WITH OBVIOUS MEANING

It is desirable that the symbols and constructs on a diagram have obvious meaning, as far as possible. For example, a diagram showing the components of a process must show *selection* and *repetition*. Some diagramming techniques do not show these. Some show them with symbols that are not obvious in meaning. With Michael Jackson diagramming, an asterisk (*) drawn in the top right-hand corner of a block means repetition, and a circle (○) means selection. In Fig. 3.23, for example, one of the blocks marked with a circle is selected. The block PRINT BUZZWORDS, marked with an asterisk, is repeated several times.

Unless a key is written on the diagram, it would not be clear to an uninitiated reader what the ○ and * mean. People who once learned to read these charts forget the meaning of the ○ and * and would forget the meaning of other abstract symbols or mnemonics.

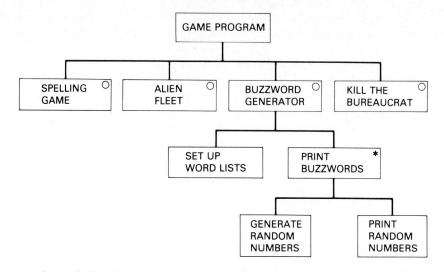

Figure 3.23 The ○ and * in the top right-hand corner of blocks on charts such as this do not have obvious meaning. The form of the diagram should be selected to make the meaning as obvious as possible to relatively uninitiated readers.

A mapmaker has the same problem. He chooses symbols that are as obvious in meaning as possible, such as these:

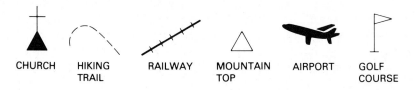

CHURCH   HIKING TRAIL   RAILWAY   MOUNTAIN TOP   AIRPORT   GOLF COURSE

In addition, just to be sure, he puts a key on the diagram explaining the symbols.

A memorable means of illustrating repetition is to use a double line, double box, or double arrowhead. This is done in music. A double line in a score means repetition:

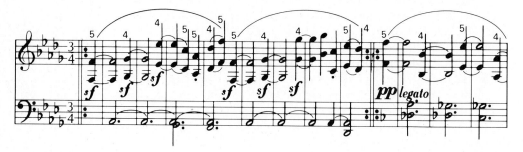

In structured diagrams, a double block or double line at the head of a bracket could mean that that block or bracket is repeated:

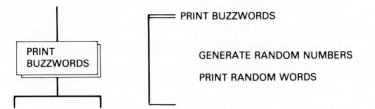

A memorable way of illustrating selection is to use a subdivided bracket:

```
┌──────── SPELLING GAME
│         ---------
│         ---------
├──────── ALIEN FLEET
│         ---------
│         ---------
├──────── BUZZWORD GENERATOR
│         ---------
│         ---------
├──────── KILL THE BUREAUCRAT
│         ---------
└         ---------
```

In this bracket, one of the four items is performed, whereas in a nonsubdivided bracket, everything is performed.

```
┌
│   PRINT REPORT HEADER
│   PRINT REPORT BODY
│   PRINT TOTALS
│   PRINT STATISTICS
└
```

If a block or bracket is conditional, it is not enough to write a condition symbol, as with some diagramming methods. The bracket should be able to show the nature of the condition:

```
┌── IF C1
│   PROCESS ACTIVE RETURNS
│   DETERMINE POTENTIAL LIABILITIES
└
```

or

```
┌── IF STOCK < 500
│   PERFORM REORDER
└
```

SUMMARY   Box 3.2 summarizes characteristics that are desirable
                               in diagramming techniques.

BOX 3.2   Summary of good diagramming techniques

Good diagramming techniques should be all of the following.

An Aid to Clear Thinking

Good diagrams help people to understand complex ideas. A diagramming notation should be designed to help thinking and communication and for computer-aided thinking. The diagrams should be an aid to teaching computer methods.

Easy to Understand

The diagrams should use constructs that are obvious in meaning and as familiar as possible. They should avoid mnemonics and symbols that are not explained on the diagram or with immediately available keys.

An Aid to End-User Communication

End users should be able to learn to read, critique, and draw the diagrams quickly, so that the diagrams form a good basis for communication between users and DP professionals.

Meaningful

It is the meaning rather than the graphic image that is valuable. The meaning should be encoded in an encyclopedia from which one or more types of diagrams can be generated. The encyclopedia will often store more information than is visible on the screen. It may be displayed by pointing to an icon and saying SHOW.

A Basis for Program Code Generation

It should be possible to generate code from the diagrams along with tools such as dictionaries, report formatters, and screen pointers. To achieve this, the diagrams must be more complete and rigorous than the diagrams of the first generation of structured techniques.

BOX 3.2 *(Continued)*

Printable on Normal-Sized Paper

Wall charts of vast size are to be avoided because they inhibit change and portability. Diagrams should be subdividable into normal-sized pages. They may be designed to spread out vertically on fan-fold paper.

Subsettable

Complex diagrams should be subsettable so that they can be subdivided into easy-to-understand components. The user should be able to extract easy-to-use subsets at a computer screen.

Navigable

The user should be able to navigate easily around complex diagrams, changing their representation, if necessary, with the techniques, such as PAGE, SCROLL, ZOOM, ZOOC, NEST, EXPAND, and SHOW, listed in Box 3.1.

Designed for Minimum Searching

A user should be able to find information with as little searching as possible. Close related information should be close together on the diagram to minimize page turning, interscreen navigation, and the following of lengthy lines.

Decomposable Into Detail

A simple overview diagram should be decomposable into successively finer levels of detail. Where possible, the detail diagram should be of the same form as the higher-level diagram. The decomposition may proceed until appropriately diagrammed program code is reached.

Designed for Screen Manipulation

The diagrams should be designed to be manipulated easily and powerfully on a workstation screen (preferably a personal computer).

(Continued)

BOX 3.2 *(Continued)*

Designed for Computer-Aided Thinking

A computer can give a designer much help in stepping through the design, using data correctly, using library functions, design verification, and so on. The computer-aided design technique should help the designer's thinking as much as possible.

Easy to Draw by Hand

Automation will not completely replace sheets of paper. The diagramming technique should facilitate quick sketching by hand with a template. Machine-drawn versions of the diagrams may improve on the hand-drawn versions by using color, shading, library techniques, motion, and computer manipulation.

Drawable on Cheap Printers

The diagrams should be drawable with desktop dot-matrix printers. A variant of the diagrams should be printable with the ASCII character set so that a mainframe line printer can print them. The ASCII variant may be relatively crude and may modify some of the conventions slightly. The need for ASCII printing should not prevent the use of well-human-factored icons and style on dot-matrix printers.

Designed With Minimum Types of Symbols

The number of graphic symbols a user must understand should be minimized. Each underlying idea should be represented by a single symbol, not by different symbols in different places. (There may have to be variations of a symbol to suit different printers or display devices.)

Assertive

The presence of a graphic symbol should denote the presence of some knowledge; the absence of the symbol should denote the lack of that knowledge. For example, the absence of a mark on a line should not denote meaning about that line (such as a one-to-one association between the blocks linked by the line). Following this principle permits a type of subsetting: producing a diagram in which some symbols are omitted in order to highlight others or to avoid clutter or to produce an overview diagram.

BOX 3.2 *(Continued)*

Based on Clear Visual Logic

There is a visual logic that makes some ways of depicting an idea better than others. Diagrams should make abstract ideas concrete by using images and spatial sense to capture ideas as logically as possible. For example, arrows should represent flow or sequence, as this is intuitively clear, but a different symbol should represent cardinality.

Logical, Not Decorative

The use of decoration that does not enhance visual logic should be avoided. The instinct to be artistic must be suppressed and replaced with an urge to maximize clarity.

Readable Using English
(Human-Language) Sentences

The symbols on a link or bracket should translate as directly as possible into a clear human-language sentence: for example:

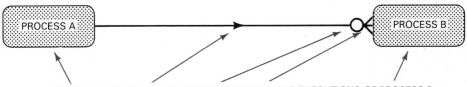

PROCESS A IS-FOLLOWED-BY ZERO, ONE-OR-MORE EXECUTIONS-OF PROCESS B

Able to Support Different Ways of
Thinking With Consistent Symbols

Different styles of diagram are appropriate for different aspects of system design. Decision trees are appropriate for certain situations, data flow diagrams for others, decomposition diagrams for others, and so on. A common family of symbols should support the different ways of thinking about systems, data, and logic.

Automatically Convertible

It is sometimes useful to convert one style of representation (one view of the world) into another. For example, decision trees, dependency diagrams, or data navigation diagrams can be converted to action diagrams. The diagramming technique should be designed so

(Continued)

BOX 3.2   *(Continued)*

that the conversion can be done by computer. The user may employ windows on a workstation screen showing the alternate representations. Different types of representations often need to be linked to represent an overall system design.

Methodologically Sound

Diagramming techniques are a visual representation of underlying methodologies. The methodologies need to be sound and to represent the most useful concepts of data analysis, structured techniques, and code generation.

4 THREE SPECIES OF DECOMPOSITION

Most structured design employs a form of decomposition. A high-level function is decomposed into lower-level functions; these are decomposed further; and so on. A tree structure shows the decomposition.

Decomposition is used with all four levels of activities: business functions, processes, procedures, and program modules.

LEVELS OF THOROUGHNESS IN DECOMPOSITION   There are three different categories of decomposition—three separate *species,* as a botanist would say about trees.

Species I

The most common type of decomposition is a tree structure, which relates to activities and not to the data which those activities use.

Species II

The second species shows the data types that are input and output to each activity. This can be much more thorough, because if it is handled by computer, the machine can check that the data consumed and produced by each node are consistent throughout the entire structure.

Species III

The third species is still more thorough. It allows only certain types of decomposition that have to obey precise rules that are defined by mathematical axioms. The resulting structure can then be completely verified to ensure that it is internally consistent and correct.

I advocate thoroughness, not just because we want to avoid errors in program specifications but also because the thorough techniques have proved in

practice to save much time and money in the long run. The thorough techniques
will lead to a higher level of automation.

DECOMPOSITION   The first species of decomposition is appropriate for
OF CORPORATE   showing the structure of a corporation. A tree-struc-
ACTIVITIES   tured chart is used to show the organization, as in
                       Fig. 4.1.

Individual divisions or units, such as CATV Bureau in Fig. 4.1, may be subdivided to show their *functional areas*. Functional areas refer to the major areas
of activity; in a corporation, they might be engineering, marketing, production,
research, and distribution.

Functions and Processes

In representing the functions and processes of a corporation, it is desirable that
they be analyzed independently of the corporate organization. The corporate
organization into divisions and departments changes periodically, but the same
fundamental functions and processes must be carried out.

    A business function is a group of activities that together support one aspect
of furthering the mission of the enterprise. They have names that are nouns or
gerunds (ending in *-ing*), for example, *purchasing, receiving, financial planning*. Figure 4.2 shows typical functional areas and functions.

    The functions can be decomposed into *processes*. A process is a specified
business activity that can be described in terms of the inputs and outputs that

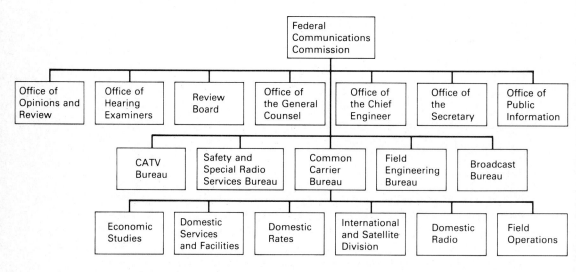

Figure 4.1   A chart decomposing an organization into its component bodies.

FUNCTIONAL AREAS	FUNCTIONS
PLANNING	MARKET ANALYSIS FINANCIAL ANALYSIS BUDGETING FORECASTING
MATERIALS	PURCHASING RECEIVING MATERIALS PLANNING QUALITY CONTROL
ACCOUNTING	CREDITORS AND DEBTORS COST ACCOUNTING CASH FLOW PROFITABILITY ANALYSIS GENERAL ACCOUNTING FUNDS MANAGEMENT
SALES	TERRITORY MANAGEMENT SELLING SALES ADMINISTRATION CUSTOMER RELATIONS

Figure 4.2   Functions and functional areas—the concern of the top level of the pyramids in Figs. 2.2 through 2.5. Functions are further decomposed into processes as in Fig. 4.3.

result from the process. A process describes *what* is accomplished, not *how* it is performed. The name of a process should be an action verb, such as:

- Create purchase requisition
- Select supplier
- Follow up order
- Calculate accounts payable summary
- Analyze supplier performance

Figure 4.3 shows functions decomposed into processes and some processes decomposed into lower-level processes.

A major area of a corporation may have hundreds of processes, with many divided into lower-level processes. The chart showing this hierarchy needs to be drawn vertically, as in Fig. 4.3, rather than horizontally, as in Fig. 4.1.

Analysis of the functions in an enterprise takes place at the top layer of the pyramid figure (see Figs. 2.2 and 2.3). The second layer of the pyramid is concerned with more detailed decomposition into processes and analysis of dependencies among processes.

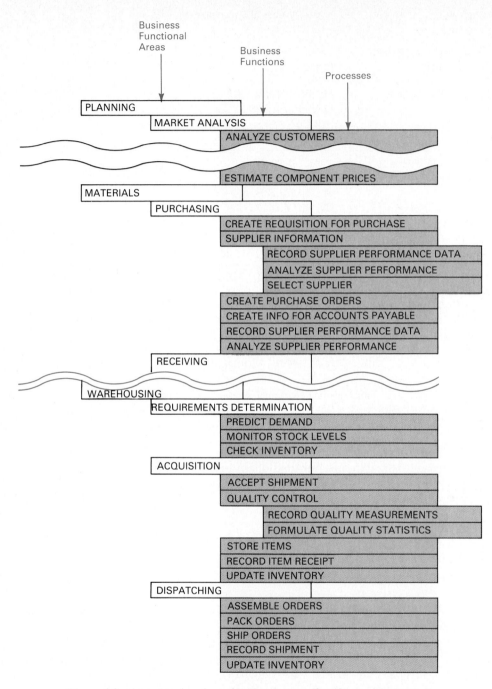

Business
Functional
Areas

Business
Functions

Processes

PLANNING
MARKET ANALYSIS
ANALYZE CUSTOMERS

ESTIMATE COMPONENT PRICES

MATERIALS
PURCHASING
CREATE REQUISITION FOR PURCHASE
SUPPLIER INFORMATION
RECORD SUPPLIER PERFORMANCE DATA
ANALYZE SUPPLIER PERFORMANCE
SELECT SUPPLIER
CREATE PURCHASE ORDERS
CREATE INFO FOR ACCOUNTS PAYABLE
RECORD SUPPLIER PERFORMANCE DATA
ANALYZE SUPPLIER PERFORMANCE

RECEIVING

WAREHOUSING
REQUIREMENTS DETERMINATION
PREDICT DEMAND
MONITOR STOCK LEVELS
CHECK INVENTORY
ACQUISITION
ACCEPT SHIPMENT
QUALITY CONTROL
RECORD QUALITY MEASUREMENTS
FORMULATE QUALITY STATISTICS
STORE ITEMS
RECORD ITEM RECEIPT
UPDATE INVENTORY
DISPATCHING
ASSEMBLE ORDERS
PACK ORDERS
SHIP ORDERS
RECORD SHIPMENT
UPDATE INVENTORY

Figure 4.3 An enterprise chart: functional areas, functions, and processes. The name of a process should normally begin with a verb. Procedures (not necessarily computerized) are designed to implement the processes.

Procedures and Program Modules

Processes, needed to run an enterprise, may be mapped into procedures that are designed to show *how* the processes are carried out. Procedures may be further decomposed into subprocedures and program modules. Program modules themselves are hierarchically decomposed into submodules. Figure 4.4 shows this ongoing decomposition from functional areas to business functions to processes to procedures to program modules.

　　Usually, however, the mapping from processes to procedures is not as direct and simple as suggested by Fig. 4.4. Decomposition into processes (level 2 of the pyramid charts) is intended to analyze *what happens* in an enterprise. The procedures level (level 3 of the pyramid charts) is intended to design procedures (automated where appropriate) *to make the business operate*. There is not always a direct correspondence between processes and procedures. Some processes are accomplished by means of a subordinate group of procedures, but sometimes there is no such clean decomposition.

　　Species I decomposition is a widely used tool for analysis and design at all four levels of the pyramid diagram. Functions are decomposed into processes, processes into subprocesses, processes into procedures, where this is appropriate (sometimes it is not). Procedures are decomposed hierarchically and eventually decomposed into program modules (level 4 of the pyramid charts). Simple decomposition is a common form of program design.

　　Box 4.1 summarizes the definitions of activities, business functions, processes, procedures and program modules.

SPECIES II DECOMPOSITION

Now let us look at the second species of decomposition, that in which the activities are related to the data they use.

A function in computing is an algorithm that takes certain inputs and produces certain outputs. We represent it mathematically as:

$$y = F(x)$$

where

> F is the function
> x is the input(s)
> y is the output(s)

(Species I decomposition, the basis of much "structured design," does not take the inputs and outputs into consideration.)

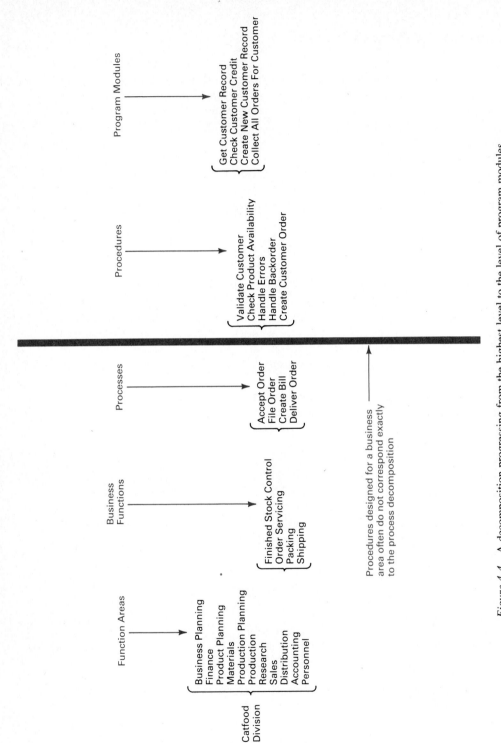

Figure 4.4 A decomposition progressing from the highest level to the level of program modules. This type of diagram shows insufficient detail at the procedure level.

processes, procedures, and program modules

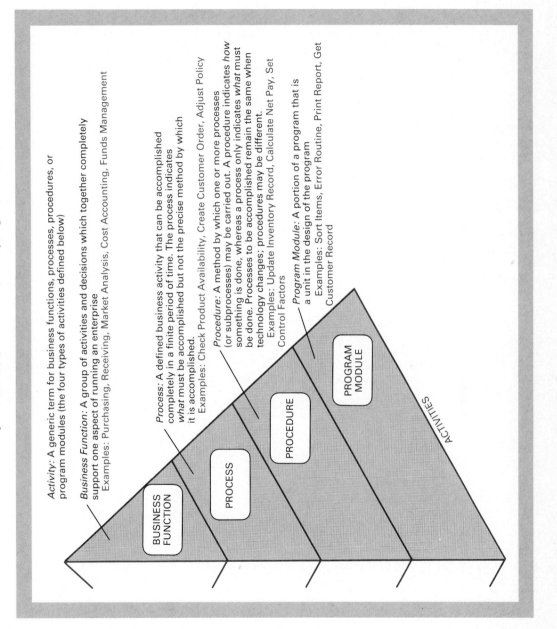

Activity: A generic term for business functions, processes, procedures, or program modules (the four types of activities defined below)

Business Function: A group of activities and decisions which together completely support one aspect of running an enterprise
Examples: Purchasing, Receiving, Market Analysis, Cost Accounting, Funds Management

Process: A defined business activity that can be accomplished completely in a finite period of time. The process indicates *what* must be accomplished but not the precise method by which it is accomplished.
Examples: Check Product Availability, Create Customer Order, Adjust Policy

Procedure: A method by which one or more processes (or subprocesses) may be carried out. A procedure indicates *how* something is done, whereas a process only indicates *what* must be done. Processes to be accomplished remain the same when technology changes; procedures may be different.
Examples: Update Inventory Record, Calculate Net Pay, Set Control Factors

Program Module: A portion of a program that is a unit in the design of the program
Examples: Sort Items, Error Routine, Print Report, Get Customer Record

BUSINESS FUNCTION

PROCESS

PROCEDURE

PROGRAM MODULE

ACTIVITIES

We could draw the function $y = F(x)$ as follows:

The variable x is the input to an activity block, labeled F, which produces an output y. This type of diagram is the basis of the HOS notation we will discuss later. It relates neatly to mathematical notation but seems unnatural to the uninitiated because the input is on the right rather than the left. It tends to lead to charts that are wide horizontally and thus difficult to print and manipulate. For most people, it seems more natural to use a vertical drawing with the input at the top and the output at the bottom:

In Chapter 3 we advocated drawing a tree structure with square brackets when designing programs. Figure 4.5 shows the right-hand part of Fig. 4.4 drawn in this way.

We can extend these brackets into a rectangle and show the data they use.

Figure 4.5 A hierarchical decomposition of the procedure VALIDATE CUSTOMER. Figure 4.6 extends this diagram to show the data used.

This is done in Fig. 4.6; the input data of each function are written at its top right corner, and the output at its bottom right corner.

CHECKING THE USE OF DATA

We can now apply some checks. We can check that the inputs to VALIDATE CUSTOMER are all used by its internal blocks and that its outputs all come from its internal blocks. We can check that no internal block uses data that do not originate somewhere, and no internal block produces data that do not go anywhere. Figure 4.7 uses arrows to show the passage of data among the functions.

Now let us work our way one step further up the tree and show ORDER SERVICING, or at least the part of it represented by the three rightmost brackets of Fig. 4.4. Figure 4.8 shows this.

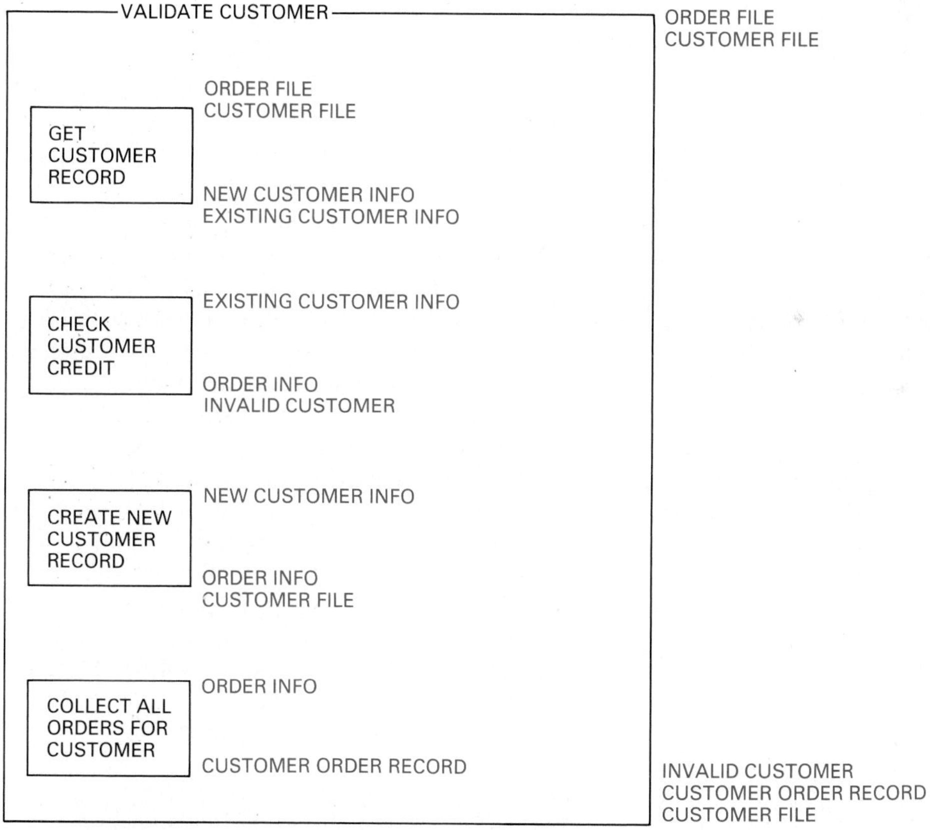

Figure 4.6 The hierarchy of Fig. 4.5 drawn to show the data inputs (top right corners) and outputs (bottom right corners).

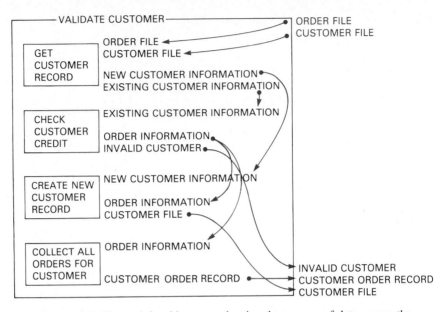

Figure 4.7   Figure 4.6, with arrows showing the passage of data among the procedures. Figure 4.5 is the left-hand part of this diagram.

By checking all the transfers of data, we can be much more thorough than with simple decomposition. The chart, however, has become complex, and we have decomposed only one of the four blocks in ORDER SERVICING and within that only one of the five blocks in ACCEPT ORDER. If we decomposed all of the blocks to the same level, the chart would be about 20 times as large and complex. Getting it correct would strain the patience of a monk.

However, failing to get it correct is expensive. It means that our specifications are wrong. It is enormously cheaper to find errors at the specification stage than after the programmers have written code.

Full expansion and checking of the blocks in Fig. 4.8 requires a computer. The analysts should be able to build up the diagram a step at a time, usually working from the highest level. They are likely to start with species I decomposition of processes and then add the data as they begin to design procedures. At the lower levels, they will discover more details about the data required, and these details need to be reflected upward to the top. The computer can check the consistency and completeness of all the data transfers.

PROCEDURE DECOMPOSITION AND DATA FLOW DIAGRAMS

Figure 4.8 shows the same information as the data flow diagrams of Chapter 3. A decomposition chart can be converted into a data flow diagram, and vice versa.

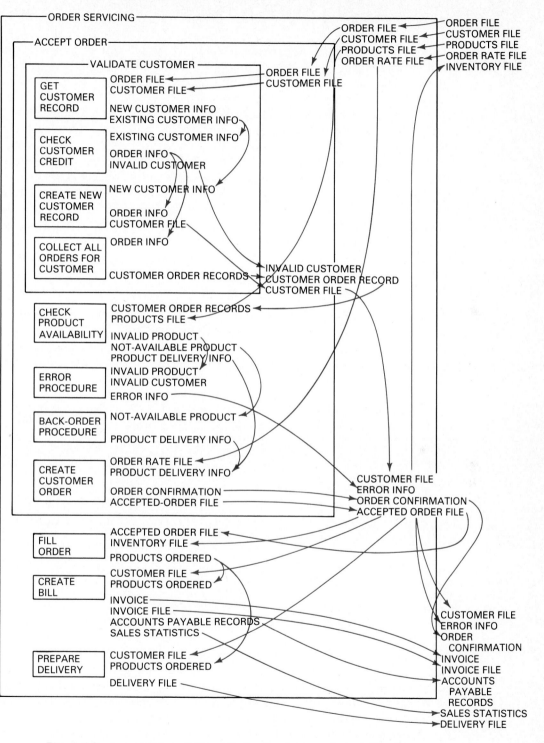

Figure 4.8 An expansion of Fig. 4.7 showing the procedures at the three right-hand levels of Fig. 4.4.

For some situations, it is easier to think of system activities in terms of data flow. For others, it is easier to think of it in terms of decomposition. Both of these, when carried through to the level needed for program design, become detailed, like Fig. 4.8 with 20 times as many blocks. Both therefore need computerized representation and checking. What is needed is a computer graphics tool that can relate the two and help the analysts fill in the detail without inconsistencies.

Data flow diagrams tend to be more useful for showing the flow of documents in an organization or the way one business event triggers other events. They give a pictorial representation of the movement of tangible data, to which the end users can relate and be trained to draw and check. As systems analysis moves to the more detailed task of program design, hierarchical structures are more useful. Hierarchical structures will be converted into program code, as we will see later.

SPECIES III
DECOMPOSITION

With decomposition as normally practiced, we can decompose an activity in any way that comes into our head. The third and most rigorous species of decomposition allows us to decompose only in certain ways, and these are defined with mathematically precise axioms.

In Fig. 4.7, for example, we have more than one type of decomposition. The first block of VALIDATE CUSTOMER is GET CUSTOMER RECORD. This is *always* performed. The second and third blocks are CHECK CUSTOMER CREDIT and CREATE NEW CUSTOMER. *Only one of these two is performed*. Which one depends on whether the order is from a new customer or an existing customer.

The originators of the HOS methodology [1, 2] concluded that *all* decomposition can be divided into *binary* decompositions. The parent provides the input data for its binary children and receives the output. Three types of binary decomposition (Fig. 4.9) are needed:

1. *Sequential*. The first activity is executed. Its results pass to the second activity, which is then executed.

2. *Independent*. Both activities are executed independently.

3. *Alternate*. *Either* the first activity *or* the second activity is executed.

Using these three binary primitives, they discovered that they could keep decomposing until program code could be generated automatically. Each binary decomposition follows rigorous mathematical axioms that enforce correctness so that the entire resulting structure can be proved to be internally correct. We thus have automatic generation of bug-free code [1].

The problem with this is that binary decompositions are so small that the

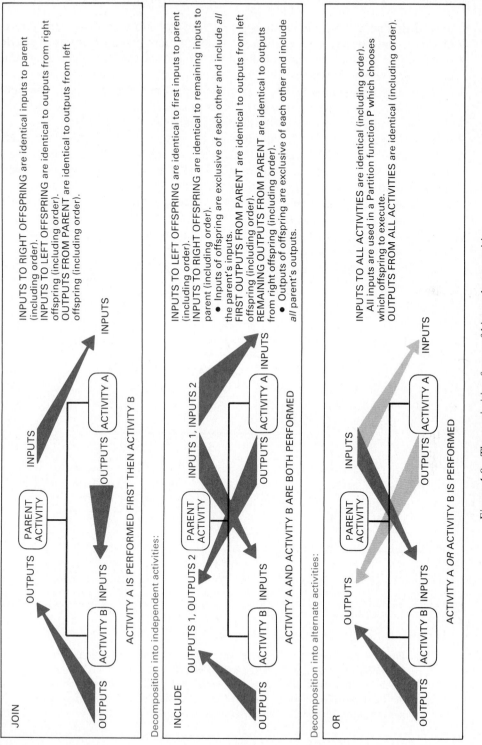

Decomposition into sequential activities:

JOIN

INPUTS TO RIGHT OFFSPRING are identical inputs to parent (including order).
INPUTS TO LEFT OFFSPRING are identical to outputs from right offspring (including order).
OUTPUTS FROM PARENT are identical to outputs from left offspring (including order).

ACTIVITY A IS PERFORMED FIRST THEN ACTIVITY B

Decomposition into independent activities:

INCLUDE

INPUTS TO LEFT OFFSPRING are identical to first inputs to parent (including order).
INPUTS TO RIGHT OFFSPRING are identical to remaining inputs to parent (including order).
● Inputs of offspring are exclusive of each other and include *all* the parent's inputs.
FIRST OUTPUTS FROM PARENT are identical to outputs from left offspring (including order).
REMAINING OUTPUTS FROM PARENT are identical to outputs from right offspring (including order).
● Outputs of offspring are exclusive of each other and include *all* parent's outputs.

ACTIVITY A AND ACTIVITY B ARE BOTH PERFORMED

Decomposition into alternate activities:

OR

INPUTS TO ALL ACTIVITIES are identical (including order).
All inputs are used in a Partition function P which chooses which offspring to execute.
OUTPUTS FROM ALL ACTIVITIES are identical (including order).

ACTIVITY A *OR* ACTIVITY B IS PERFORMED

Figure 4.9 Three primitive forms of binary decomposition.

overall design task is tedious. It is like trying to build a complex structure out of small Lego pieces. The solution is to design more powerful forms of decomposition that are themselves built from the primitives and are hence completely checkable. This is rather like building macroinstructions in programming.

Figures 4.10 and 4.11 show examples of HOS decomposition. The inputs to each block are on its right and the outputs are on its left.

This more precise form of decomposition has several effects. First, it is built in a computer-assisted fashion, step by step, with the computer checking for syntax errors and periodically analyzing the chart to detect any errors in decomposition or use of data. Appropriately skilled analysts can create complex specifications much more quickly than with hand drawing.

Second, the specification that results is free of internal errors, ambiguities, omissions, and inconsistencies.

Third, the decomposition can be continued to a level of detail from which bug-free code is generated automatically.

Fourth, when changes have to be made, they are made on the terminal screen, and all the consequential changes that should result from any modifica-

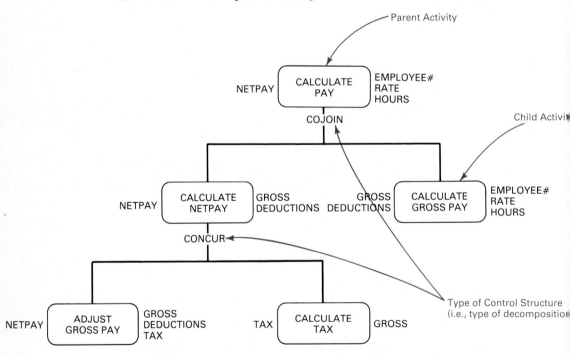

Figure 4.10 Decomposition done with HOS. Each decomposition must be of a defined type (such as COJOIN and CONCUR in this diagram) that obeys precise mathematical rules. The input variables to each activity are shown to the right and the output variables to the left. (A clearer drawing format is needed than that used in today's HOS charts.)

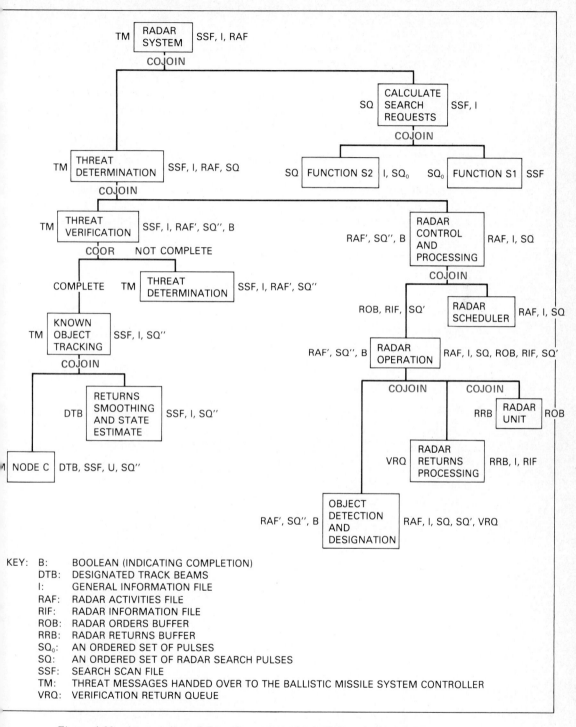

Figure 4.11 An overview of the radar system of a ballistic missile defense system, done with species III decomposition, which gives axiomatic checking of the decomposition [3, 4].

tion are indicated. The program can then be regenerated. Maintenance, in other words, is easier and faster.

Fifth, the technique seems alien and sometimes difficult to many traditional analysts and programmers. Bright analysts and new graduates often learn it very quickly, but much retraining is needed if a large DP team is to adopt it.

COMMENTARY   When the systems analysis profession has matured beyond its present stage, I expect that most decomposition will progress to species II, with data usage being represented and analyzed with computerized tools. Much will progress to species III, with axiomatic control of the decomposition. Species III decomposition will probably progress far beyond that of HOS today, with a powerful library of tools and predesigned control structures.

REFERENCES

1. Details available from Higher Order Software, Inc., Cambridge, Mass. The software tool USE.IT automates this methodology.

2. J. Martin, *System Design from Provably Correct Constructs*. Englewood Cliffs, N.J.: Prentice-Hall, 1985.

3. W.R. Hackler and A. Samarov, *An AXES Specification of a Radar Scheduler* (Technical Report No. 23). Cambridge, Mass.: Higher Order Software, Inc., 1979.

4. W.R. Hackler, *An AXES Specification of a Radar Scheduler* (Proceedings of the Fourteenth Hawaii International Conference on System Sciences, vol. 1). Honolulu: Western Periodicals Company, 1981.

5   A CONSISTENT DIAGRAMMING NOTATION

I have stressed that an enterprise should establish a set of standards for data processing diagrams. The standards should be the basis of the training given both to data processing professionals and to end users. Enterprisewide standards are essential for communication among persons involved with computers, for establishing corporate or interdepartmental data models and procedures, and for managing the move into computer-aided design (CAD/CAP, CASA/CAP, or whatever is the favored acronym).

Many corporations have adopted diagramming conventions from methodologies of the past that today are inadequate because they are narrowly focused, ill structured, ignorant of data-base techniques, unaware of fourth-generation languages, too difficult to teach to end users, clumsy and time-consuming, inadequate for automation, or, as is usually the case, incapable of tackling problems in their entirety.

This chapter summarizes the constructs we need to be able to draw. Similar constructs are needed on many different types of diagrams. A consistently drawn set of constructs can be used on the following basic tools:

- Decomposition diagrams (Chapter 7)
- Dependency diagrams (Chapter 8)
- Data flow diagrams (Chapter 9)
- Action diagrams (Chapter 6)
- Program structure diagrams for which we employ action diagrams (Chapter 6)
- Data analysis diagrams (Chapter 10)
- Data structure diagrams (Chapter 10)
- Entity-relationship diagrams (Chapter 11)
- Data navigation diagrams (Chapter 12)
- Decision trees and tables (Chapter 14)

- State transition diagrams and tables (Chapter 15)
- Dialog design diagrams (Chapter 16)

This chapter discusses the constructs and how they are drawn. These constructs will appear in various types of diagrams in subsequent chapters.

Box 5.1 lists principles that should apply to diagramming standards.

Figure 5.1 shows the family of icons used throughout the standards.

STRUCTURED PROGRAM DESIGN Structured programs are organized hierarchically. There is only one root module. Execution must begin with this root module. Any module can pass control to a module at the next lower level in the hierarchy—a parent module passes control to a child module. Program control enters a module at its entry point and must leave at its exit point. Control returns to the invoking (parent) module when the invoked (child) module completes execution.

A tree-structured diagram is used to draw the program modules that obey this orderly set of rules. As we saw in Chapter 4, tree structures can be drawn in various ways. It is common to draw them as a set of blocks with the root block at the top and each parent above its children. A neater way to show the flow of control is to draw them with brackets. Children are within, and to the right of, their parent bracket:

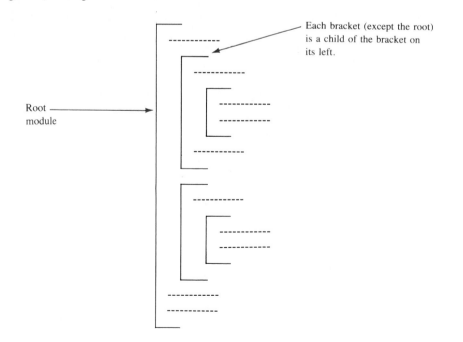

**BOX 5.1　Principles that should apply
to diagramming standards**

1. PRINCIPLES OF DIAGRAMMING STANDARDS

- Analysts, programmers, and end users should be provided with a set of diagramming techniques that are aids to clear thinking about different aspects of analysis, design, and programming.
- The various diagramming tools should use the minimum number of icon types.
- They should be as easy to learn as possible.
- Conversion between diagrams should be automatic whenever possible.
- The diagramming techniques should be a corporatewide standard, firmly adhered to.

2. AUTOMATION OF DIAGRAMMING

- The diagrams should be the basis of computer-aided system analysis and computer-aided programming (CASA/CAP).
- Higher-level design diagrams should convert automatically to action diagrams where relevant.
- The family of diagrams should be a basis for code generation.
- The diagrams should be easy to change and file at the computer screen.
- The diagrams should relate to data models.
- The diagrams convey *meaning,* which is stored in a system encyclopedia. The encyclopedia often stores more detail than is shown on any one screen.
- One design or program often needs more than one type of diagram. The associated diagrams should appear in windows and be linked visually.
- The diagrams and associated encyclopedia should constitute the system documentation.

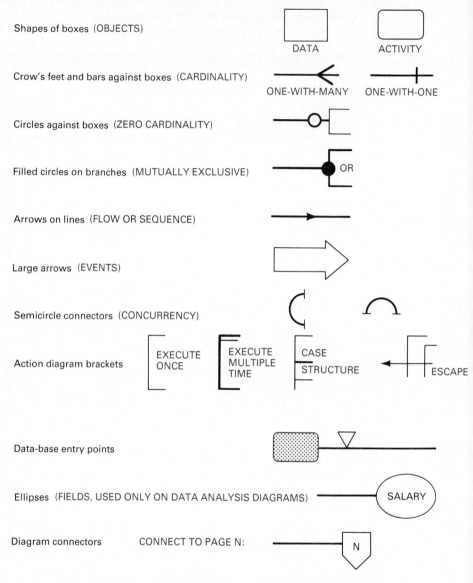

Shapes of boxes (OBJECTS)   DATA   ACTIVITY

Crow's feet and bars against boxes (CARDINALITY)   ONE-WITH-MANY   ONE-WITH-ONE

Circles against boxes (ZERO CARDINALITY)

Filled circles on branches (MUTUALLY EXCLUSIVE)   OR

Arrows on lines (FLOW OR SEQUENCE)

Large arrows (EVENTS)

Semicircle connectors (CONCURRENCY)

Action diagram brackets   EXECUTE ONCE   EXECUTE MULTIPLE TIME   CASE STRUCTURE   ESCAPE

Data-base entry points

Ellipses (FIELDS, USED ONLY ON DATA ANALYSIS DIAGRAMS)   SALARY

Diagram connectors   CONNECT TO PAGE N: N

Figure 5.1   The symbols used on many different types of diagrams.

In creating structured programs, four basic constructs are used.

- SEQUENCE   Items are executed in the stated sequence.
- CONDITION   A set of operations is executed only if a stated condition applies.
- CASE   One of several alternate sets of operations is executed.

- REPETITION   A set of operations is repeated, the repetition being terminated on the basis of a stated test. There are two types of repetition control. In one (DO WHILE), the termination test is applied *before* the set of operations is executed; in the other (DO UNTIL), the terminated test is applied *after* the set of operations is executed.

Amazingly, some of the diagramming techniques used for representing structured programs cannot show these four basic constructs.

The four constructs can be shown very simply with brackets:

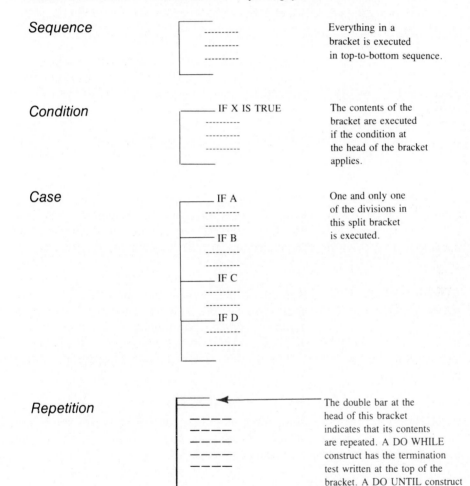

Sequence

Everything in a
bracket is executed
in top-to-bottom sequence.

Condition

IF X IS TRUE

The contents of the
bracket are executed
if the condition at
the head of the bracket
applies.

Case

IF A

IF B

IF C

IF D

One and only one
of the divisions in
this split bracket
is executed.

Repetition

The double bar at the
head of this bracket
indicates that its contents
are repeated. A DO WHILE
construct has the termination
test written at the top of the
bracket. A DO UNTIL construct
has the termination test written
at the bottom of the bracket.

The words used in fourth-generation languages can be appended to the brackets. The diagram is thus edited until it becomes an executable program. Figure 6.12 shows an executable program drawn in this way.

This type of diagram is called an *action diagram*. At its initial stage, it can be a tree structure representing a high-level overview or decomposition. It is successively extended until it becomes an executable program. This can be done in a computer-aided fashion, with software adding the words of a particular computer language. Action diagrams can be automatically generated from decomposition diagrams, dependency diagrams, data flow diagrams, data navigation diagrams, decision trees, state transition diagrams, and dialog diagrams.

Action diagrams are discussed in more detail in the following chapter.

BOXES

Many types of diagrams use blocks to represent activities or data. To distinguish between activities and data, activities are drawn as round-cornered boxes and data are drawn as square-cornered boxes.

LINES

Most diagrams have lines interconnecting the boxes. The lines represent associations in diagrams of data, decomposition, flow, time dependencies, or relationships in other diagrams.

COMPUTERIZED EXPANSION

Not all of the information about a *box* or *line* is shown on the diagram, necessarily. The user of a computerized diagramming tool can point to a *box* or *line* and say: SHOW DETAIL. A pop-on window may display the detail stored about the box or line. The window is sometimes a diagram of a different type.

ARROWS

Sometimes the lines connecting boxes have arrows on them to indicate *flow* or *sequence*. Flow implies that activities are performed in sequence:

An arrow is drawn in the middle of a line connecting boxes rather than at the end because the ends of the line are used for cardinality symbols.

CROW'S FEET

The term *cardinality* refers to how many of one item is associated with another. There can be one-with-one and one-with-many cardinality. Sometimes numbers may be used to place upper or lower limits on cardinality.

A crow's-foot connector from a line to a box is drawn like this:

It means that one or more instances of B can be associated with one instance of A. It is referred to as a *one-with-many association*.

ONE-WITH-ONE CARDINALITY

On diagrams of data, one-with-one cardinality is drawn with a small bar across the line:

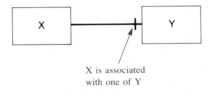

X is associated
with one of Y

ZERO CARDINALITY

A zero as part of the cardinality symbol means that a quantity of zero of that block is also an option:*

CUSTOMER has zero, one, or many TRANSACTIONS

EMPLOYEE has zero or one WIFE

*In some European practice a circle is placed at the opposite end of the line. This is confusing and violates the simple, clear representation of cardinality. Such practice should be stopped.

A line may have cardinality indicators in both directions:

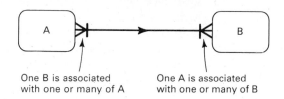

One B is associated
with one or many of A

One A is associated
with one or many of B

On data diagrams, it is recommended that a line representing a relationship between data entities should *always* have the cardinality symbols drawn at both ends. It is sloppy diagramming to draw a line connecting to a data box with no cardinality symbol.

On activity diagrams, the cardinality is usually one-with-one; because of this, the one-with-one symbol is often omitted. A line with no cardinality symbol implies one-with-one (as on a typical data flow diagram, for example).

The zero cardinality symbol could be at either end of a line with an arrow on it.

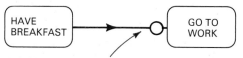

HAVE BREAKFAST may be followed by GO TO WORK

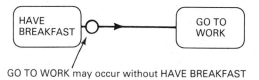

GO TO WORK may occur without HAVE BREAKFAST

In each case, the zero is placed against the box that may not exist.

MAXIMUM AND MINIMUM

The cardinality indicators express a maximum and a minimum:

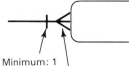

Minimum: 1
Maximum: Many

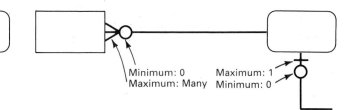

Minimum: 0
Maximum: Many

Maximum: 1
Minimum: 0

The maximum is always placed next to the box it refers to.

More detailed information about cardinality may be stored in the encyclo-pedia associated with the diagram. It might say, for example, that the maximum is 25 or that the maximum and minimum are both 3.

Where the maximum and minimum are both 1, two 1 bars may be placed on the line:

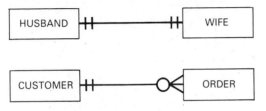

The two bars may be read as meaning "one and only one." Often a single 1 bar is used to mean "one and only one."

Figure 5.2 summarizes the representation of minimum and maximum car-dinality.

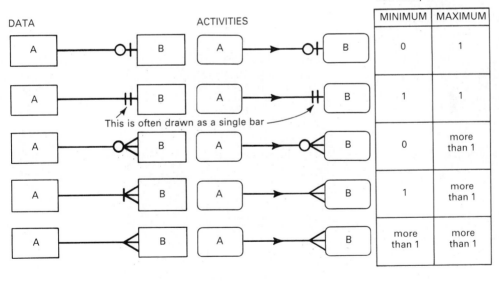

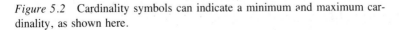

Figure 5.2 Cardinality symbols can indicate a minimum and maximum car-dinality, as shown here.

CONDITIONS

Zero cardinality has a special role to play. It means that something may or may not exist. With activities, it means that an activity may or may not be performed.

On activity diagrams, a *condition* is associated with zero cardinality. The condition may be shown on the link. In some cases a complex network of conditions is required between two blocks. This may be shown on a different diagram. A flow diagram may become too cluttered if conditions are written on it, so they can be shown in pop-on windows, possibly using an action diagram.

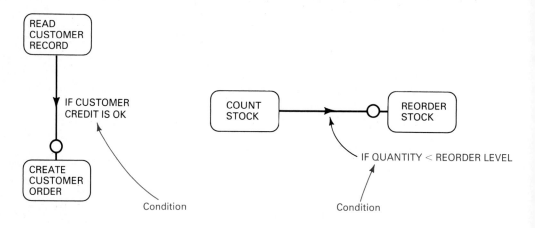

ALTERNATE PATHS

When an activity may be triggered by several activities, a zero may be placed on the paths from these activities:

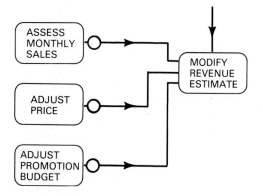

This diagram says that neither ASSESS MONTHLY SALES nor ADJUST PRICE nor ADJUST PROMOTION BUDGET has to exist in order for MODIFY REVENUE ESTIMATE to occur.

MUTUAL EXCLUSIVITY

Sometimes a block is associated with one of a group of blocks. This is indicated with a branching line with a filled-in circle at the branch:

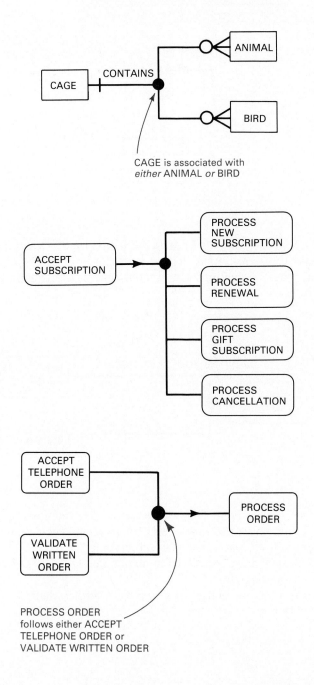

CAGE is associated with *either* ANIMAL *or* BIRD

PROCESS ORDER follows either ACCEPT TELEPHONE ORDER or VALIDATE WRITTEN ORDER

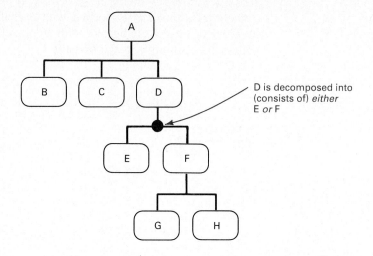

You might think of the solid circle as being a small letter *o* standing for "or."

A mutual exclusivity circle, like a cardinality circle, has conditions associated with it. These conditions are written on, or associated with, the lines leaving the circle:

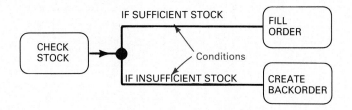

When we convert dependency diagrams, data navigation diagrams, or other diagrams into action diagrams ready for creating executable code, the condition statement will appear on the action diagrams.

Figure 5.3 shows the possible combinations of two activities and their translation to action diagrams.

The case structure of action diagrams is a similar shape to the branching mutual exclusivity line:

FLOW OR DEPENDENCY DIAGRAM   EQUIVALENT ACTION DIAGRAM

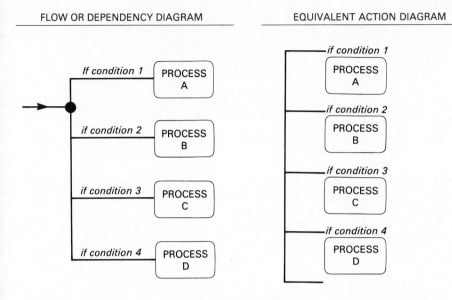

LABELING OF LINES

On some types of diagrams, the lines connecting boxes should be labeled. Lines between activity boxes are unidirectional. There may be lines in both directions between *activity* boxes, but these should be separate lines, each with its own particular meaning.

Lines between *data* boxes, on the other hand, are bidirectional. The line could be read in either direction:

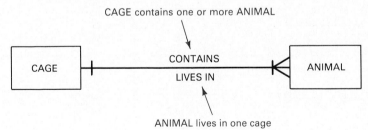

It is usually necessary to label only one direction of such a line.

A label *above* a horizontal line is the name of the relationship when the line is read from left to right. A label *below* a horizontal line is the name when the line is read from right to left.

In the choice of two activities A and B, the following possibilities exist.

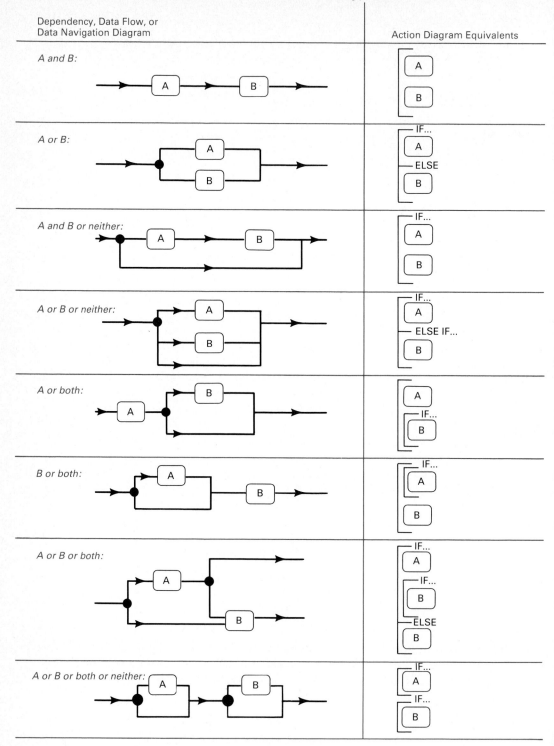

Figure 5.3 The possibilities that exist in the choice of two activities A and B.

As the line is rotated, the label remains on the same side of the line:

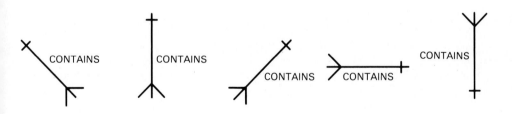

Thus the label to the right of a vertical line is read when going *down* the line. The label on the left of a vertical line is read when going *up* the line.

READING LINKS LIKE SENTENCES

Lines between boxes give information about the relationship between the boxes. This information ought to read like an English sentence, for example:

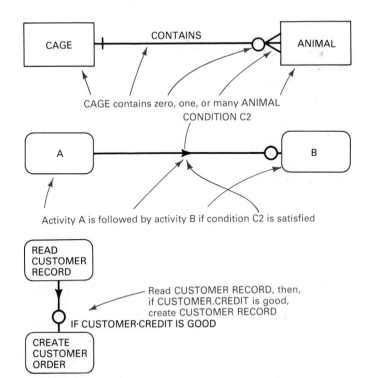

ARROWS ON LINES

An arrow on a line between activity boxes means that the activities occur in sequence:

Here process B follows process A. This may be because B is dependent on A. Often the dependency exists because data flows from A to B.

In the following diagrams, A, B, C, and D occur in that sequence.

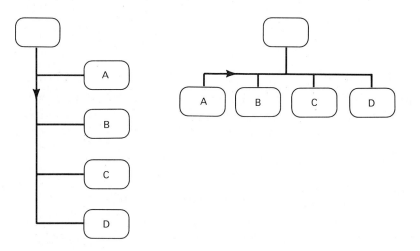

High-level decomposition diagrams are usually unconcerned with sequence. They use a tree structure to show how a function is composed of lower-level functions. Lower-level decomposition diagrams may need to show sequence. They may show how an activity is composed of subactivities that are executed in a given sequence. To show this, an arrow pointing in the direction of the sequence is used. This direction should be drawn from top to bottom on a vertical tree or from left to right on a horizontal tree.

It is usually better to show sequence on a dependency or flow diagram than on a decomposition diagram:

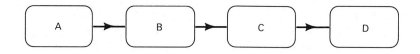

LARGE ARROWS

A large arrow on a diagram is used to show that an event occurs:

This may be used on a dependency diagram, data flow diagram, or state transition diagram.

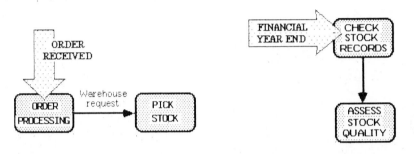

CONCURRENCY

For the first four decades of computing, almost all computers performed their operations sequentially. A major difference between the fourth and fifth generations of computers is likely to be that a fifth-generation machine will have several processors and will execute operations in parallel where this is possible.

At the time of writing, a large uniprocessor mainframe that executes 10 mips (millions of instructions per second) costs about $1 million. A 32-bit microcomputer chip executing 1 mips costs about $50. This startling difference in cost has caused research organizations everywhere to ask, ''How could a mainframe be constructed from many microcomputers that operate in parallel?'' Even if parallelism resulted in substantial inefficiency, a highly parallel computer could be much more cost-effective than a high-speed uniprocessor.

As we look to the future, the arguments for parallelism become stronger because the one-mips microcomputer is likely to be mass-produced at much lower costs, probably dropping to less than $1 per microcomputer for high-quantity orders. To facilitate the building of parallel computing engines, the chip that forms the basic building block will contain more than just a microcomputer. It will contain memory and input/output channels with mechanisms for queuing and handshaking to control exchange of data. The INMOS *transputer* is a chip that contains a 32-bit processor, 32,000 bits of memory, and four input/output channels with control mechanisms [1]. Two input/output channels are used for connecting transputers into loop structures; three channels are used when connecting them into hierarchies (tree structures); four channels are used when connecting them into matrices. The mass-production of transputers at low cost will help to usher in the age of parallel machines. In ten years' time we may ask not how many kilobytes of memory a machine has but how many kiloprocessors. In the nearer future we may use personal computers with two or even more processors.

It is difficult to take advantage of parallel architectures when using computer languages that are essentially sequential, as almost all computer languages have been. There has been little success in writing COBOL or FORTRAN compilers for parallel computers. Relatively recently, new languages have emerged that can exploit parallel hardware architectures. Some are data-base or knowledge-base languages in which searches, joins, or other relational operations can exploit concurrent machine operations. Some are programming languages that can specify concurrent actions. Some are specification languages that indicate that certain actions can occur concurrently.

DIAGRAMMING CONCURRENCY

Where parallel processing is possible, we need a construct on our diagrams that indicates that specified activities can happen concurrently.

The language OCCAM [1, 2] is a tight programming language that can express concurrency. It is used for writing programs for multimicroprocessor configurations or transputer systems. To control the order of execution of processes, OCCAM uses three fundamental mechanisms in addition to the conventional WHILE and IF constructions:

- SEQ indicates that operations are carried out in *sequence*.
- ALT indicates that one and only one operation is carried out of several *alternate* operations.
- PAR indicates that operations can be carried out in *parallel*.

SEQ and ALT are represented in the brackets discussed earlier, ALT being a case structure. PAR requires a new diagramming construct. We will indicate that brackets can be executed concurrently by linking them with a semicircular arc:

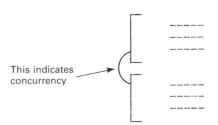

This indicates concurrency

You might think of the arc as being a *C* standing for "concurrency."

The basic constructs SEQ, ALT, and PAR are, then, drawn as follows:

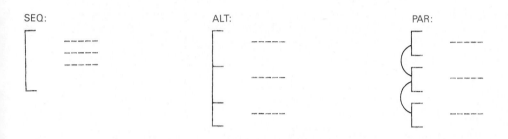

Whereas OCCAM is designed for machine programming at a low level, the HOS specification language is designed for systems analysts who begin with a high-level overview of the systems they are designing [3, 4]. This specification language has the three forms of decomposition mentioned in Chapter 4: JOIN, OR, and INCLUDE. These again express *sequence, alternates,* and *concurrency.* Where they are binary decompositions, they can be drawn as follows:

Figure 5.4 shows, on the left, an HOS overview of a procedure. It employs JOINs, INCLUDEs, and an OR. The right of the figure shows the same procedure drawn with brackets, with two concurrency indicators.

A decomposition can be drawn with diagram symbols rather than with the words JOIN, INCLUDE, and OR:

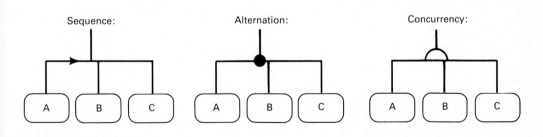

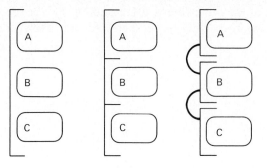

In some cases the concurrency symbol is on one bracket or block only, indicating that this bracket or block relates to parallel activities. This one subroutine may initialize and use a parallel array of processors. In OCCAM, for example, we may have the following:

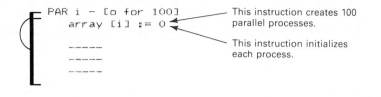

Whereas the other types of constructs in this book have been used extensively, the concurrency indicator has not as yet because of the essentially serial nature of today's programming. Concurrency will be vitally important in future system design.

LEVELS OF DETAIL

As indicated in the pyramid diagrams of Chapter 2, analysis and design can occur at different levels of detail. It is important to distinguish between the different levels, for example, between processes and procedures and between entity types and stored record types. Different degrees of shading may be used to make this distinction, as shown in Fig. 5.5.

Shading can easily be done by computer. It would not be done on handdrawn diagrams. On hand-drawn diagrams, a symbol may be used on the top left-hand corner of the paper to indicate the level in the pyramid:

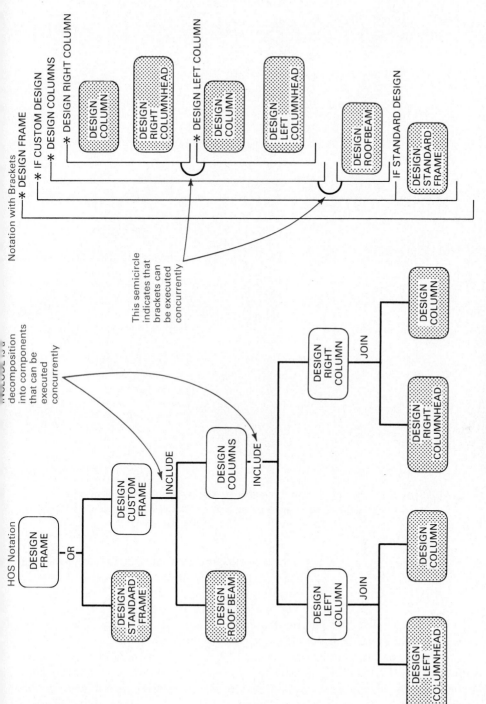

Figure 5.4 Diagrams illustrating concurrency.

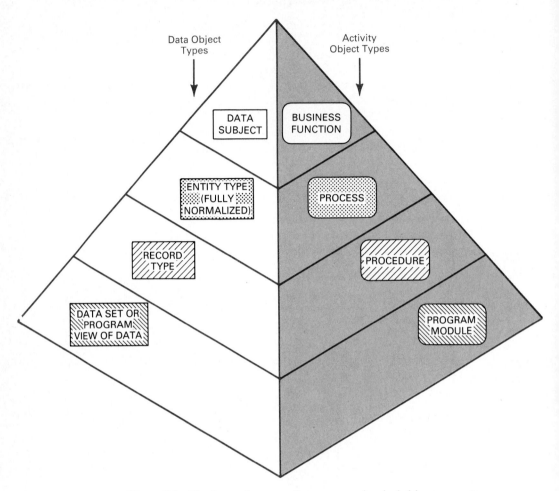

Figure 5.5 The boxes drawn on diagrams may be shaded by a computer as shown here to indicate which level of analysis and design they apply to.

CONVERSION OF DIAGRAMS TO EXECUTABLE CODE

There is a correspondence among the differing diagramming types. They need to be associated in order to automate as fully as possible the tasks of the analyst and programmer. It is this drive toward computer-aided design that makes it so important to have consistent notation among the different types of diagrams.

A data navigation diagram (Chapter 12) is drawn using an entity-relationship diagram (Chapter 11). A data navigation diagram can be converted automatically into an action diagram (Chapter 6). Similarly, decomposition diagrams (Chapter 7), dependency diagrams (Chapter 8), data flow diagrams

(Chapter 9), decision trees (Chapter 14), state transition diagrams (Chapter 15), and dialog design diagrams (Chapter 16) can be automatically converted to action diagrams. An action diagram is edited in a computer-aided fashion until it becomes executable code. This computer-aided progression from high-level overview diagrams or data administrator's data models to executable code makes it possible to increase the productivity of the systems analyst by a large amount.

Figure 5.6 shows the relationship between diagramming techniques and the forms of conversion to action diagrams. Code generation can occur from action diagrams and representations of data, screens and reports, as indicated in Fig. 2.4.

Later chapters contain examples of the automated conversion to action diagrams and then to executable code.

HAND-DRAWN DIAGRAMS

The diagrams in this book are intended to be created with a modern workstation or a dot-matrix printer. When they are drawn by hand, a template like that in Fig. 5.7 should be used.

ASCII Character Diagrams

Sometimes diagrams have to be drawn on a line printer or printer with an ASCII character set. In this case, the crow's foot has only two toes and is represented with <, >, ∨, or ∧:

Square-cornered and round-cornered boxes can be represented as boxes with + or o, respectively, at their corners:

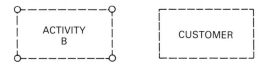

ASCII diagrams are not likely to be as elegant as drawings done with a graphics screen and dot-matrix printer.

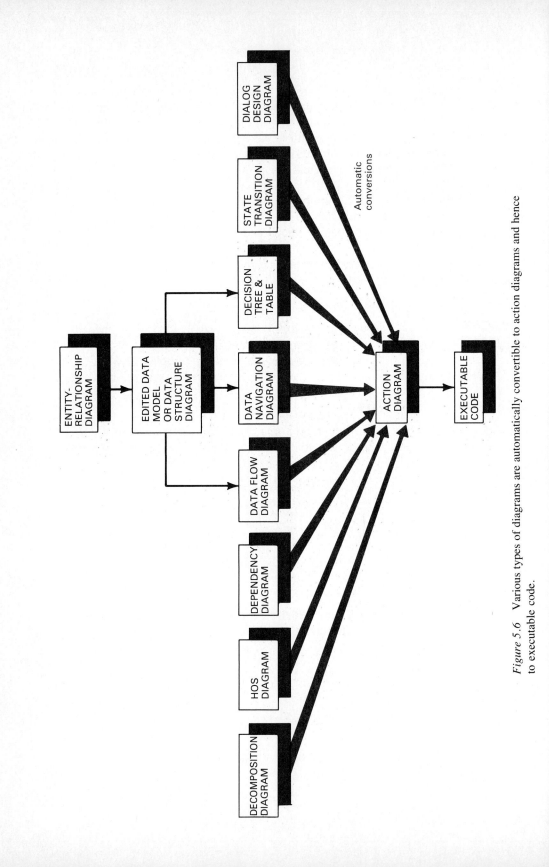

Figure 5.6 Various types of diagrams are automatically convertible to action diagrams and hence to executable code.

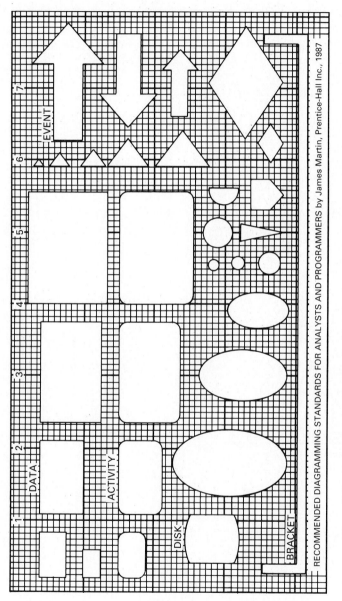

Figure 5.7 A template for drawing the diagrams in this book. It is recommended that the plastic be thicker than that of the traditional IBM template.

RECOMMENDED DIAGRAMMING STANDARDS FOR ANALYSTS AND PROGRAMMERS by James Martin, Prentice-Hall Inc., 1987

DIAGRAM CONNECTORS

A pentagonal arrow is used as a connector to connect lines to a distant part of a diagram. The connector symbol may be used to connect to other pages. This is often unnecessary with computerized graphics because the user scrolls across large complete diagrams.

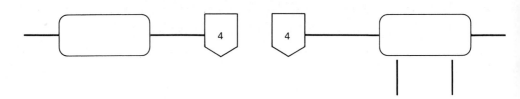

THREE DOTS

Three dots in front of a name on a box or a line of an action diagram indicate that the item can be expanded with the EXPAND command.

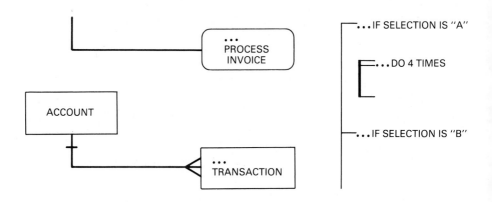

When a large diagram is contracted, the three dots are automatically inserted to show that it may be expanded to its original form.

LINES SHOULD BE HORIZONTAL OR VERTICAL

Lines between boxes should be drawn horizontally and vertically. This assists with the labeling conventions, avoids distorted crow's feet, and enables the computer to employ a palette of symbols that do not need to be rotated.

Diagrams containing hierarchies should be drawn with root boxes at the top and left, where possible. One-to-many lines should go downward and to the right. Hierarchical patterns in data become familiar to the analyst as having the following type of shape:

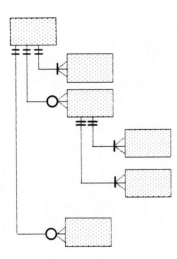

Computerized tools used to synthesize complex data models can draw them in this way automatically.

On diagrams with activity boxes, the arrows representing flows or time sequences should go downward or from left to right wherever possible:

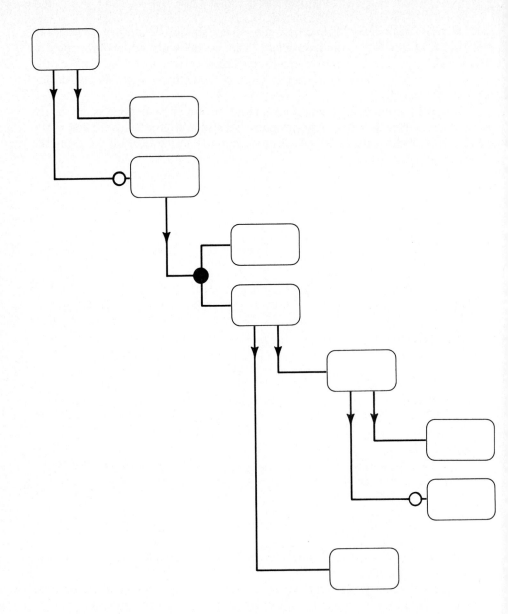

USE OF COLOR   Color should be used to convey meaning. It should
                         not be used for mere decoration. The instinct to be
artistic must be suppressed and replaced with an urge to maximize clarity.

    Analysts or programmers should be able to use colors of their own choice
on parts of the diagram they select. They may use it for the following purposes:

- To highlight items of special importance
- To highlight areas that need more work
- To mark areas to be worked on by different people
- To have mnemonic value (different colors can be associated with different subjects)
- To highlight items to which the user's attention should be directed
- To distinguish between blocks or areas of different types

In addition to (or instead of) color, different shadings and patterns may be employed.

MANIPULATION OF LARGE DIAGRAMS

Large diagrams may be manipulated as follows. It is suggested that the command words be standard on the diagramming tools.

- **Paging**   **LEFT, RIGHT, UP, DOWN, HOME, JUMP**
  Reveals a different page of a large diagram.

- **Scrolling**   **SCROLL, CENTER**
  Moves across a diagram. Scrolling is best achieved with a mouse. If the user selects CENTER and points to a block, the diagram will be scrolled so that block is at the center.

- **Zooming**   **ZOOM IN, ZOOM OUT, FULL ZOOM**
  Expands or shrinks the diagram without changing it. Full zoom shows the entire diagram shrunk to fit one screen.

- **Zoocing**   **ZOOC IN, ZOOC OUT, FULL ZOOC**
  Zooc stands for *zoom and change* or *zoom and clarify*. It expands or shrinks a diagram, like a zoom, but adjusts it for readability or clarification.

- **Nesting**   **EXPAND, CONTRACT**
  Changes to a more or less detailing diagram *of the same form*. For example, it may reveal blocks within blocks. A diagram can be expanded only if it has previously been contracted. Three dots indicate this.

- **Detailing**   **SHOW, HIDE**
  Changes to a more or less detailed representation *of a different form*. Pointing to an icon and commanding SHOW reveals detail about that icon that is in the encyclopedia. This may be shown in a separate window. It may be text, a table, or a different type of diagram.

NESTING

To make large diagrams easy to display and understand, they should be nested. A block or a line of an action diagram can be enlarged into a diagram that shows its contents. The reverse process hides the contents of a block or line. The commands EXPAND and CONTRACT may be used for this purpose. EXPAND produces a diagram *of the same type*.

When a line or block has detail that can be revealed with the EXPAND command, three dots are visible at the start of the line or name:

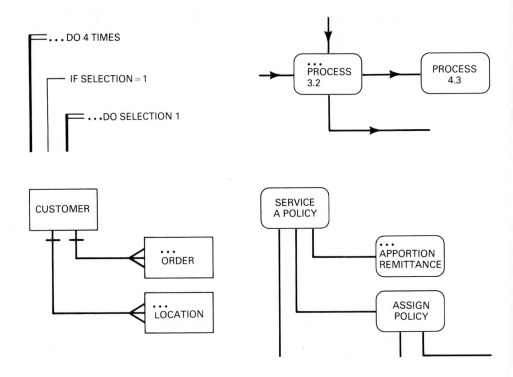

WINDOWS

The use of windows on a workstation screen has an important effect on diagramming. A pop-on window can be displayed to show the details of any component of a diagram. This means that diagrams can be clear and uncluttered. A substantial level of detail may appear in the window, e.g., dictionary listings, text comments, an action diagram showing code, structures, or conditions.

Multiple types of diagrams are often needed for one design or program. These may occupy different scrollable windows. Color or reverse video may be used to visually associate items in different windows.

In a hierarchical diagram (action diagram, decomposition diagram, hierarchies in an entity-relationship diagram, data analysis diagram, or decision tree), the user may perform nesting by pointing at a parent block and using the command EXPAND or CONTRACT.

In a mesh-structured diagram (data flow diagram, dependency diagram, entity-relationship diagram, state transition diagram, dialog design diagram), the user may select several blocks and say CONTRACT. The system then shrinks them into one block. The command EXPAND reveals the hidden blocks.

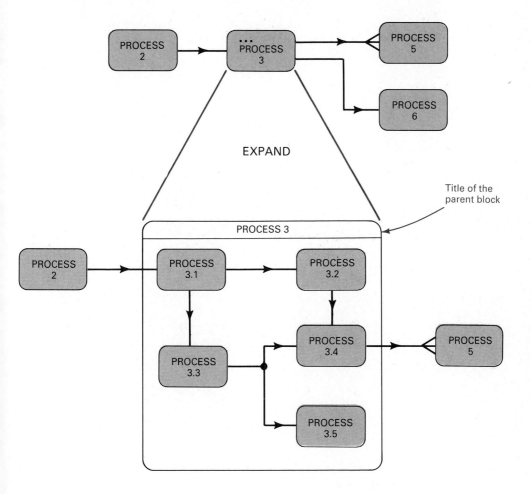

SHOWING AND HIDING DETAIL

EXPAND and CONTRACT refer to nesting in which the *type of diagram remains the same*. SHOW and HIDE refer to showing or hiding properties *(different kinds of detail)*.

In the following illustration, the arrow indicating a derived data item is expanded to show a decision tree:

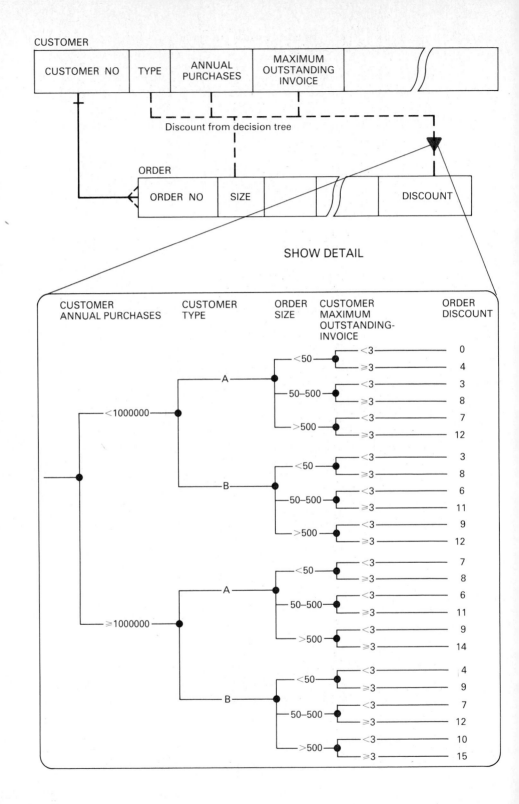

SHOW DETAIL

REFERENCES

1. Transputer and OCCAM manuals are available from INMOS Corporation, P.O. Box 16000, Colorado Springs, CO 80935 Phone: (303) 630-4000.

2. R. Taylor and P. Wilson, ''Process-oriented Language Meets Demands of Distributed Processing,'' *Electronics,* Nov. 30, 1982.

3. Manuals on USE.IT, which is a tool employing the HOS specification language, are available from Higher Order Software, Inc., Cambridge, MA 02140. Phone: (617) 661-8900.

4. J. Martin, *System Design from Provably Correct Constructs*. Englewood Cliffs, N.J.: Prentice-Hall, 1985.

6 ACTION DIAGRAMS

OVERVIEW VERSUS DETAILED LOGIC DIAGRAMMING Of the diagramming techniques that evolved in the 1970s and earlier, some are usable for the *overview* of program structure and some are usable for the *detailed* program logic. Structure charts, HIPO diagrams, Warnier-Orr diagrams, and Michael Jackson charts draw overall program structures but not the detailed tests, conditions, and logic. Their advocates usually resort to structured English or pseudocode to represent the detail. Flowcharts and Nassi-Shneiderman charts show the detailed logic of a program but not the structural overview.

There is no reason why the diagramming of the overview should be incompatible with the diagramming of the detail. Indeed, it is highly desirable that these two aspects of program design employ the same type of diagram because complex systems are created by successively filling in detail (top-down design) and linking together blocks of low-level detail (bottom-up design). The design needs to move naturally between the high levels and low levels of design. The low level should be a natural extension of the high level. *Action diagrams* achieve this. They give a natural way to draw program overviews like structure charts, HIPO or Warnier-Orr diagrams, *and* detailed logic like flowcharts or Nassi-Shneiderman charts. They were originally designed to be as easy to teach to end users as possible and to assist end users in applying fourth-generation languages.

Glancing ahead, Figs. 6.2 and 6.3 show simple examples of action diagrams. Figure 6.8 shows an extension of Fig. 6.2.

BRACKETS A program module is drawn as a bracket:

```
   ┌ --------
   │ --------
   │ --------
   │ --------
   └
```

Brackets are the basic building blocks of action diagrams. The bracket can be of any length, so there is space in it for as much text or detail as is needed.

Inside the bracket is a sequence of operations. A simple control rule applies to the bracket. You enter it at the top, do the things in it in a top-to-bottom sequence, and exit at the bottom.

Inside the bracket there may be other brackets. Many brackets may be nested. The nesting shows the hierarchical structure of a program. Figure 6.1 shows the representation of a hierarchical structure with brackets.

Some brackets are *repetition* brackets. The items in the bracket are executed several times. The repetition bracket has a double line at its top:

```
   ┌═══════   FOR ALL TRANSACTIONS
   │ -----------
   │ -----------
   │ -----------
   │ -----------
   └
```

When one of several processes is to be used (mutually exclusive selection), a bracket with several divisions is used:

```
   ┌──── PROCESS NEW SUBSCRIPTION
   │
   ├──── PROCESS RENEWAL
   │
   ├──── PROCESS CANCELLATION
   └
```

This is the programmer's case structure. One, and only one, of the divisions in this bracket is executed.

ULTIMATE DECOMPOSITION

Figure 6.2 illustrates an action diagram overview of a program structure. It can be extended to show conditions, case structures, and loops of different types; it can show detailed program logic. Figure 6.3 expands the process in Fig. 6.2 called VALIDATE SUB ITEM. Figures 6.2 and 6.3 could be merged into one

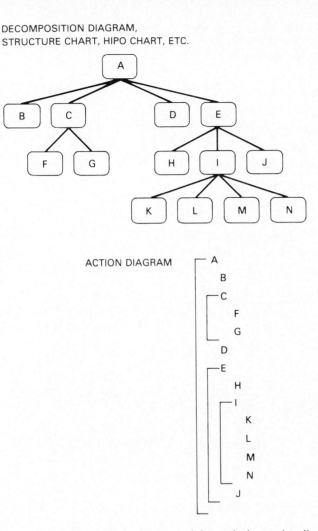

DECOMPOSITION DIAGRAM,
STRUCTURE CHART, HIPO CHART, ETC.

ACTION DIAGRAM

Figure 6.1   A hierarchical block structure and the equivalent action diagram.

chart. (Glancing ahead, Fig. 6.7 shows *executable* program code written in a fourth-generation language.)

This diagramming technique can thus be extended all the way from the highest-level overview to working code in a fourth-generation language. When it is used on a computer screen, the developers can edit and adjust the diagram and successively fill in detail until they have working code that can be tested interpretively. We refer to this as *ultimate decomposition*.

As we will see later, the process of ultimate decomposition can be linked to data-base planning and design.

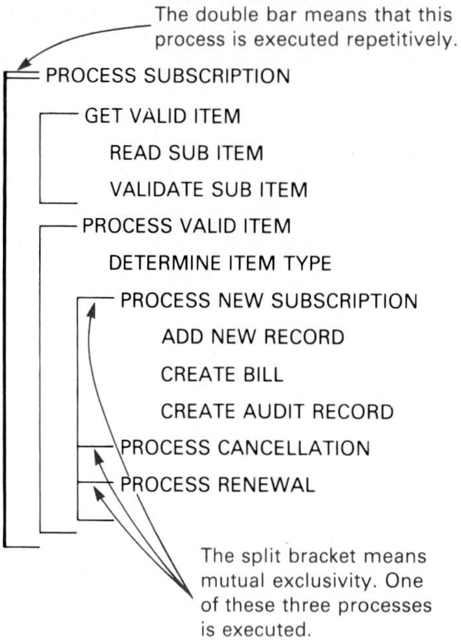

The double bar means that this
process is executed repetitively.

PROCESS SUBSCRIPTION

   GET VALID ITEM

      READ SUB ITEM

      VALIDATE SUB ITEM

   PROCESS VALID ITEM

      DETERMINE ITEM TYPE

      PROCESS NEW SUBSCRIPTION

         ADD NEW RECORD

         CREATE BILL

         CREATE AUDIT RECORD

      PROCESS CANCELLATION

      PROCESS RENEWAL

The split bracket means
mutual exclusivity. One
of these three processes
is executed.

Figure 6.2   A high-level action diagram. This action diagram can now be expanded into a chart showing the detailed program logic. VALIDATE SUB ITEM from this chart is expanded into detailed logic in Fig. 6.3.

CONDITIONS

Often a program module or subroutine is executed only if a certain condition applies. In this case the condition is written at the head of a bracket:

```
┌────── IF CUSTOMER# IS VALID
│  ----------
│  ----------
│  ----------
└──────
```

Conditions are often used to control mutually exclusive choices:

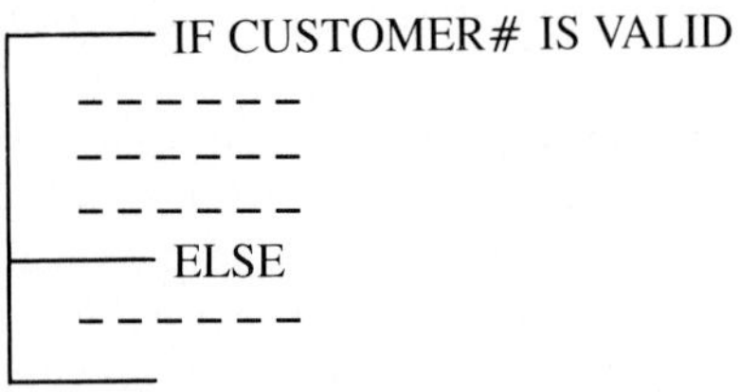

```
┌────── IF CUSTOMER# IS VALID
│  - - - - - -
│  - - - - - -
│  - - - - - -
├────── ELSE
│  - - - - - -
└──────
```

This has only two mutually exclusive conditions, an IF and an ELSE. Sometimes there are many mutually exclusive conditions, as follows:

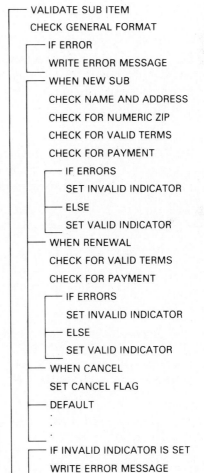

```
┌──────── WHEN KEY = "1"
│  ─ ─ ─ ─ ─
│  ─ ─ ─ ─ ─
├──────── WHEN KEY = "2"
│  ─ ─ ─ ─ ─
│  ─ ─ ─ ─ ─
├──────── WHEN KEY = "3"
│  ─ ─ ─ ─ ─
│  ─ ─ ─ ─ ─
├──────── WHEN KEY = "4"
│  ─ ─ ─ ─ ─
│  ─ ─ ─ ─ ─
└──
```

```
┌── VALIDATE SUB ITEM
│   CHECK GENERAL FORMAT
│   ┌── IF ERROR
│   │     WRITE ERROR MESSAGE
│   └──
│   ┌── WHEN NEW SUB
│   │     CHECK NAME AND ADDRESS
│   │     CHECK FOR NUMERIC ZIP
│   │     CHECK FOR VALID TERMS
│   │     CHECK FOR PAYMENT
│   │     ┌── IF ERRORS
│   │     │     SET INVALID INDICATOR
│   │     ├── ELSE
│   │     │     SET VALID INDICATOR
│   │     └──
│   ├── WHEN RENEWAL
│   │     CHECK FOR VALID TERMS
│   │     CHECK FOR PAYMENT
│   │     ┌── IF ERRORS
│   │     │     SET INVALID INDICATOR
│   │     ├── ELSE
│   │     │     SET VALID INDICATOR
│   │     └──
│   ├── WHEN CANCEL
│   │     SET CANCEL FLAG
│   ├── DEFAULT
│   │     .
│   │     .
│   └──
│   ┌── IF INVALID INDICATOR IS SET
│   │     WRITE ERROR MESSAGE
└───┴──
```

Figure 6.3 An action diagram showing the detailed logic inside the process VALIDATE SUB ITEM. This diagram, showing detailed logic, is an extension of the overview diagram of Fig. 6.2.

LOOPS

A loop is represented with a repetition bracket with the double line at its top.

When many people first start to program, they make mistakes with the point at which they test a loop. Sometimes the test should be made *before* the actions of the loop are performed, and sometimes the test should be made *after*. This difference can be made clear on brackets by drawing the test either at the top or the bottom of the bracket:

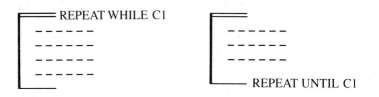

If the test is at the head of the loop, as with a WHILE loop, the actions in the loop may never be executed if the WHILE condition is not satisfied. If the test is at the bottom of the loop, as with an UNTIL loop, the actions in the loop are executed at least once. They will be executed more than once if the condition is fulfilled.

SETS OF DATA

Sometimes a procedure needs to be executed on all the items in a set of items. It might be applied to all transactions or all records in a file, for example:

```
┌═══════ FOR ALL TRANSACTIONS
│  - - - - - -
│  - - - - - -
│  - - - - - -
│  - - - - - -
└
```

Action diagrams have been used with fourth-generation languages such as NOMAD, MANTIS, FOCUS, RAMIS, and IDEAL. They are a good tool for teaching end users to work with these languages. Some such languages have a FOR construct with a WHERE clause to qualify the FOR, for example:

```
┌═══════ FOR EACH TRANSACTION WHERE CUSTOMER# > 5000
│  ----------
│  ----------
│  ----------
└
```

SUBPROCEDURES   Sometimes a user needs to add an item to an action diagram that is itself a procedure that may contain actions. We call this a subprocedure or subroutine and draw it with a round-cornered box. A subprocedure might be used in several procedures. It will be exploded into detail, showing the actions it contains, in another chart.

Subprocedures Not Yet Designed

In some cases, the procedure designer has sections of a procedure that are not yet thought out in detail. He can represent this as a box with rounded corners and a right edge made of question marks:

COMMON   Some procedures appear more than once in an action
PROCEDURES   diagram because they are called (invoked) from more than one place in the logic. These procedures are called *common procedures*. They are indicated by drawing a vertical line down the left-hand side of the procedure box:

The use of procedure boxes enables an action diagrammer to concentrate on the parts of a procedure with which he is familiar. Another person may, perhaps, fill in the details in the boxes. This enables an elusive or complex procedure design to be worked out a stage at a time.

The use of these boxes makes action diagrams a powerful tool for designing procedures at many levels of abstraction. As with other structured techniques, top-down design can be done by first creating a gross structure with such boxes, while remaining vague about the contents of each box. The gross structure can then be broken down into successive levels of detail. Each explosion of a box adds another degree of detail, which might itself contain actions and boxes.

Similarly, bottom-up design can be done by specifying small procedures as action diagrams whose names appear as boxes in higher-level action diagrams.

ESCAPES

Certain conditions may cause a bracket or group of brackets to be terminated. They may cause the termination of the bracket in which the condition occurs, or they may cause the termination of several brackets. Terminations, or escapes, are drawn with an arrow to the left through one or more brackets:

It is important to note that an escape structure allows only a forward skip to the exit point of a bracket. This restriction keeps the structure simple and does not allow action diagrams to degenerate into unstructured "spaghetti" logic.

An escape is different from a GO TO instruction. It represents an orderly close-down of the brackets escaped from. Some fourth-generation languages have an escape construct and no GO TO instruction. The escape command has names such as EXIT, QUIT, and BREAK.

GO TO

When a language has a well-implemented escape, there is no need for GO TO instructions. However, some languages have GO TO instructions and no escape. Using good structured design, the GO TO would be employed to emulate an escape. Any attempt to branch to a distant part of the program should be avoided.

It has nevertheless, been suggested that a GO TO should be included in the action diagram vocabulary. This can be done by using a dashed arrow to replace the solid escape arrow:

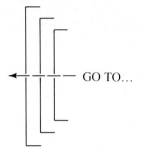

In the interests of structured design, we have not included this construct in our recommended list of action diagram features.

NEXT ITERATION   In a repetition bracket, a *next-iteration* construct is useful. With this, control skips the remaining instructions in a repetition bracket and goes to the next iteration of the loop. A next-iteration construct (abbreviated NEXT) is drawn as follows:

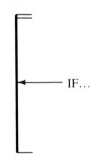

The arrow does not break through the bracket, as it does with an escape construct.

FOURTH-GENERATION LANGUAGES   When fourth-generation languages are used, the wording on the action diagram may be the wording that is used in coding programs with the language. Some examples of this follow:

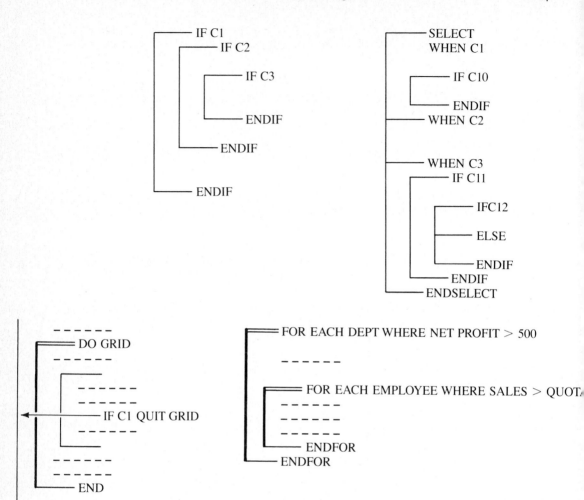

Figure 6.4 shows an action diagram for a procedure using control state-ments from the language IDEAL [1].

DECOMPOSITION TO PROGRAM CODE

Figure 6.5 shows a high-level decomposition of a game program. With action diagrams we can decom-pose this until we have program code. The action diagram gives more room for explanation than we have in boxes on decomposition diagrams. Instead of saying PRINT RANDOM WORDS, it says PRINT RANDOM WORD FROM EACH OF THE THREE LISTS.

Figure 6.6 decomposes the part of the diagram labeled BUZZWORD GENERATOR. The inner bracket is a repetition bracket that executes 22 times.

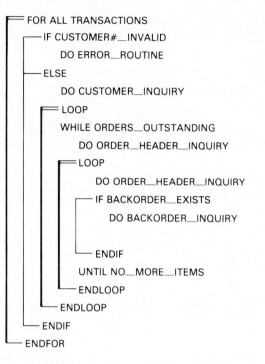

Figure 6.4 Action diagrams can be labeled with the control statement of fourth-generation language and form an excellent way to teach such languages. This example uses statements from the language IDEAL from ADR [1].

This is inside a bracket that is terminated by the operator pressing the ESC *(escape)* key. The last statement in this bracket is WAIT, indicating that the system will wait after executing the remainder of the bracket until the operator presses the ESC key. This gives the operator as much time as he wants to read the printout.

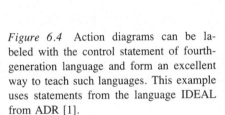

Figure 6.5 A high-level decomposition of a game program.

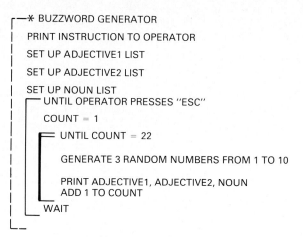

Figure 6.6   An expansion of the buzzword generator portion of Fig. 6.5.

Figure 6.7 decomposes the diagram further into an executable program. This program is written in the fourth-generation language MANTIS [2].

TITLES VERSUS CODE STRUCTURE

At the higher levels of the design process, action diagram brackets represent the names of procedures and subprocedures. As the designer descends into program-level detail, the brackets become *program constructs*—IF brackets, CASE brackets, LOOP brackets, and so on.

A bracket that shows a title rather than an action to be implemented or a program instruction may be drawn as a dotted or dashed line. It may have a character preceding the title, such as *, &, or C, to indicate that the title line should be treated as a comment by the compiler. Different compilers used different characters for this purpose.

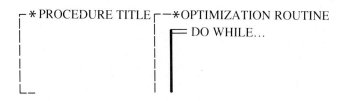

Title brackets may be single IF-ELSE, case structure, or repetition brackets.

The designer may use a mix of title brackets and program brackets such

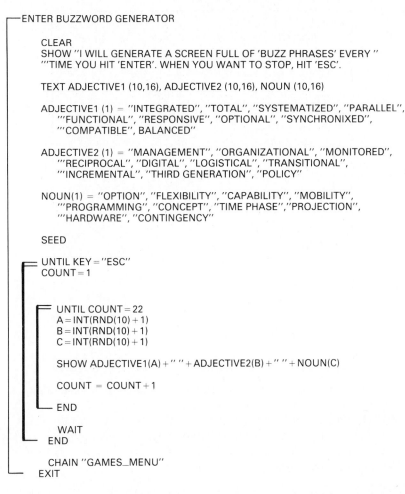

ENTER BUZZWORD GENERATOR

CLEAR
SHOW "I WILL GENERATE A SCREEN FULL OF 'BUZZ PHRASES' EVERY "
"'TIME YOU HIT 'ENTER'. WHEN YOU WANT TO STOP, HIT 'ESC'.

TEXT ADJECTIVE1 (10,16), ADJECTIVE2 (10,16), NOUN (10,16)

ADJECTIVE1 (1) = "INTEGRATED", "TOTAL", "SYSTEMATIZED", "PARALLEL",
   "'FUNCTIONAL", "RESPONSIVE", "OPTIONAL", "SYNCHRONIXED",
   "'COMPATIBLE", BALANCED"

ADJECTIVE2 (1) = "MANAGEMENT", "ORGANIZATIONAL", "MONITORED",
   "'RECIPROCAL", "DIGITAL", "LOGISTICAL", "TRANSITIONAL",
   "'INCREMENTAL", "THIRD GENERATION", "POLICY"

NOUN(1) = "OPTION", "FLEXIBILITY", "CAPABILITY", "MOBILITY",
   "'PROGRAMMING", "CONCEPT", "TIME PHASE","PROJECTION",
   "'HARDWARE", "CONTINGENCY"

SEED

UNTIL KEY = "ESC"
COUNT = 1

UNTIL COUNT = 22
A = INT(RND(10) + 1)
B = INT(RND(10) + 1)
C = INT(RND(10) + 1)

SHOW ADJECTIVE1(A) + " " + ADJECTIVE2(B) + " " + NOUN(C)

COUNT = COUNT + 1

END

WAIT
END

CHAIN "GAMES_MENU"
EXIT

Figure 6.7 An expansion of the action diagram of Fig. 6.6 into program code. This is an executable program in the fourth-generation language MANTIS [2]. Successive decomposition of a diagram until it becomes executable code is called *ultimate decomposition.*

that by displaying the title brackets only (with action diagramming software), an overview structure of the program is seen.

The designer may also use comments to clarify the design. The comment line starts with an asterisk. The software may be instructed to display or to hide the comments.

The program-construct brackets may be labeled with appropriate control words. These may be the control words of a particular programming language, or they may be language-independent words.

Figure 6.8 shows the program constructs with language-independent con-

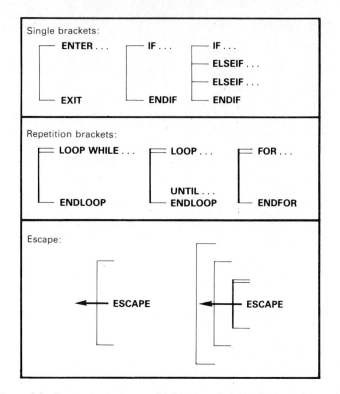

Figure 6.8   Program constructs with language-independent control words.

trol words. Figure 6.9 shows the same constructs with the words of the fourth-generation language IDEAL. It is desirable that any fourth-generation language have a set of clear words equivalent to Fig. 6.8, and it would help if standard words for this existed in the computer industry.

CONCURRENCY   As discussed in Chapter 5, where brackets may be executed concurrently, they are to be joined with a semicircular link:

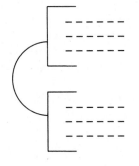

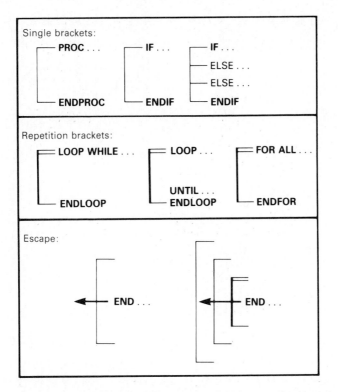

Figure 6.9 Program constructs with the control words of the fourth-generation language IDEAL [1].

A bracket that relates to a parallel operation on an array processor has the concurrency symbol attached to the bracket:

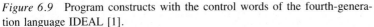

PAR i = [o FOR 32]
echo (kb [i], pr [i])

INPUT AND OUTPUT DATA   The brackets of the action diagram are quick and easy to draw. If the user wants to show the data that enter and leave a process, the bracket is expanded into a rectangle, as shown in Fig. 6.10. The data entering the process are noted at the top right corner of the block. The data leaving are noted at the bottom right corner.

Rectangles can be nested, as they were in Fig. 6.10. We then have species II decomposition as described in Chapter 4. This type of decomposition is de-

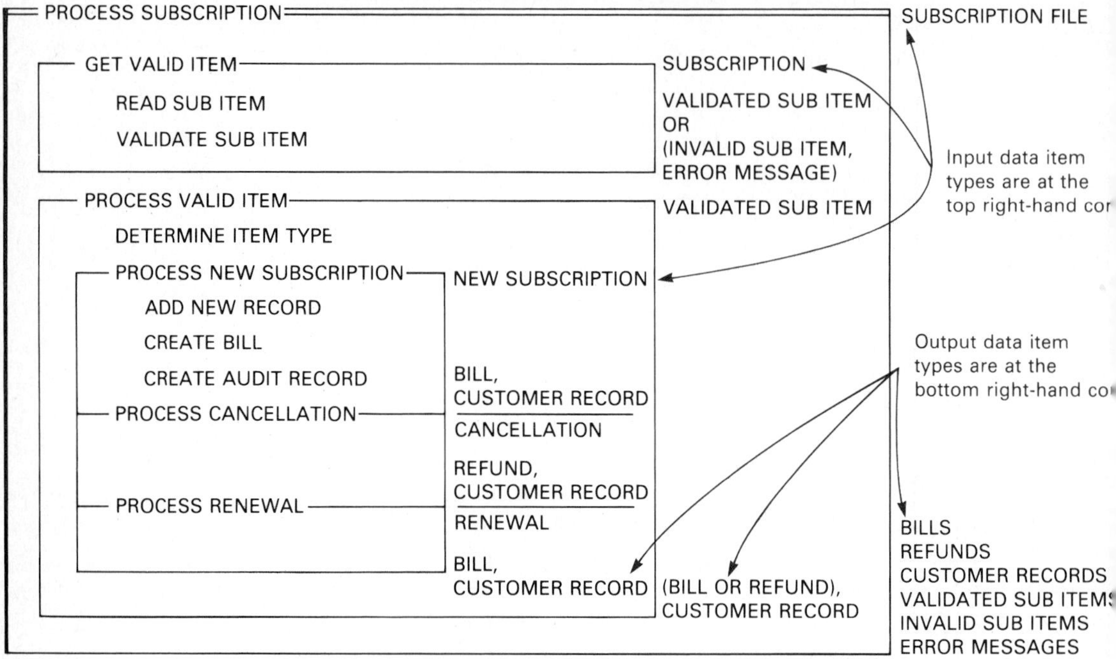

Figure 6.10 The bracket format of Fig. 6.2 is here expanded into the rectangular format used to show the data-item types that constitute input and output for each process. This is designed for computerized cross-checking.

signed for computerized checking to ensure that all of the inputs and outputs balance.

The square brackets may be thought of as a shorthand way of drawing rectangles like those in Fig. 6.10.

A diagramming technique, today, should be designed for both quick manual manipulation and computerized manipulation. Users and analysts will want to draw rough sketches on paper or argue at a chalkboard using the technique. They will also want to build complex diagrams at a computer screen, using the computer to validate, edit, and maintain the diagrams, possibly linking them to a dictionary, data-base model, or the like. The tool acts rather like a word processor for diagramming, making it easy for users to modify a diagram. Unlike a word processor, it can perform complex validation and cross-checking on the diagram.

The design of simple programs does not need automated correlation in inputs and outputs, nor does it need diagrams like Fig. 6.10 that show the inputs and outputs. In the design of complex specifications, automated correlation of inputs and outputs among program modules is essential if mistakes are to be avoided.

In showing input and output data, Fig. 6.10 contains the information on a data flow diagram. It can be converted into a layered data flow diagram, as in Fig. 6.11. Unlike a data flow diagram, it can be directly extended to show the program structure, including conditions, case constructs, and loop control.

It is highly desirable that a programmer sketch the structure of programs with action diagram brackets. These can be drawn on the programmers coding sheet. I have often found that coders make logic errors in the use of loops, END statements, case structures, EXITs, and the like, in programs written with fourth-generation languages such as FOCUS, RAMIS, IDEAL, and NATU-RAL. When they are taught to draw action diagram brackets and fit the code to them, these structure errors become apparent. The control statements can be fitted to the brackets.

Software, which can run like word processing software, on personal computers, can be used for building, editing, and modifying action diagrams and fitting code to them.

ACTION DIAGRAM EDITORS

There exist for personal computers action diagram editors that speed up the production and modification of programs and help to eliminate common types of bugs. The control words of various programming languages can be added to the action diagrams by the computer. It is relatively quick to convert code from one language to another.

The brackets used can be selected from a menu and can be stretched, edited, cut and pasted, and duplicated. The computer can apply a variety of integrity checks.

Large programs can be displayed in overview form. Code can be contracted to hide the details and then reexpanded at will.

Experience with action diagram editors has shown that end users can employ them to sketch their systems and procedures they need. When this occurs, action diagrams form a useful communication vehicle between users and systems analysts. The design so created has successively greater detail added to it until it becomes executable code.

Professional programmers' experience in designing and coding systems has shown that skilled use of an action diagram editor substantially lowers the time taken to create and debug complex code.

Experience in the maintenance area shows that one person can understand and modify another person's code much more quickly when action diagrams are used.

CONTRACT AND EXPAND

A very useful feature of an action diagram editor is the ability to contract large action diagrams, hiding much of the detail. The user selects a bracket and

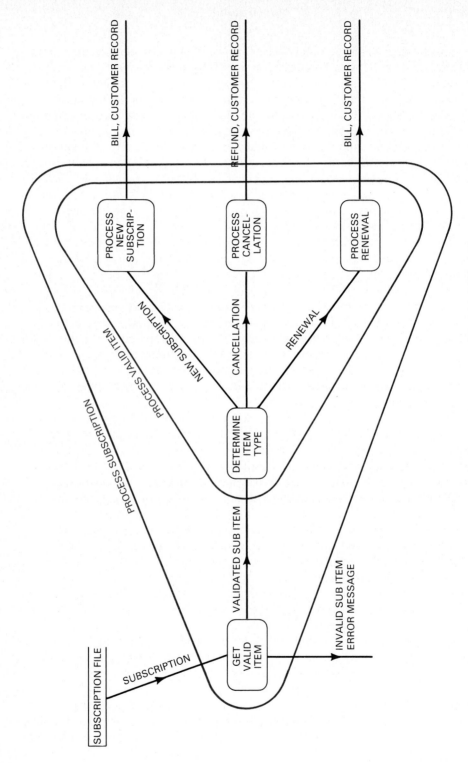

Figure 6.11 A data flow diagram corresponding to Fig. 6.10.

uses the command CONTRACT. The bracket shrinks so that only its top line is seen. Any nested brackets within the contracted bracket disappear. To show the user that information has been hidden, three dots are inserted in front of the text line of the contracted bracket.

In Fig. 6.12 the user sets the cursor on a portion of a case structure and says CONTRACT. The resulting contracted code contains a line beginning with three dots. In Fig. 6.13 the user selects this line and commands EXPAND.

CONTRACT may be used several times to create hierarchies of contraction. EXPAND then reveals lines that themselves can be expanded.

Contracting and expanding permits large programs to be manipulated with ease.

AUTOMATIC DERIVATION OF ACTION DIAGRAMS

Action diagrams can be derived automatically from correctly drawn decomposition diagrams (Chapter 7), dependency diagrams (Chapter 8), data flow diagrams (Chapter 9), data navigation diagrams (Chapter 12), HOS charts (Chapter 4), decision trees (Chapter 14), state transition diagrams (Chapter 15), and dialog diagrams (Chapter 16). (See Fig. 5.4.) If a computer algorithm is used for doing this, it needs to check the completeness or integrity of the dependency diagram or navigation diagram. This helps to validate or improve the analyst's design.

Looking ahead, Fig. 7.5 gives examples of decomposition diagrams and their corresponding action diagrams, Fig. 8.1 gives examples of dependency diagrams and their corresponding action diagrams, Fig. 12.2 gives examples of data navigation diagrams and their corresponding action diagrams, Figs. 14.2 and 14.4 illustrate the conversion of a decision tree to an action diagram, Figs. 15.2 and 15.10 show a state transition diagram converted to an action diagram, and Figs. 16.1 and 16.2 show a dialog design diagram automatically converted to an action diagram.

It should be noted that many types of drawings that analysts create cannot be converted *automatically* to action diagrams. When this is the case, it represents a serious defect in the methodology. It is usually desirable to abandon methodologies that do not permit automatic conversion to action diagrams or their equivalent.

CONVERSION OF ACTION DIAGRAMS TO CODE

Different computer languages have different commands relating to the constructs drawn on action diagrams. If the action diagram is being edited on a computer screen, a menu of commands can be provided for any particular language. Using the language IDEAL, for example, the designer might select the word LOOP for the top of a repetition bracket, and the software automatically puts ENDLOOP at the bottom of the bracket and

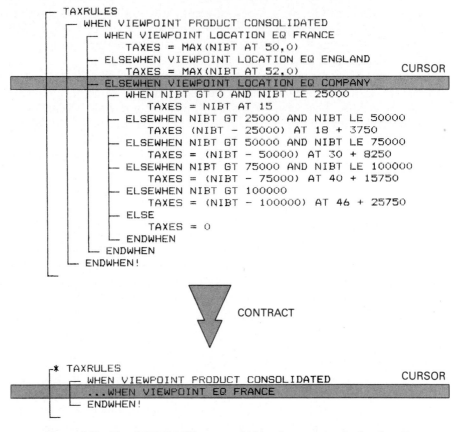

CONTRACT

Figure 6.12 The CONTRACT command hides the contents of a bracket. To show that there is hidden information three dots are placed at the start of the contracted line.

asks the designer for the loop control statement. The designer might select IF, and the software creates the following bracket:

```
┌─ IF
├─ ELSE
└─ ENDIF
```

The user is asked to specify the IF condition.

Such structures with the commands for a given language may be automatically generated from a dependency diagram or data navigation diagram. The objective is to speed up as much as possible the task of creating error-free code.

With different menus of commands for different languages, a designer may

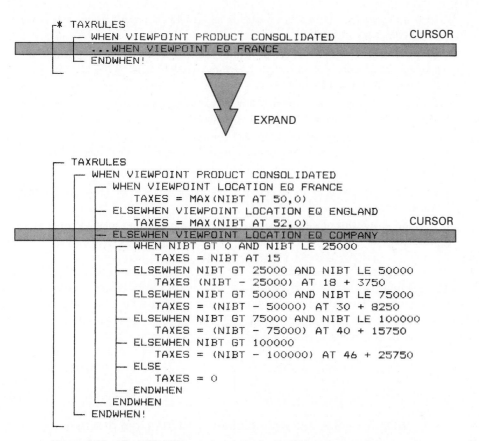

Figure 6.13 The EXPAND command can be applied to lines beginning with three dots. It reveals their hidden contents. This and Fig. 6.12 show the use of CONTRACT and EXPAND. With these commands, large designs can be reduced to summary form.

switch from one language to another if necessary. This facilitates the adoption of different languages in the future.

ADVANTAGES

Action diagrams were designed to solve some of the problems with other diagramming techniques. They were designed to have the following properties:

1. They are quick and easy to draw and to change.
2. They are good for manual sketching and for computerized editing.
3. A single technique extends from the highest overview down to coding-level detail (ultimate decomposition).

4. They draw all the constructs of traditional structured programming and are more graphic than pseudocode.

5. They are easy to teach to end users; they encourage end users to extend their capability into examination or design of detailed process logic. They are thus designed as an information center tool.

6. They can be printed on normal-width paper rather than wall charts, making them appropriate for design with personal computers.

7. Data navigation diagrams (Chapter 12) can be converted *automatically* into action diagrams. These can include compound relational operations (Chapter 13).

8. Action diagrams are designed to link to a data model.

9. They work well with fourth-generation languages and can be tailored to a specific language dialect.

10. They are designed for computerized cross-checking of data usage on complex *specifications*.

Some aspects of this list did not exist when the early structured techniques were designed: computerized editing of an analyst's diagrams, computerized cross-checking, data models, compound relational data-base operations, use of personal computers for design, fourth-generation languages, strong end-user involvement in computing, and information center management.

Chapter 12 extends action diagramming techniques to show data-base operations. Box 6.1 summarizes the diagramming conventions of action diagrams.

BOX 6.1   Summary of notation used in action diagrams

Brackets

The bracket encloses a set of activities which are to be performed. It may represent an organizational unit, a process, a program, a subroutine, or a block of code.

Title Bracket

⌐*BILLING RUN

A bracket that shows a title, rather than an action or program statement, has an asterisk attached to its top bar.

BOX 6.1   *(Continued)*

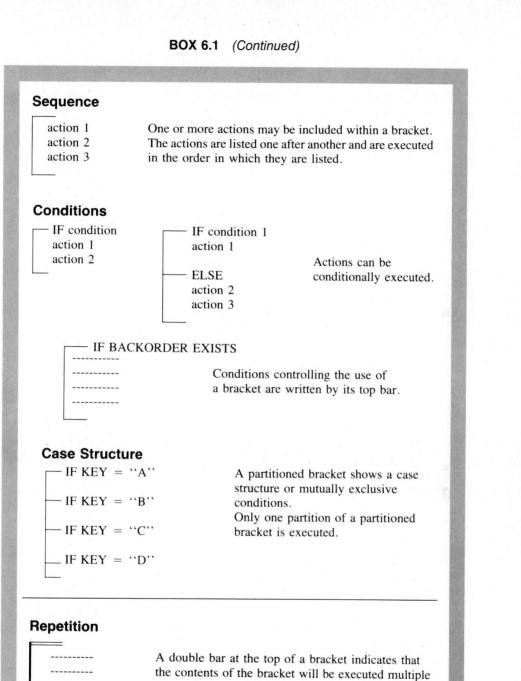

Sequence

action 1
action 2
action 3

One or more actions may be included within a bracket. The actions are listed one after another and are executed in the order in which they are listed.

Conditions

IF condition
action 1
action 2

IF condition 1
action 1

ELSE
action 2
action 3

Actions can be conditionally executed.

IF BACKORDER EXISTS

Conditions controlling the use of a bracket are written by its top bar.

Case Structure

IF KEY = "A"

IF KEY = "B"

IF KEY = "C"

IF KEY = "D"

A partitioned bracket shows a case structure or mutually exclusive conditions.
Only one partition of a partitioned bracket is executed.

Repetition

A double bar at the top of a bracket indicates that the contents of the bracket will be executed multiple times; for example, it is used to draw a program loop.

(Continued)

BOX 6.1 *(Continued)*

DO WHILE N > O   Conditions controlling a DO WHILE loop
are written at the top of the bracket,
showing that the condition is tested before
the contents of the bracket are executed.

DO   Conditions controlling a DO UNTIL loop are
written at the bottom of the bracket,
showing that the condition is tested after
the contents of the bracket are executed.

UNTIL NO MORE ITEMS

FOR ALL . . .

FOR EACH . . .
WHERE . . .

Nesting

Brackets are nested to show a hierarchy—
a form of tree structure.

BOX 6.1 *(Continued)*

Rectangle Format

The bracket may be expanded into a rectangle. The inputs to the activities in the rectangle are written at its top right-hand corner; the outputs are written at its bottom right-hand corner.

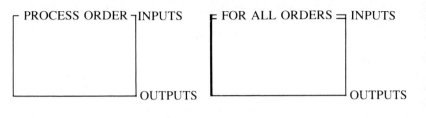

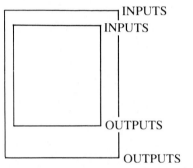

The rectangle format is designed for use with a computer which assists in drawing and cross-checks the inputs and outputs.

Exits

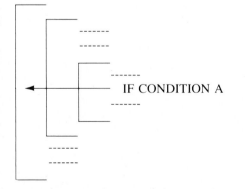

An arrow to the left through one or more brackets indicates that the brackets it passes through are terminated if the condition written by the arrow is satisfied. Control passes to the action immediately following the terminated bracket.

(Continued)

BOX 6.1 *(Continued)*

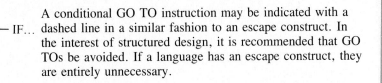

A conditional GO TO instruction may be indicated with a dashed line in a similar fashion to an escape construct. In the interest of structured design, it is recommended that GO TOs be avoided. If a language has an escape construct, they are entirely unnecessary.

Next Iteration

A NEXT structure is an arrow in a repetition bracket that does not break through the bracket. If the condition by the arrow is fulfilled, control transfers to the next iteration of the loop.

Subprocedures

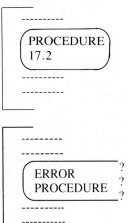

A round-cornered box within a bracket indicates a procedure diagrammed elsewhere.

A round-cornered box with its right edge made from question marks indicates a procedure not yet thought out in more detail.

Common Procedures

A procedure box with a vertical line drawn through the left side indicates a common procedure— that is, a procedure that appears multiple times in the action diagram.

BOX 6.1 *(Continued)*

Concurrency

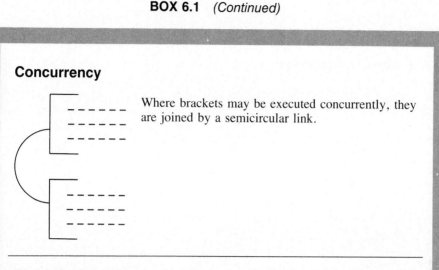

Where brackets may be executed concurrently, they are joined by a semicircular link.

The following relate to data-base action diagrams, which are discussed in Chapters 12 and 13.

Simple Data Action

READ | CUSTOMER

A rectangle containing the name of a record type or entity type is preceded by a simple data access action: CREATE, READ, UPDATE, or DELETE.

Compound Data Action

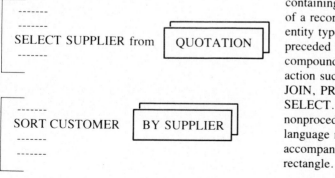

SELECT SUPPLIER from | QUOTATION

SORT CUSTOMER | BY SUPPLIER

A double rectangle containing the name of a record type or entity type is preceded by a compound data access action such as SORT, JOIN, PROJECT, or SELECT. Words of a nonprocedural language may accompany the double rectangle.

(Continued)

BOX 6.1 *(Continued)*

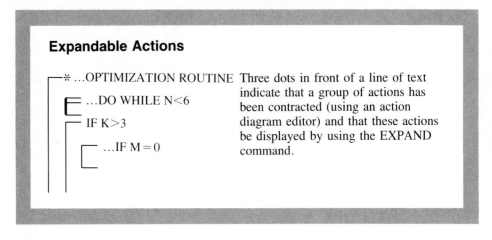

Expandable Actions

—⁎ ...OPTIMIZATION ROUTINE   Three dots in front of a line of text
indicate that a group of actions has
...DO WHILE N<6   been contracted (using an action
diagram editor) and that these actions
IF K>3   be displayed by using the EXPAND
...IF M = 0   command.

REFERENCES

1. IDEAL manual available from Applied Data Research, Inc. Princeton, N.J.

2. The example in Figs. 6.6 and 6.7 is adapted from a program in the *MANTIS User's Guide,* Cincom Systems, Inc., Cincinnati, Ohio, 1982.

7 DECOMPOSITION DIAGRAMS

One of the simplest of analysts' diagrams is the decomposition diagram. A high-level organization or activity is decomposed into lower-level organizations or activities. The lower we go in this hierarchy, the greater the detail revealed.

Tree structures are used to show the decomposition and can be drawn in the various ways described in Chapter 3.

In decomposition diagrams, a parent block is composed of its offspring blocks. It could be described as a "composed-of" diagram. The offspring together completely describe the parent. In some other tree structures, this is not true. In some program structure diagrams, a parent block invokes its child blocks but may itself contain functions that are not in the child blocks; the child blocks are, in effect, subroutines.

Most structured design employs a form of decomposition. A high-level representation of an activity is decomposed into lower-level, more detailed activities; these are decomposed further; and so on.

Decomposition diagrams can be applied to any of the activities defined in Box 4.1: business functions, processes, procedures, and program modules. The diagrams are sometimes called "function decomposition diagrams," "process decomposition diagrams," and so on. In addition, decomposition diagrams are sometimes drawn to show the structure of files, menus, tables of contents, and reports.

Decomposition diagrams may show functions decomposed into processes. They may show procedures decomposed into program modules. Often they are confined to one level of the DP pyramid (Fig. 2.1) and show processes decomposed into subprocesses or procedures decomposed into subprocedures until elementary processes or procedures that cannot be decomposed further are reached.

In many corporations, activities have never been charted. When they are listed and related to the data they use, it is usually clear that much duplication exists. Each area of a corporation tends to expand its activities without knowledge of similar activities taking place in other areas. Each department tends to create its own paperwork. This does not matter much if the paperwork is processed manually. However, if it is processed by computer, the proliferation of separately designed paperwork is harmful because it greatly increases the cost of programming and maintenance. A computerized corporation ought to have different procedures from a corporation with manual paperwork. Most of the procedures should be on-line, with data of controlled redundancy and minimum diversity of application programs. The entry of data in a terminal replaces the need to create multiple carbon copies of forms that flow among locations. Information becomes instantly available, and procedures should be changed to take advantage of this.

Charts showing decomposition of activities in an enterprise become large. They will be changed and added to many times and so need to be kept in a computerized form. Small charts can be extracted from the overall computerized chart to show the corporation and its business functions, an overview of one functional area, a detailed breakdown of one process, and so on.

End users and user management relate well to charts such as Figs. 4.1, 4.2, and 4.3. They can be encouraged to draw such charts and, where useful, decompose them into the detail necessary for planning computer programs.

THREE FORMATS

Three formats are used for decomposition diagrams. They are illustrated in Fig. 7.1.

The horizontal format has been the most common in the past. It has the disadvantage that it tends to spread out horizontally when it has a large number of items. The vertical format of Fig. 7.1 tends to spread out vertically, so it is easy to print with a cheap desktop printer.

The action diagram format of Fig. 7.1 is the most compact and has the advantage that more items of a large diagram can be seen on a workstation screen at one time. The other two formats are decorative but, apart from visual appeal, add nothing to the action diagram format. Persons used to manipulating the different formats with a PC editor tend to prefer working with the action diagram format because they can see more items at once and because lengthier wording can be used for the items.

PARENT AND LEAF NODES

In a "composed-of" diagram, the parent nodes give, in effect, titles for the activities they encompass. They are therefore shown on the action diagram with title brackets. The activities implemented are the elementary activities, which are the leaf nodes (terminal nodes) of the tree.

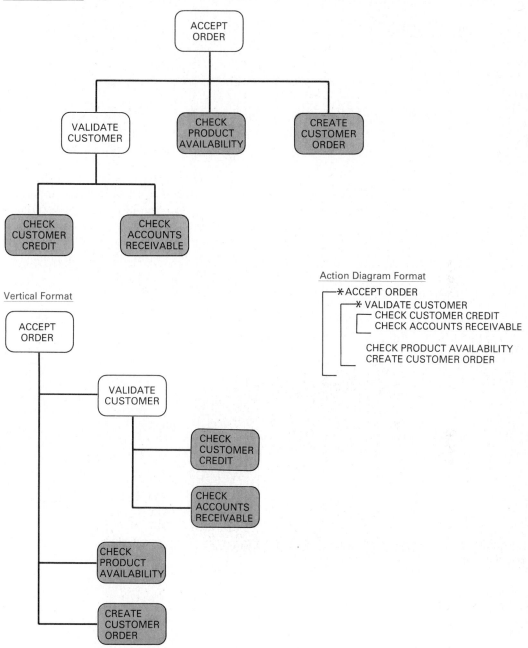

Figure 7.1 A decomposition diagram drawn in horizontal format, vertical format, and action diagram format. The parent nodes (unshaded) are, in effect, titles for the activities they encompass. They are shown with title brackets in the action diagram.

A program written for the activities in Fig. 7.1 would do the elementary activities

CHECK CUSTOMER CREDIT
CHECK ACCOUNTS RECEIVABLE
CHECK PRODUCT AVAILABILITY
CREATE CUSTOMER ORDER

Clearly, more detail needs to be added to this to show what happens if customer credit is bad, accounts receivable are unacceptable, or the product is not available. This detail is easier to add to the action diagram format.

ADDITIONAL CONSTRUCTS ON DECOMPOSITION DIAGRAMS

Simple tree-structured decompositions, as in Fig. 7.1, are the most commonly used. They are good enough for creating an overview of an enterprise's functions and processes. However, they are not good enough for diagramming the details of procedures. We need to add to the tree structures a means of representing conditions, mutually exclusive links, cardinality, and so forth.

Optionality

A certain branch of a tree may be optional. The items on it may or may not exist. We show this with the circle representing zero cardinality as described in Chapter 5:

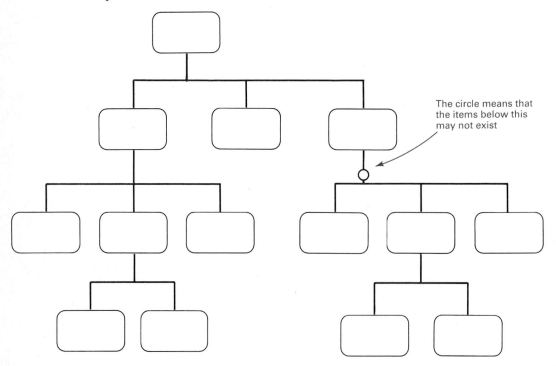

The circle means that the items below this may not exist

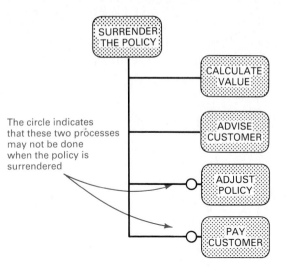

Conditions

A condition may be associated with a link to show under what conditions certain blocks are omitted:

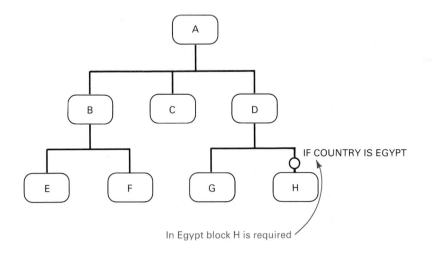

Conditions are often best displayed in a separate *detail* window. This is especially true when branching lines are drawn or when compound sets of conditions are used.

Mutual Exclusivity

Sometimes *either* one item *or* another is permissible but not both, or one item from a group is permissible. This is indicated with the filled-in circle on a branching line:

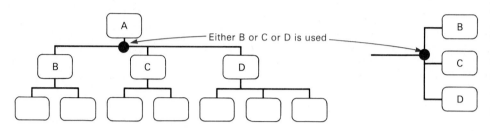

A branch without a circle means mutual *inclusivity;* that is, if one of the items branched to is used, the others are also used.

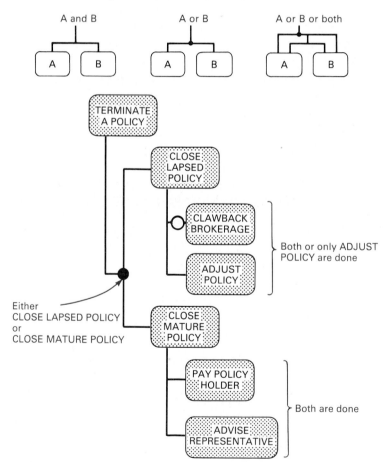

With optionality and mutual exclusivity symbols, it is desirable that conditions be associated with the appropriate part of the diagram. When the vertical format is used, the condition may be written above the block in question:

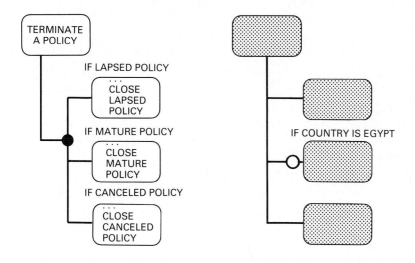

Again, where details of conditions are too complex or lengthy to put on the diagram, they may appear in a separate window describing the link.

Cardinality

Commonly, a facility is decomposed into other *single* facilities. An organization consists of single suborganizations; a business function consists of single subfunctions. Sometimes, however, we need to state that a facility is decomposed into subfacilities that occur several times. There is a one-with-many relationship between an activity and a component of that activity. This is shown using a crow's foot to indicate one-with-many cardinality:

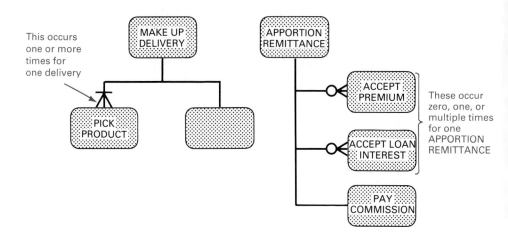

Sequence

Sometimes it is desirable to indicate in a decomposition diagram that activities occur in a given sequence. This is done with an arrow on the line to which the activities are connected. The sequence is normally from left to right (on a tree that progresses *down* the page) or from top to bottom (on a tree that progresses *across* the page).

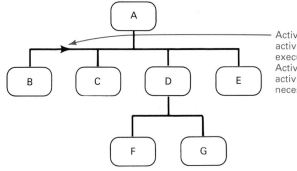

Activity A consists of activities B, C, D, and E executed in that sequence. Activity D consists of activities F and G, not necessarily in sequence.

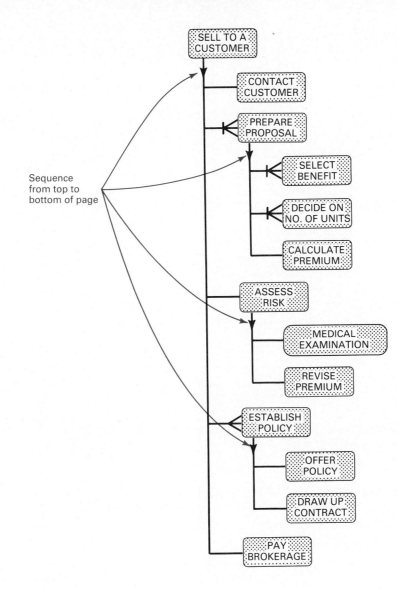

Concurrency

An activity may be decomposed into offspring that can be executed at the same time. This is indicated with the semicircle used for concurrency.

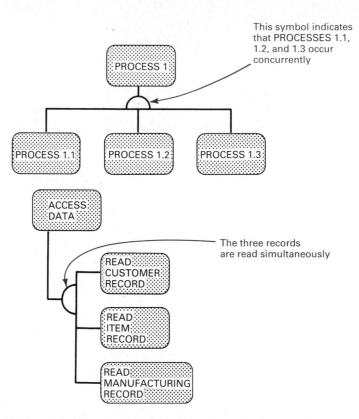

This symbol indicates that PROCESSES 1.1, 1.2, and 1.3 occur concurrently

The three records are read simultaneously

As discussed in Chapter 4, there are three fundamental types of decomposition, into

- Sequential activities
- Independent activities (which can occur concurrently)
- Alternate activities

We draw these as follows:

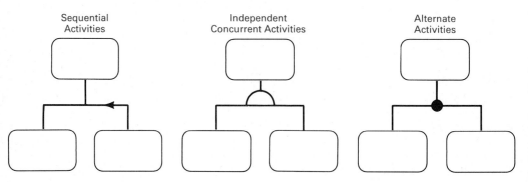

Sequential Activities

Independent Concurrent Activities

Alternate Activities

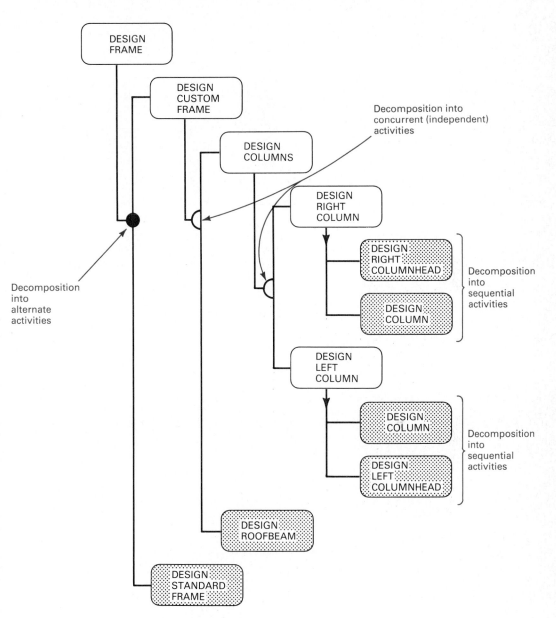

Figure 7.2 A diagram with sequential, concurrent, and alternate decomposition. The horizontal format and action diagram format of this are shown in Fig. 5.2.

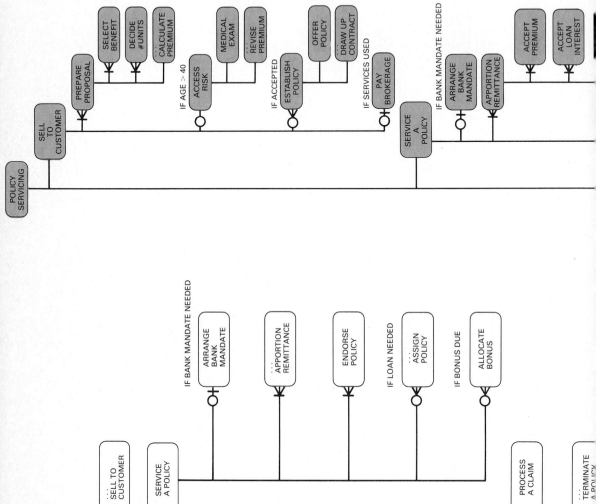

VICING. Three dots in several of the boxes indicate that parts of the diagram have been contracted (on a workstation screen). Figure 7.4 shows the diagram when these processes are reexpanded.

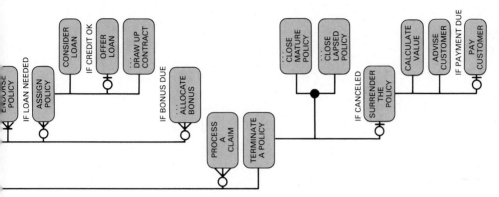

Figure 7.4 Three dots in some of the boxes in this decomposition indicate that the boxes can be further expanded on a workstation screen. The ability to use CONTACT and EXPAND commands is very useful with large diagrams.

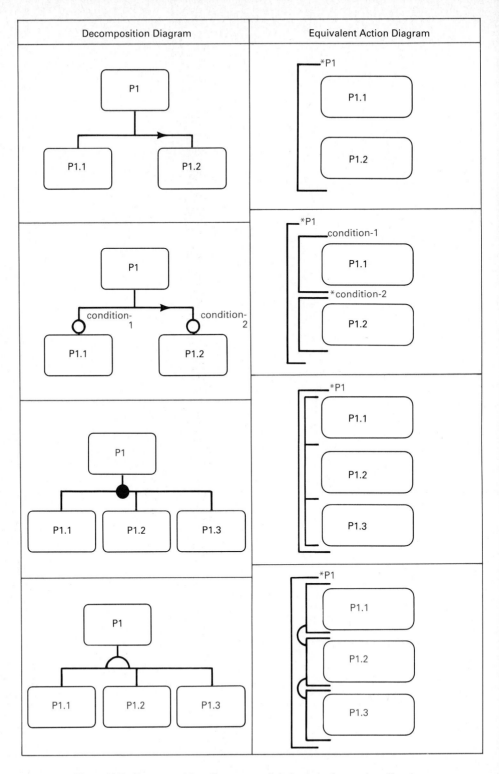

Figure 7.5   Decomposition diagrams and their equivalent action diagrams.

Decomposition Diagram	Equivalent Action Diagram

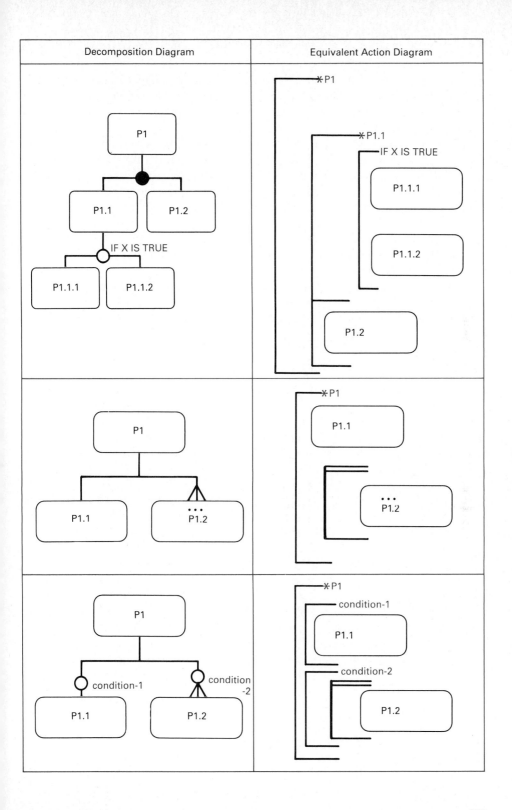

As discussed in Chapter 4, the HOS specification language uses these three types of decomposition and refers to them as JOIN, INCLUDE, and OR constructs. Figure 7.2 shows a decomposition diagram with *sequential, concurrent,* and *alternate* decomposition.

If independent activities are shown on a decomposition diagram, a computer may or may not execute them concurrently. Most of today's computers are serial machines that perform sequential execution of actions that could be done concurrently. Because of this, most analysts have not thought about the possibility of concurrent operations and draw decomposition diagrams with no concurrency indicators. Today it is not expensive to put several processors inside a personal computer, for example, so the usefulness of concurrent operations ought to be considered. Thinking often begins with visual conceptualization and clear diagrams.

If a design that shows concurrency is executed on a purely serial machine, the activities indicated as concurrent will in fact be executed one after the other. The diagram can be a logical statement; physical execution is somewhat different.

Contraction and Expansion

With a computerized editor, a large dependency diagram may be contracted by pointing to any parent block and using the CONTRACT command. Three dots are placed in that block to show that it has undisplayed children. Pointing to a block with three dots and saying EXPAND reveals its contents. This is illustrated in Figs. 7.3 and 7.4.

ULTIMATE DECOMPOSITION

If an appropriate set of constructs is used, procedures can be decomposed until executable code is derived. This is particularly so with the code of some fourth-generation languages.

Decomposing all the way to executable code is called *ultimate decomposition*. Action diagrams are designed for decomposition into executable code.

Decomposition diagrams can be automatically converted to action diagrams, as illustrated in Fig. 7.5. A CAD tool that does this should provide the designer with the capability to window between these two forms of diagrams so that a change in one can be reflected in the other. The action diagram can be edited with computerized assistance to generate executable code.

8 DEPENDENCY DIAGRAMS

A decomposition diagram shows how activities fit into a hierarchy. It does not show that certain activities are dependent on other activities. A time dependency exists between two activities if one cannot be carried out until the other has completed. This is shown on a dependency diagram.

If process B cannot be performed until process A has been completed, we draw this as follows:

Dependencies among activities can apply to functions, processes, or procedures, hence the terms ''function dependency diagram,'' ''process dependency diagram,'' and ''procedure dependency diagram.''

The following could be a process or a procedure dependency diagram:

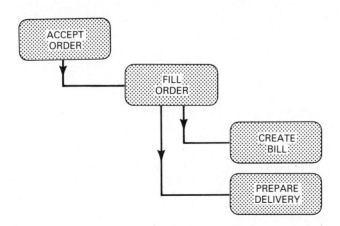

**THREE TYPES OF
DEPENDENCIES**   One activity may be dependent on another activity
for three types of reasons.

1. Resource Dependency

Activity A produces or modifies some tangible resource; activity B uses this resource. For example, DELIVER ORDER cannot occur before PICK GOODS, because there would be nothing to deliver. This type of dependency occurs only between resource handling activities.

2. Data Dependency

Activity A creates or updates some data; activity B uses the data. For example, CREATE BACKORDER cannot occur until ACCEPT ORDER has occurred because CREATE BACKORDER needs certain data from the ACCESS ORDER process.

3. Constraint Dependency

An execution of some step in activity B depends on a constraint that was set in activity A or the testing of a condition that was set in activity A.

This type of dependency is to be avoided because it suggests tight coupling between activities. It should be replaced with a data dependency so that the constraint or condition set in activity A results in data being passed to activity B.

The activity boxes should be regarded as separate and disjointed, with no entanglements between them except for the common use of data or tangible items.

**FLOWS OR
SHARED ACCESS**   There are two types of interaction among dependent
activities, flows and shared access to common storage.

With resource dependencies, tangible goods may flow from one activity to another. Alternatively, the first activity may put goods in a warehouse, and the dependent activity take them from the warehouse.

With data dependencies, data may flow from one activity to another. Alternatively, the first activity may put data into on-line storage, and the dependent activity takes them from the storage. Many dependent activities may share the same on-line files or data base.

**INDEPENDENCE
OF MECHANISMS**   We have distinguished between *processes* and *procedures*. Diagrams with processes show *what* must
happen to make the enterprise function but not *how*

this happens in terms of detail mechanisms. Diagrams with procedures show *how* and are concerned with the mechanisms. We could call the former *mechanism-independent diagrams*. They are sometimes called "logical" diagrams, but this word has other connotations.

Mechanism-independent diagrams are not concerned with whether data flow directly from one process to another or whether they are passed via shared on-line storage. Such diagrams enable us to diagram business processes without considering whether a data base is used or even whether a computer is used. End users tend to relate well to mechanism-independent diagrams that illustrate their business processes.

As we descend into more detail, we need to consider the use of data bases. At this stage in the design, dependency diagrams (or data flow diagrams, which are a specific form of dependency diagram) become inadequate. We need the greater details of data navigation diagrams and action diagrams, discussed later.

CONSTRUCTS ON DEPENDENCY DIAGRAMS

As with other types of diagrams we can use the constructs of Chapter 5 to provide more information on dependency diagrams.

Optionality

One process may give rise to another process only when certain conditions apply. We show optionality with a circle on the link between processes or procedures. The circle may be labeled with a condition:

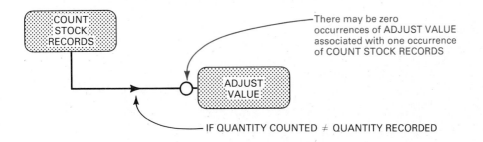

Often the condition is not written on the diagram because it is a high-level view of dependencies and the diagram needs to be uncluttered by detail. Complex conditions may be shown in a separate window.

A circle may be at either end of the line connecting blocks. Suppose the line goes from process A to process B. If the circle is by process B, the dependent process B may not occur. If the circle is by process A, process B may occur without process A having happened:

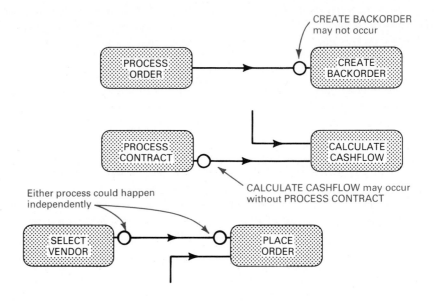

Multiple Dependencies

Sometimes one activity is dependent on several other activities. Lines from the preceding activity boxes join and enter the dependent activity box:

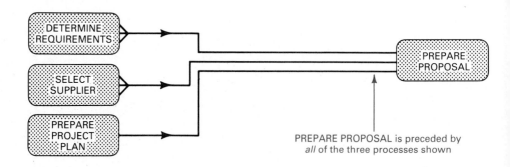

Conversely, one activity may give rise to many others:

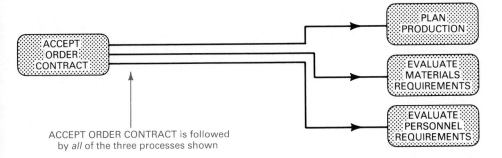

ACCEPT ORDER CONTRACT is followed
by *all* of the three processes shown

Mutual Exclusivity

Sometimes one or other of two activities must be performed, but not both. Sometimes one of several activities must be performed. These *mutually exclusive* choices of activity are shown by a solid circle on a branching line—the OR circle used earlier:

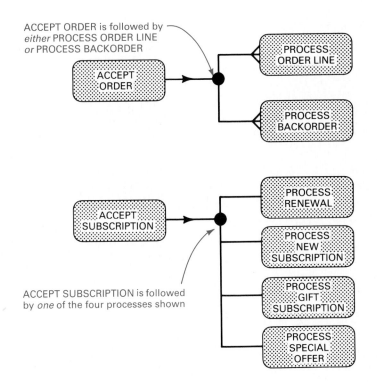

In this case, one activity is followed by alternate activities. One activity can also be dependent on alternate activities. For example, a depot may order stock of a particular product in three possible circumstances. One, a routine process MONITOR STOCK indicates that the stock has dropped below a reorder level. Two, a CREATE BACKORDER process has been initiated because a customer order cannot be filled. Three, a delivery is being loaded and PICK STOCK reveals unexpectedly that there are insufficient stocks. No other process can cause more stock to be ordered. These three processes are independent:

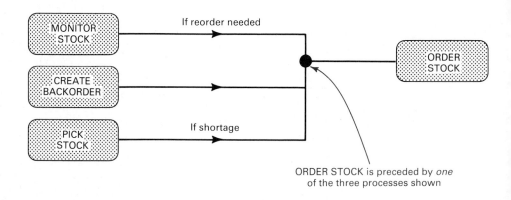

ORDER STOCK is preceded by *one* of the three processes shown

Conditions may be written on the mutually exclusive links.

Cardinality

In the foregoing diagrams, the dependent process is executed *once* after the preceding process. In some diagrams, we want to show that it may be executed several times:

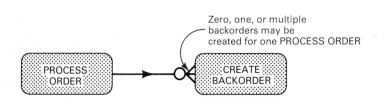

Zero, one, or multiple backorders may be created for one PROCESS ORDER

Similarly, a dependent process may follow several executions of a preceding process:

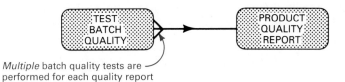

Multiple batch quality tests are
performed for each quality report

Less common is a one-with-many association at both ends of a link:

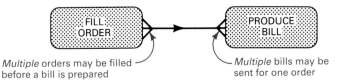

Multiple orders may be filled
before a bill is prepared

Multiple bills may be
sent for one order

Start and End of Repetition Sequences

In some cases, a one-with-many association is used in conjunction with a many-with-one, and the two need to be associated. They form the beginning and end of a repetition construct (loop). To show that they are associated, they are numbered:

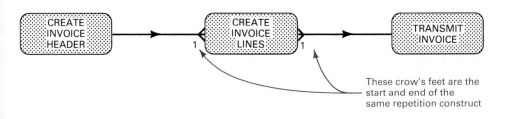

These crow's feet are the
start and end of the
same repetition construct

Recursion

On rare occasions a process is drawn that depends upon itself. Decomposing an order into a bill of materials may result in subassemblies having to be decomposed into lower-level subassemblies or components. Decomposing a complex project into activities may result in activities themselves being further decomposed:

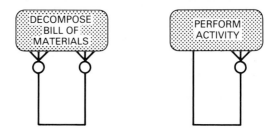

The diagram on the right is, in effect, a tree structure in which every block in the tree has the same label: PERFORM ACTIVITY. The diagram on the left is, in effect, a network structure (plex structure) in which every block is labeled DECOMPOSE BILL OF MATERIALS.

Parallel Links

Occasionally, two or more links join the same two activity blocks. If these go in the same direction, this might indicate that the processes have been insufficiently or incorrectly decomposed. Links going in opposite directions between two processes occur in feedback loops or control mechanisms:

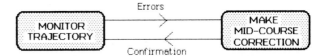

Events

Some processes are triggered by other processes. This is often the case, but need not be so. Some are triggered by events. For example, the receipt of a payment may trigger a process. A process may be triggered by a customer telephoning to make a booking, a security alarm going off, the financial year ending, a bank's closing time being reached, or a demand for information. All are events external to the processes. We may talk about *event-triggered* processes and *process-triggered* processes.

A large arrow on a diagram is used to show that an event occurs:

This may be used on a dependency diagram, data flow diagram, or other type of diagram such as a state transition diagram.

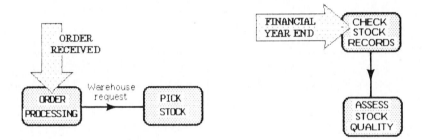

Some processes may be either event-triggered or process-triggered. For example, ALLOCATE PAYMENT in the following diagram may be triggered either by the event PAYMENT ARRIVES or by the process PRODUCE IN-VOICE:

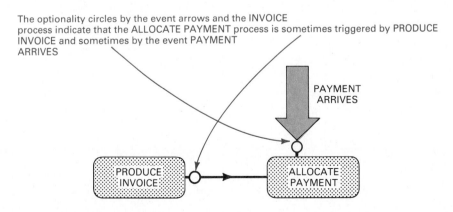

The optionality circles by the event arrows and the INVOICE process indicate that the ALLOCATE PAYMENT process is sometimes triggered by PRODUCE INVOICE and sometimes by the event PAYMENT ARRIVES

In some cases, both a preceding process and an event must occur before a given process takes place. In this case, the event arrow links to the dependency arrow:

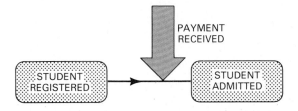

Concurrency

Activities on a dependency diagram can often be executed concurrently. This can be indicated (where useful) by means of the concurrency symbol used in previous chapters:

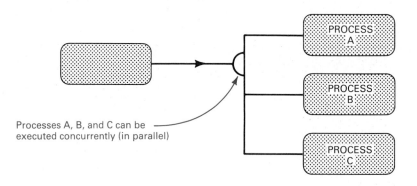

Processes A, B, and C can be executed concurrently (in parallel)

When high-level functions or processes are used, it is clear when they are independent, and so the concurrency symbol is not needed. With procedures that may be executed on machines, the concurrency symbol is valuable and will become of greater necessity as multiprocessing becomes more common.

After two or more groups of parallel activities have occurred, it is sometimes necessary to resynchronize, that is, for the parallel streams to meet and become one. This shown by lines from each stream meeting at one process:

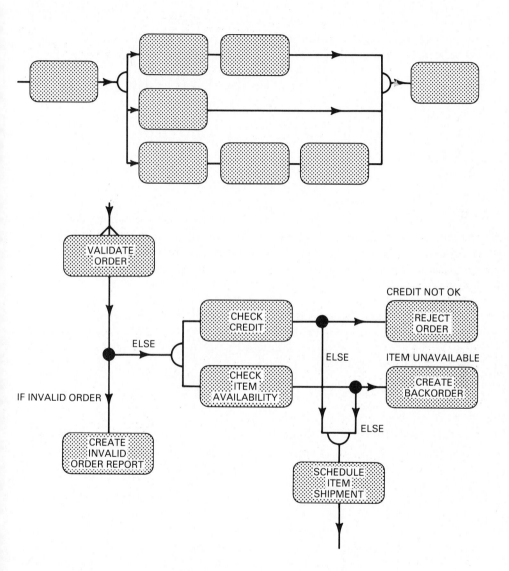

Clear termination of the concurrent streams of activities is needed for automatic conversion of the dependency diagram into an action diagram.

CONVERSION TO ACTION DIAGRAMS   A dependency diagram can be converted automatically into an action diagram. An action diagram that shows sufficient detail can be thought of as a skeleton of a program. The skeleton is filled in to produce an executable program. This process can be done in a fast computer-aided fashion.

Action diagrams are discussed in detail in Chapter 6; Fig. 8.1 illustrates the automatic conversion of dependency diagrams to action diagrams. A CAD tool that performs this conversion should allow the designer to window between the dependency diagram and the action diagram and modify either.

A PROCESS–ENTITY MATRIX   It is not practical or desirable to show every dependency among processes. A process may use data or resources that were created by another process months before. To sell goods, it is necessary to hire salespeople, but these two activities would not normally be linked on a dependency diagram. Dependency diagrams are used to show processes with a close relationship that must be analyzed in order to understand how the enterprise functions.

There are often dependencies that are not drawn between processes that use the same data. This shared usage of data-base records is illustrated on a matrix chart like that in Fig. 8.2, which shows entity types and processes that create, retrieve, update, or delete data about the entities. Although one process may use data that another process creates or updates, these processes may be sufficiently unconnected in time or sequence that they would not be combined on one dependency diagram.

DIAGRAMMING STYLE   Complex mesh-structured diagrams can be difficult to read if not drawn well. To make a dependency diagram clear, the arrows should point down or to the right where possible.

An activity with no arrows entering it from another activity is called a *root* or *level 1* activity. A group of activities are associated with a level 1 activity. The level 1 activity should be at the top left of the group. Similarly, an activity with no arrows *leaving* it should be at the bottom or right.

If a level 1 activity and the lines connecting it are removed, any remaining activity with no arrows entering it is called a *level 2* activity. This may be at the top left of the remaining group.

Using this rule, a computer algorithm can redraw or ''clean up'' a dependency diagram with casually positioned boxes:

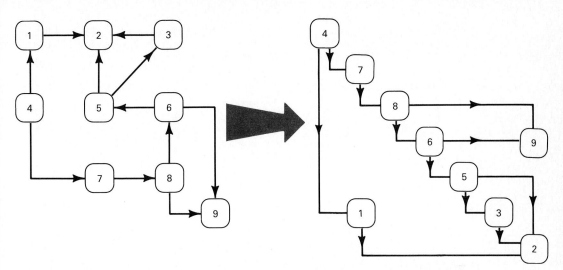

An intelligent analyst can usually do a better job than a computer of clarifying a messy diagram. There is often a main line path through the diagram that the analyst understands, as well as exception activities that the analyst will place to one side. The above diagram might be better drawn like this:

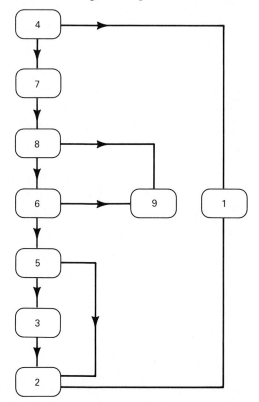

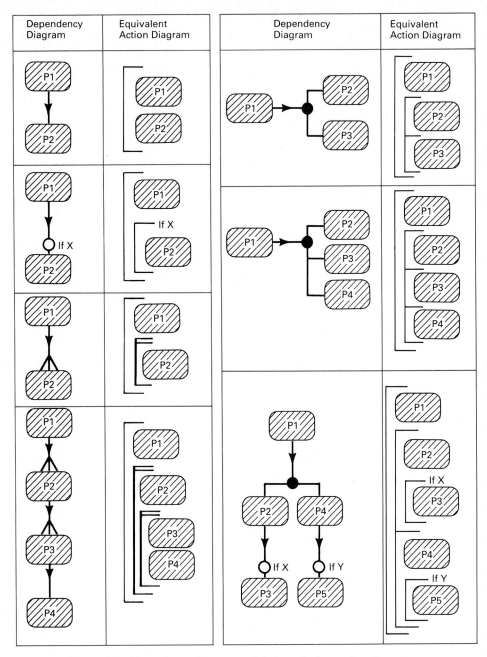

Figure 8.1 Dependency diagrams and their equivalent action diagrams.

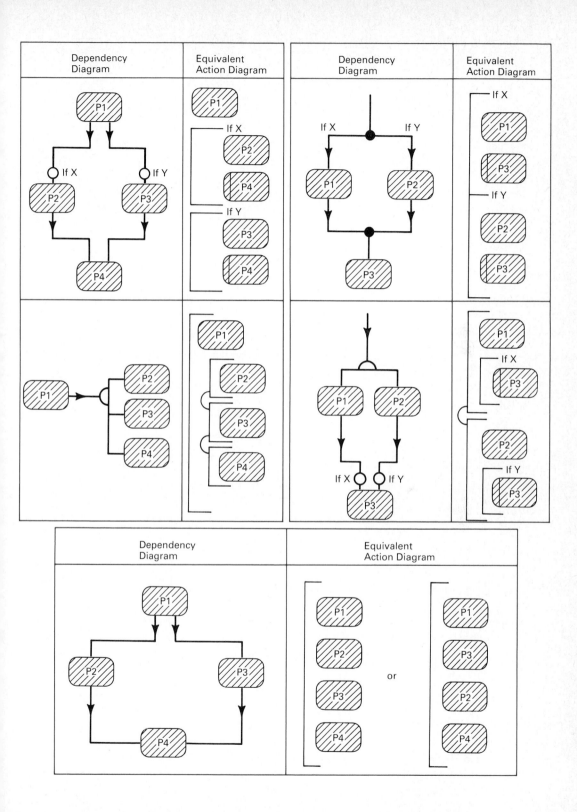

PROCESS \ ENTITY TYPE	Customer	Order	Vendor	Product	Invoice	Material	Cost	Part	Raw Material Inventory	Finished Goods Inventory	Employee	Sales Territory	Budget	Plan	Were in Process	Facility	Open Requirements	Machine Tools	Payroll
Enter Customer Order	R	C	R	R			U			U									
Control Customer Order	R	R	R	R		R	R			R					U				
Create Invoice	R	R		R	C			R											
Plan Production				R			R	R	R	R	R				U		R	R	
Update Finished Goods Inventory				R						U									
Prepare Bills of Material		R		R		R		R							U		U		
Update Parts Inventory									R	R	R				U				
Control Purchase Orders			R	R		R	R	R	R	R									
Create Routings															R	R		R	
Monitor Shop Floor Activities		R		R		R			R	R	R							R	
Plan Capacity		R							R	R		U			R			R	
Update General Ledger		R			R	R													
Evaluate Product Cost		R		R			R	R				U					R	R	
Produce Operating Statements													R	R	R				
Produce Accounts Receivable Report	R	R											R						
Produce Accounts Payable Report			R				R	R								R			
Produce Asset Accounting Report									R	R						R		R	
Create Marketing Budget	R	R					R						R	U					
Create Payroll											R								C

Figure 8.2 A process—entity type matrix. (C, create; R, read; U, update; D, delete.)

Many dependency and data flow diagrams are unruly bird's nests. Perhaps the work of redrawing them was too great. Computerized tools give the capability to move blocks easily and have the lines with arrows reconnect them automatically. Analysts should be encouraged to use this facility to make their diagrams as clear as possible.

Figures 8.3 and 8.4 show dependency diagrams with the arrows going downward and to the right.

DIAGRAMS SHOWING DATA

It is necessary to link the design of data in an enterprise (the normalized data models) with the design of processes. We can add information to a dependency diagram to show what records or normalized groupings of data it uses.

Figure 8.4 shows a *procedure* dependency diagram for an Order Acceptance Procedure. This diagram shows the record types employed. The record

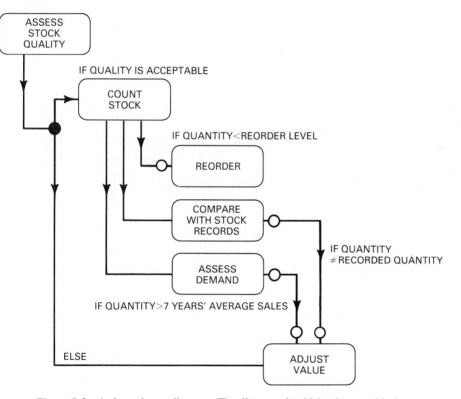

Figure 8.3 A dependency diagram. The diagram should be drawn with the arrows pointing down or to the right wherever possible. The root of the diagram (a box with no arrows entering it) should be at the top left.

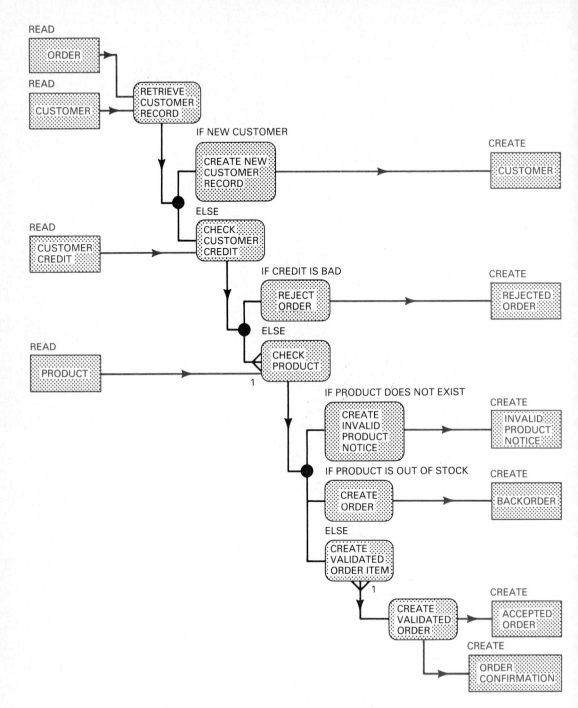

Figure 8.4 A dependency diagram showing the data record types used (in red).

types that are read are on the left; those that are created or updated are on the right (the data arrows go from left to right).

The arrows going from one procedure box to another can be marked with the data that pass between those procedures. If the diagram is marked in this way, it is in effect, a data flow diagram (the subject of the next chapter).

9 DATA FLOW DIAGRAMS

A data flow diagram is similar to a dependency diagram except that it shows data stores and data passing between activities. Often the best way to create a data flow diagram is first to draw a dependency diagram (which shows only the activities) and then add information about data stores and data flow to it.

A dependency diagram is commonly used at level 2 of the DP pyramid, showing the business processes and their associations. A data flow diagram is commonly used at level 3 for the design procedures:

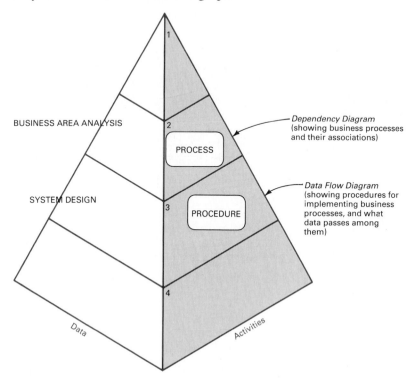

COMPONENTS OF A DATA FLOW DIAGRAM

Figure 9.1 shows a typical data flow diagram (DFD). It shows how four procedures are linked to form a sales distribution system.

Data flow diagrams have four main components:

- Round-cornered boxes representing activities (usually procedures).
- Links between boxes like those in a dependency diagram. The links have an arrow showing the flow of data between activities. The arrow is labeled with the name of the data.
- An open-ended rectangle showing a data store.
- A double-line square showing an external source or destination of data.

Data flow diagrams as traditionally drawn do not show constructs that were described in Chapter 8 (cardinality, conditions, etc.). It is valuable to draw these on data flow diagrams in a similar fashion to dependency diagrams. This facilitates automatic conversion to action diagrams.

We will first discuss data flow diagrams as traditionally drawn (using the notation of Gane and Sarson [1], then illustrate data flow diagrams that incorporate the constructs just mentioned.

The black part of Fig. 9.1 is like a dependency diagram (the one at the beginning of Chapter 8) except that it labels the data flows. The red part of Fig. 9.1 shows the data stores.

DATA FLOW

The *data flow* traces the flow of data through a system of procedures. Direction of data flow is indicated by an arrow. The data are identified by name, alongside the corresponding arrow; for example:

PRODUCTS ORDERED

In effect, the data flow shows how the procedures are connected.

PROCEDURE

A *procedure* operates on (or transforms) data. For example, it may perform arithmetic or logic operations on data to produce some result. Each procedure is represented by a round-cornered box on the DFD. The name of the procedure is written inside the box; for example:

VALIDATE CUSTOMER

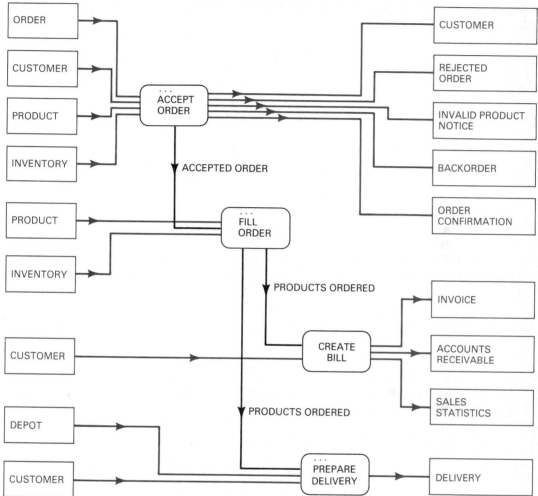

SALES DISTRIBUTION SYSTEM

Figure 9.1 A data flow diagram for a sales distribution system. The black part shows procedures and data passing between procedures. The red part shows the data stores used by the procedures. The three dots at the start of a procedure label indicate that the procedure has been designed in more detail and that an expanded version of the procedure may be displayed. Figure 9.2 shows the ACCEPT ORDER procedure in more detail.

No other information about what the procedure does is shown in the DFD.

Normally data flows in and out of each procedure. Often there are several data flows in and out of a procedure; for example:

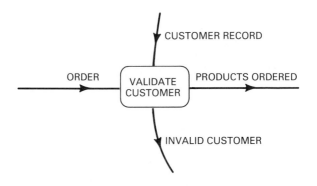

DATA STORE

A *data store* represents a repository of data. It has often been drawn on DFDs as a pair of parallel lines closed at one end. The name of the data store is written between the lines; for example:

PRODUCTS FILE

The square-cornered box used for data objects in general is appropriate for drawing this repository of data.

Each data store is connected to a procedure box by means of a data flow. The direction of the data flow arrow shows whether data are being read from the data store into the procedure or produced by the procedure and then output to the data store.

In the following example, error information is produced by the ERROR PROCEDURE and written out to ERROR FILE:

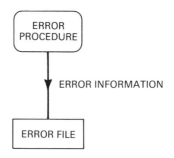

TERMINATOR　　　　A *terminator* shows the origin of data used by the system and the ultimate recipient of data produced by the system. The origin of data is called a *source,* and the recipient of data is called a *sink*. A rectangular box or double square, as shown below, is used to represent a terminator in a DFD:

Terminators actually lie outside the DFD.

NESTING　　　　Data flow diagrams, like dependency diagrams, are commonly *nested*. One box on a diagram may be a high-level procedure. Another data flow diagram shows what happens inside that box.

Figure 9.1, for example, shows a sales distribution system. The top box is called ACCEPT ORDER. The details of ACCEPT ORDER are shown in another data flow diagram, Fig. 9.2. The three-dot notation is used in Fig. 9.1 to indicate that the boxes can be *expanded* into a more detailed representation.

This nesting process is called *leveling*. Often it is done so that any one data flow diagram has no more than six or seven procedure boxes. More complex data flow diagrams are difficult to read. On complex systems, many levels of nesting may be used.

GANE AND SARSON NOTATION　　　　Gane and Sarson [1] adopted slightly different diagramming conventions for data flow diagrams from those popularized by Yourdon and De Marco [2, 3]. In some ways, the Gane and Sarson notation is better. Figure 9.3 summarizes the two.

Gane and Sarson draw a process as a rounded rectangle; Yourdon and De Marco draw it as a circle. In computerized drawing, it is easier to link *multiple* arrows to a round-cornered box than a circle:

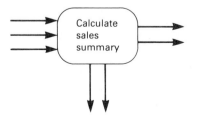

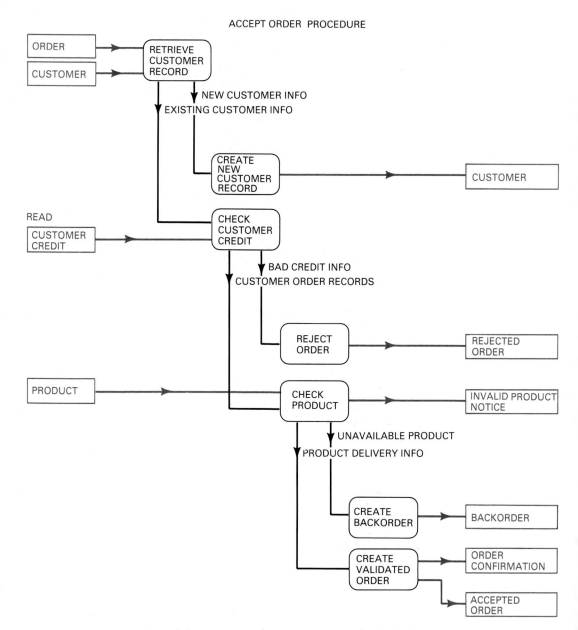

ACCEPT ORDER PROCEDURE

ORDER

CUSTOMER

RETRIEVE
CUSTOMER
RECORD

NEW CUSTOMER INFO
EXISTING CUSTOMER INFO

CREATE
NEW
CUSTOMER
RECORD

CUSTOMER

READ

CUSTOMER
CREDIT

CHECK
CUSTOMER
CREDIT

BAD CREDIT INFO
CUSTOMER ORDER RECORDS

REJECT
ORDER

REJECTED
ORDER

PRODUCT

CHECK
PRODUCT

INVALID PRODUCT
NOTICE

UNAVAILABLE PRODUCT
PRODUCT DELIVERY INFO

CREATE
BACKORDER

BACKORDER

CREATE
VALIDATED
ORDER

ORDER
CONFIRMATION

ACCEPTED
ORDER

Figure 9.2   The top activity in Fig. 9.1 (ACCEPT ORDER) is expanded here
into a more detailed data flow diagram.

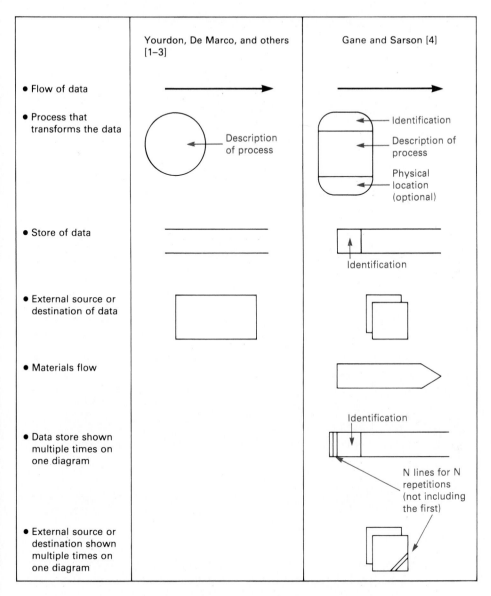

Figure 9.3 Symbols used on data flow diagrams.

At the top of Gane and Sarson's block, a block number or other identifier
is drawn:

At the bottom, the designer may draw the physical location where the
process takes place or the name of the computer program that executes the
process:

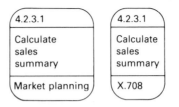

The data store is drawn with a block at the left that may contain its number
or identification. It may relate to a data model:

An external source or destination of data is drawn with a double square:

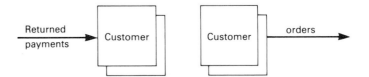

To simplify the mesh of lines on a drawing, a data store or external source
or destination may appear several times. If a data store appears twice, a vertical
line is drawn at the left side of its block. If an external block appears twice, a
diagonal line is drawn in its bottom right corner:

If either of these appears three times, two such lines are drawn:

If they appear N times, $N - 1$ such lines are drawn.

Data flow diagrams are useful for showing the flow of materials as well as computer data. It is important to indicate what are computer data and what are not. Gane and Sarson use thick arrows for showing the flow of materials.

Sometimes computer data accompany materials. Gane and Sarson draw the two together, as shown in Fig. 9.4.

USE OF COMPUTER GRAPHICS

Data flow diagrams for complex projects become large, unwieldy, and difficult to maintain. The use of computer graphics solves these problems. When such tools are used, a developer creates diagrams on a workstation screen, updating the set of charts for the project that are available to all developers.

Various computerized versions of data flow diagramming exist, including some elegant PC tools. Figure 9.5 is a data flow diagram created on a PC screen with the EXCELERATOR software from InTech [4].

Here are the advantages of using computerized graphics:

- Significant cost and time savings
- Reduction in labor needed to redraft graphics development
- Encouragement of repositioning the blocks to clarify the diagram
- Significant labor reduction for documentation updates during maintenance
- Elimination of proofreading and potential for error introduction on diagram updates

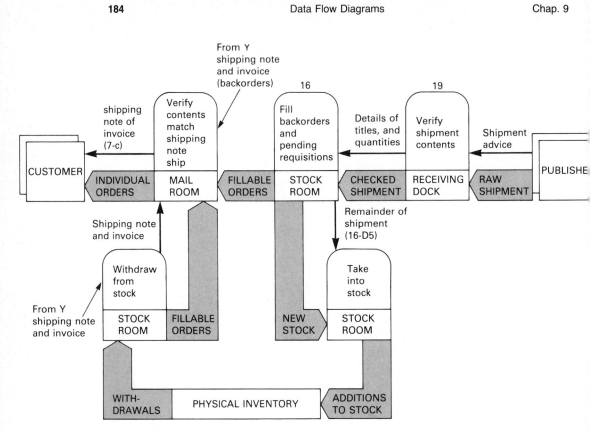

Figure 9.4 Gane and Sarson diagram showing physical flows (thick arrows) as well as data flows (thin arrows).

- Capability to produce very large data flow diagrams, as in long-range system planning
- Linkage to an encyclopedia with a methodology that aids other aspects of system design and code generation

Style in Diagramming

There is a notable difference in diagramming style between Figs. 9.1 and 9.2 and Fig. 9.5. Figure 9.5 jumbles up the boxes in a seemingly random fashion. As discussed in Chapter 8, it is desirable to position the boxes on a diagram to make it as clear as possible. A computerized tool ought to give the maximum help in making the diagrams as clear as possible.

It makes the diagram clearer to separate the data from the activities and to make the data boxes a different color from the activity boxes.

INSUFFICIENT PRECISION   Data flow diagrams are a very valuable tool for charting flows of documents and computer data. However, as commonly drawn, they have insufficient precision for computer-aided design.

Tools are available for drawing data flow diagrams on a computer screen. However, we want the computer to be more than merely a drawing tool; we want three types of help from it:

1. We want it to check the accuracy of the design in any way possible.
2. We want it to link the design to a computerized encyclopedia and data model.
3. Most important, we want it to convert our diagrams into code structures on action diagrams, for the automation of the programming task.

CROSS-CHECKING   In many cases, data flow diagrams have been used badly. Large, complex specifications have been created with the help of such diagrams, but the task of cross-checking all of the inputs and outputs of data was not done adequately.

The authors of some data flow diagrams protest that when they draw the early, high-level diagrams, they cannot yet know the detail that will emerge when designing the later diagrams. It is always true that the early diagrams are sketches, not yet detailed or precise. However, later, when the detail is worked out, it ought to be reflected in the higher levels so that these levels become correct.

With a computerized tool, this can be done automatically. The detailed inputs and outputs of the lower-level layers can be reflected in the higher-level layers. Amazingly, some computerized tools do not do this. They are merely drawing aids, not linked to integrity checks.

LINKAGE TO A DATA MODEL   The lower-level charts of a complex system often show, in total, many data items. If all of these data items were individually shown on the top-level charts, the charts would be very cluttered. The top-level charts may therefore show an aggregate data name that encompasses many of the lower-level names. The top-level chart may, for example, show MANUFACTURING DATA BASE as input; the next level shows JOB RECORD, which is part of MANUFACTURING DATA BASE; the lowest level shows MACHINE-TOOL#, START-TIME, etc., which are part of JOB RECORD. This is called *data layering*.

We need drawing conventions to show how the data are layered. Different ways to draw structured data are shown in later chapters.

If detailed data flow diagrams are drawn without thorough understanding

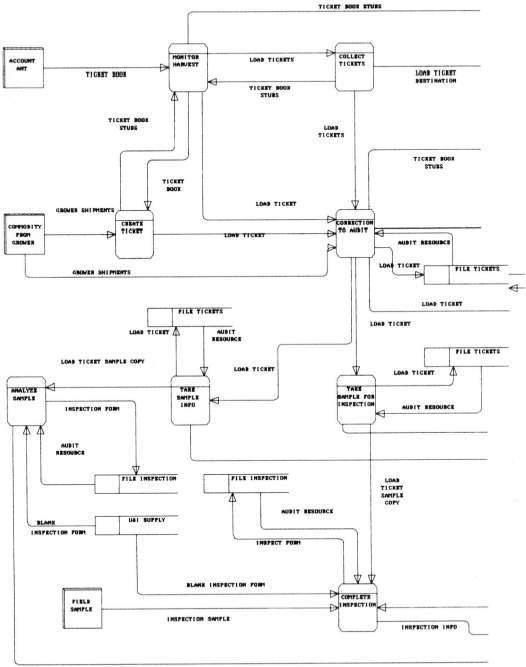

Figure 9.5 Data flow diagram produced and maintained on a personal computer with EXCELERATOR from InTech [4]. EXCELERATOR links data flow and other diagrams to its data dictionary.

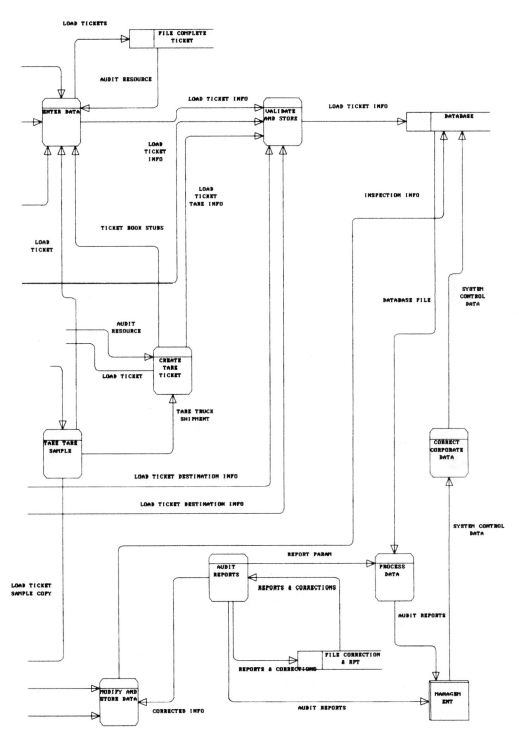

Figure 9.5 (Continued)

187

and structuring of the data, problems will result. Data analysis and data modeling, discussed later, need to go hand in hand with data flow diagramming.

ADDITIONAL CONSTRUCTS

Data flow diagram are commonly drawn without the constructs illustrated with dependency diagrams in Chapter 8: optionality, conditions, cardinality, mutual exclusivity, recursion, and concurrency. It is useful to employ these constructs with data flow diagrams also. This facilitates automated conversion to action diagrams.

Figure 9.2 was drawn without these constructs. It is redrawn in Fig. 9.6 using the constructs where applicable. It can now be converted into the action diagram of Fig. 9.7.

When thinking about procedures, an analyst (or end user) constantly thinks about conditions and repetition. When is something done and when is it not? Which things have to be done repetitively—for every customer, for every item on an order, and so on? Data flow diagrams are much more useful if they can express conditions, repetition, mutually exclusive paths, and the like.

When a computerized tool is used, essentially the same software can be used for dependency diagrams and data flow diagrams. Data flow diagrams allow the user to express more detail in terms of data.

The designer may begin by sketching a dependency diagram showing the procedures. He may automatically translate that into an action diagram. This helps him to see whether the links between procedures appear correct. He may adjust the diagrams at this level, then think about the data used and add these to the diagram, creating a data flow diagram. He may employ a data model or data storage diagram to help with this (discussed in the following chapters). Again, at the data flow diagram stage, he may examine the equivalent action diagram. The rectangular format of action diagram may be used to show data inputs and outputs for the various procedures and to check that they balance.

CONVERSION TO CODE

The common technique of drawing a structure chart from a data flow diagram and creating structured English from this [1, 2, 3] is inadequate for the age of computer-aided design. Drawing a structure chart, creating structured English, and converting the structured English to program code are error-prone, nonrigorous, manual processes.

Instead of these, a data flow diagram ought to be drawn with the techniques of dependency diagrams and converted *automatically* to an action diagram, as illustrated in Fig. 8.1. An action diagram can then be edited on the computer screen to produce executable code.

With an appropriate CAD tool, the designer can window between the data flow diagram and the action diagram, adjusting either and linking the design to

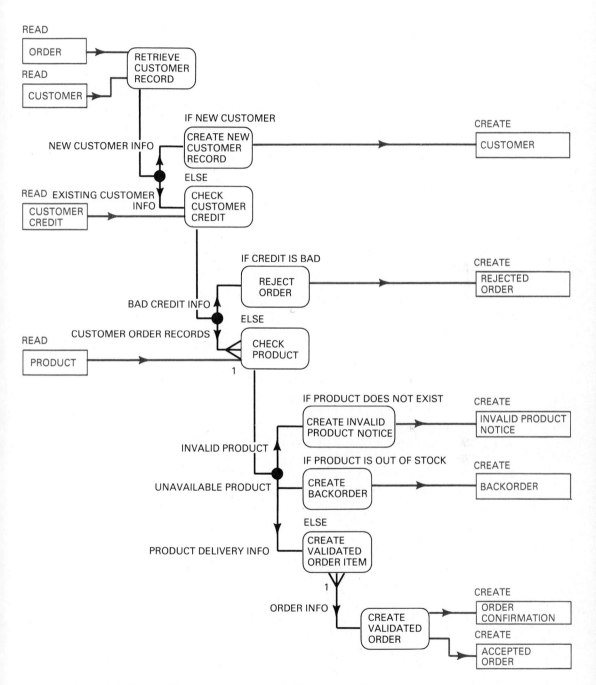

Figure 9.6 Figure 9.2 redrawn to show conditions, mutually exclusive associations, repetition, and the like.

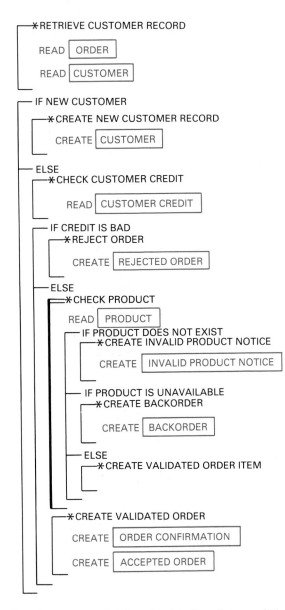

Figure 9.7 An action diagram generated from the data flow diagram of Fig. 9.6. A rectangular-format action diagram could show the data passing between procedures. Automatic generation of action diagrams from data flow diagrams helps the designer to think out the data flow diagram more clearly. The action diagram would then be edited and added to on the workstation screen, with control words of a selected language being added automatically.

a centrally maintained data model. The action diagram can be linked to fourth-generation languages to produce executable code.

REFERENCES

1. C. Gane and T. Sarson, *Structured Systems Analysis: Tools and Techniques.* New York: IST, Inc., 1977.

2. E. Yourdon and L. Constantine, *Structured Design.* New York: Yourdon, Inc., 1978.

3. T. De Marco, *Structured Analysis and System Specification.* New York: Yourdon, Inc., 1978.

4. EXCELERATOR from InTech, 5 Cambridge Center, Cambridge, MA 02142.

10 DATA ANALYSIS AND DATA STRUCTURE DIAGRAMS

Many structured techniques represent data as tree structures (hierarchies). The data on purchase orders, bank statements, restaurant menus, and most computer printouts can be represented as tree structures. However, some computer input and output data are not hierarchical. Such data can be drawn as tree structures only if certain data items are shown redundantly or if there are non-tree-structured associations linking the trees. Nonhierarchical data structures are referred to as *plex* or *network* structures.

Plex- (network-)structured data are extremely important in the data-base environment. This chapter and the next illustrate the ways in which data-base structures are drawn. This chapter illustrates bubble charts and drawings of record structures. The following chapter illustrates entity-relationship charts and data models.

BUBBLE CHARTS

Bubble charts provide a way of drawing and understanding the associations among data items. This understanding is necessary in order to create records that are clearly structured. Bubble charts form the input to a data-modeling process that creates stable data structures. This process is automated.

Bubble charts are a useful way to teach end users and analysts about associations in data. They should employ bubble charts when they start to create logical data-base structures. As they become more expert, they may avoid drawing them and represent the same information as input to an automated tool that synthesizes the data structure [1].

The most elemental piece of data is called a *data item*. It is sometimes also called a *field* or a *data element*. It is the atom of data, in that it cannot be subdivided into smaller data types and retain any meaning to users. You cannot split the data item called SALARY, for example, into smaller data items that by themselves are meaningful to end users.

In a bubble chart, each type of data item is drawn as an ellipse:

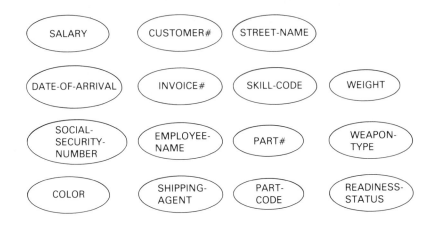

A data base contains hundreds (sometimes thousands) of types of data items. Several thousand types of data items may be used in the running of a big corporation.

To computerize the activities of a corporation, the data items it uses must be defined, cataloged, and organized. This is often difficult and time-consuming because data have been treated rather sloppily in the past. What is essentially the same data item type has been defined differently in different places, represented differently in computers, and given different names. Data-item types that were casually thought to be the same are found to be not quite the same.

The data administrator has the job of cleaning up this confusion. Definitions of data-item types must be agreed on and documented. Much help from end users is often needed in this process.

ASSOCIATIONS BETWEEN DATA ITEMS

A data item by itself is not of much use. For example, a value of SALARY by itself is uninteresting. It becomes interesting only when it is associated with another data item such as EMPLOYEE-NAME, thus:

A data base, therefore, consists not only of data items but also of associations among them. There are a large number of data-item types, and we need a map showing how they are associated. This map is sometimes called a *data model*.

ONE-WITH-ONE AND ONE-WITH-MANY ASSOCIATIONS There are two kinds of links that we shall draw between data items, a one-with-one association and a one-with-many association. A one-with-one association from data-item type A to data-item type B means that *at each instant in time, each value of A has one and only one value of B associated with it*. There is a one-with-one mapping from A to B. If you know the value of A, you can know the value of B.

There is only one value of SALARY associated with a value of EMPLOYEE# at one instant in time; therefore, we can draw a one-with-one link from EMPLOYEE# to SALARY. It is drawn as a small bar across the link:

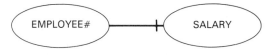

You may think of the bar as being a number 1.

It is said that EMPLOYEE# *identifies* SALARY. If you know the value of EMPLOYEE#, you can know the value of SALARY.

A one-with-many link from A to B means that *one value of A has one or many values of B associated with it*. This is drawn with a crow's foot.

While an employee can only have one salary at a given time, he might have, for instance, zero, one, or many girlfriends. Therefore, we would draw a zero beside the crow's-foot:

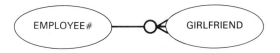

For one value of the data-item type EMPLOYEE# there can be zero, one, or many values of the data-item type GIRLFRIEND.

We can draw both of the above situations on one bubble chart:

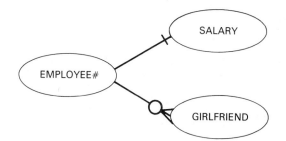

This bubble chart *synthesizes* the two previous charts into one chart. From this one chart we could derive either of the two previous charts.*

The two previous charts might be two different user views, one user being interested in salary and the other in girlfriends. We have created one simple data structure that incorporates these two user views. This is what the data administrator does when building a data base, but the real-life user views are much more complicated than this illustration, and there are many of them. The resulting data model sometimes has hundreds or even thousands of data-item types.

The one-with-one symbol is extremely important in the processes of normalizing and synthesizing data—the basis of data analysis.

TYPES AND INSTANCES   The terms with which we describe data can refer to *types* of data or to *instances* of those data. EMPLOYEE-NAME refers to a type of data item. FRED SMITH is an *instance* of this data-item type. EMPLOYEE may refer to a type of record. There are many instances of this record type, one for each person employed. The diagrams in this chapter show *types* of data, not instances. A data model shows the associations among *types* of data.

The bubble chart shows data-item types. There are many occurrences of each data-item type. In our example, there are many employees, each with a salary and with zero, one, or many girlfriends. You might imagine a third dimension to the bubble charts showing the many values of each data-item type:

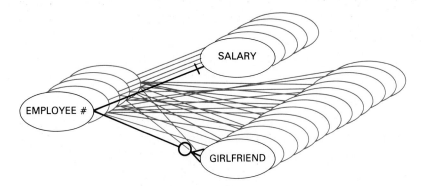

*Many analysts draw the one-with-one and one-with-many associations as single-headed and double-headed arrows, respectively:

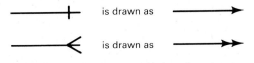

I have used this notation in earlier books, but I avoid them here because arrows tend to suggest a flow or time sequence and are used extensively for this in other types of diagrams.

In discussing data we ought to distinguish between types and instances. Sometimes abbreviated wording is used in literature about data. The words DATA ITEM or RECORD are used to mean DATA-ITEM TYPE or RECORD TYPE.

REVERSE ASSOCIATIONS   Between any two data-item types there can be a mapping in both directions. This gives four possibilities for forward and reverse association. If the data-item types are MAN and WOMAN and the relationship between them represents marriage, the four theoretical possibilities are as follows:

1. Conventional marriage:

2. Polygyny:

3. Polyandry:

4. Group marriage:

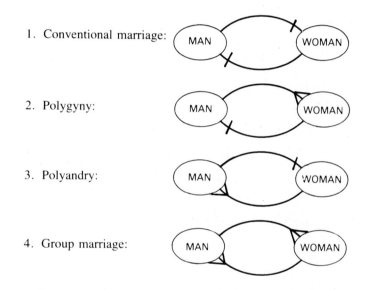

The reverse associations are not always of interest. For example, with the following bubble chart

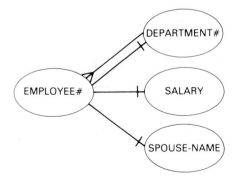

we want the reverse association from DEPARTMENT# to EMPLOYEE# because users want to know what employees work in a given department. However, there is no link from SPOUSE-NAME to EMPLOYEE# because no user wants to ask, ''What employee has a spouse named Gertrude?'' If a user wanted to ask, ''What employees have a salary over $25,000?'' we might include a crow's-foot link from SALARY to EMPLOYEE#.

KEYS AND ATTRIBUTES

Given the bubble chart method of representing data, we can state three important definitions:

1. Primary key
2. Secondary key
3. Attribute

A *primary key* is a bubble with *one or more one-with-one links* going to another bubble. Thus in Fig. 10.1, A, C, and F are primary keys.

A primary key may uniquely identify many data items.

Data items that are not primary keys are referred to as *nonprime attributes*. All data items, then, are either primary keys or nonprime attributes. In Fig. 10.1, B, D, E, G, H, and I are nonprime attributes. Often the word *attribute* is used instead of *nonprime attribute*. Strictly, the primary key data items are attributes also. EMPLOYEE# is an attribute of the employee.

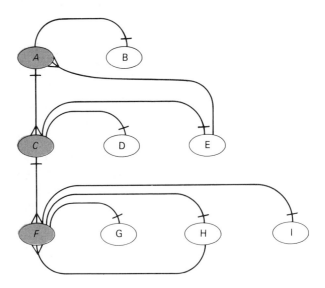

Figure 10.1   Bubble chart showing one-with-one and one-with-many associations among data-item types.

The names of data-item types that are primary keys are underlined in the bubble charts and drawings of records. We can define a nonprime attribute as follows: A *nonprime attribute* is a bubble with *no one-with-one links* going to another bubble.

Each primary key uniquely identifies one or more data items. Ones that are not other primary keys are attributes.

A *secondary key* does not uniquely identify another data item. One value of a secondary key is associated with one or many values of another data item. In other words, there is a crow's-foot link from it to that other item. A *secondary key* is a *nonprime attribute* with *one or more crow's-foot links* to another data item. In Fig. 10.1, E and H are secondary keys.

For emphasis, these three fundamental definitions are repeated in the following box.

A *primary key* is a bubble with one or more one-with-one links going to another bubble.

A *nonprime attribute* is a bubble with no one-with-one link going to another bubble.

A *secondary key* is an attribute with one or more one-with-many links going to another bubble.

DATA-ITEM GROUPS

When using a data base, we need to extract various views of data from one overall data-base structure. The bubble charts representing these different views of data can be merged into one overall chart. In the bubble chart that results from combining many user views, the bubbles are grouped by primary key. Each primary key is the unique identifier of a group of data-item types. It has one-with-one links to each nonprime attribute in that group.

The data-item group needs to be structured carefully so that it is as stable as possible. We should not group together an ad hoc collection of data items. For structuring the data-item group, there are formal rules that are part of the normalization process [1].

RECORDS

The data-item group is commonly called a *record*, sometimes a *logical record* to distinguish it from whatever may be stored physically. A record is often drawn as a bar containing the names of its data items, as in Fig. 10.2.

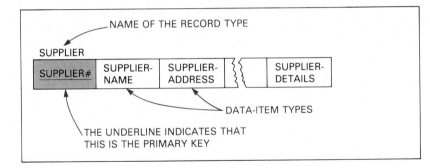

Figure 10.2   Drawing of a record.

The record in Fig. 10.2 represents the following bubble chart:

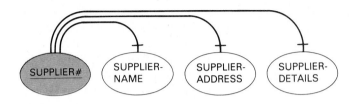

It may be useful to split the SUPPLIER-ADDRESS data item into component data items.

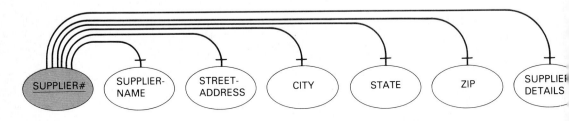

This is useful only if the components may be individually referenced.

Figure 10.3 shows the record redrawn to show that STREET-ADDRESS, CITY, STATE, and ZIP are collectively referred to as SUPPLIER-ADDRESS but are not by themselves a record with a primary key.

CONCATENATED KEYS   Some data-item types cannot be identified by any one single data-item type in a user's view. They need a primary key (unique identifier) composed of more than one data-item type in combination. This is called a *concatenated key*.

| SUPPLIER# | SUPPLIER-NAME | SUPPLIER-ADDRESS | | | | SUPPLIER-DETAILS |
| | | STREET-ADDRESS | CITY | STATE | ZIP | |

Figure 10.3   The record in Fig. 10.2 redrawn to show the decomposition of
SUPPLIER-ADDRESS. These components do not by themselves constitute a
record or data-item group with a primary key.

Several suppliers may supply a part and each charge a different price for
it. The primary key SUPPLIER# is used for identifying information about a
supplier. The key PART# is used for identifying information about a *part*.
Neither of those keys is sufficient for identifying the *price*. The price is dependent on both the supplier and the part. We create a new key to identify the
price, which consists of SUPPLIER# and PART# joined together (concatenated). We draw this as one bubble:

The two fields from which the concatenated key is created are joined with a +
symbol.
    The concatenated key has one-to-one links to the keys SUPPLIER# and
PART#. The resulting diagram is as follows:

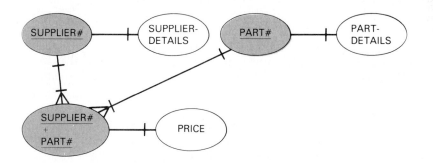

By introducing this form of concatenated key into the logical view of data,
we make each data item dependent on one key bubble. Whenever a concatenated key is introduced, the designer should ensure that the items it identifies are
dependent on the whole key, not on a portion of it only.
    In practice it is sometimes necessary to join together more than two data-
item types in a concatenated key. For example, a company supplies a product

to domestic and industrial customers. It charges a different price to different *types of customers,* and the price varies from one *state* to another. There is a *discount* giving different price reductions for different quantities purchased. The *price* is identified by a combination of CUSTOMER-TYPE, STATE, DIS-COUNT, and PRODUCT. Thus:

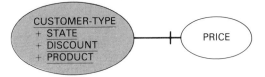

The use of concatenated keys gives each data-item group in the resulting data model a simple structure in which each nonprime attribute is fully dependent on the key bubble and nothing else:

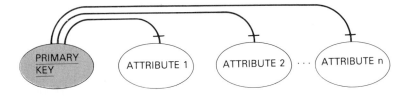

DERIVED DATA   Certain data items are derived by calculation from other data items. For example, TOTAL-AMOUNT on an invoice may be derived by adding the AMOUNT data items on individual lines. A derived data-item type may be marked on a bubble chart by shading its ellipse. Boldfaced or colored lines may be drawn to the derived data-item type from the data-item types from which it is derived. Figure 10.4 illustrates this.

Where possible, the calculation for deriving a data item should be written on the diagram, as in Fig. 10.4. Sometimes the computation may be too complex, and the diagram refers to a separate specification. It might refer to a decision tree or table such as Fig. 10.2, which shows a derived data item.

Derived data items may or may not be stored with the data. They might be calculated whenever the data are retrieved. To store them requires more storage; to calculate them each time requires more processing. As storage drops in cost, it is increasingly attractive to store them. The diagrams initially drawn are *logical* representations of data that represent derived data without saying whether or not it is stored. This is a later, physical decision.

There has been much debate about whether derived data-item types should be shown on diagrams of data or data models. In my view they should be

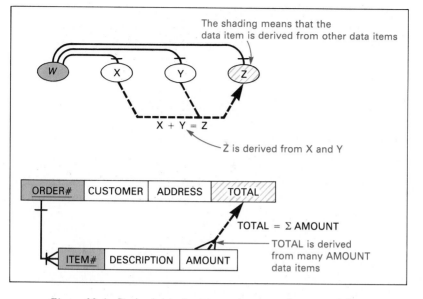

Figure 10.4 Derived data-item types shown on diagrams of data.

shown. Some fourth-generation or nonprocedural languages cause data to be derived automatically once statements like those in Fig. 10.4 are made describing the derivation.

OPTIONAL DATA ITEMS

Sometimes a data-item type may or may not exist. For one value of A, there may be zero or one value of B. This is indicated by putting a circle on the cardinality indicator:

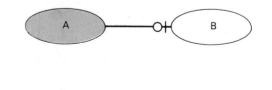

For example,

If the optional bubble is a nonprime attribute (rather than a primary key), it may be treated like any other nonprime attribute when synthesizing the data model.

Optionality applies to one-with-many associations also:

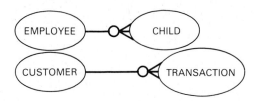

DATA ANALYSIS

When data analysis is performed, the analyst examines the data-item types that are needed and draws a diagram of the dependencies among the data items. The one-with-one and one-with-many links that we have drawn on bubble charts are also drawn between records, as in Fig. 10.4.

Figures 10.5 through 10.7 illustrate data analysis. Figure 10.5 shows a sales contract. The data-item types on this contract are charted in Fig. 10.6. The bubble chart of Fig. 10.6 is redrawn as a record diagram in Fig. 10.7.

THE HOUSE OF MUSIC INC.
A Collins Corporation
Main Office
108 Old Street, White Cliffs, IL 67309
063 259 0003

SALES CONTRACT

Contract No. 7094

SOLD BY		DATE	
Mike		6/10/83	

Name   Herbert H. Matlock

Address   1901 Keel Road

City   Ramsbottom, Illinois   Zip   64736

Phone   063 259 3730   Customer #   18306

REMARKS:

10 yrs. parts and labor on the Piano
1 yr. parts and labor on pianocorder

Delivery Address:

DESCRIPTION	PRICE	DISCOUNT	AMOUNT
New Samick 5'2" Grand Piano model G-1A			
# 820991 with Marantz P-101 # 11359			9500.00
		TOTAL AMOUNT	9500.00
		TRADE IN ALLOWANCE	2300.00
		SALES TAX	
		DEPOSIT	1000.00
		FINAL BALANCE	6200.00

PLEASE NOTE: All sales pending approval by management and verification of trade-in description.

If this contract is breached by the BUYER, the SELLER may take appropriate legal action, or, at its option, retain the deposit as liquidated damages.

Buyer's Signature

Figure 10.5   Sales contract. The data-item types on this document and their associations are diagrammed in Figs. 10.6 and 10.7.

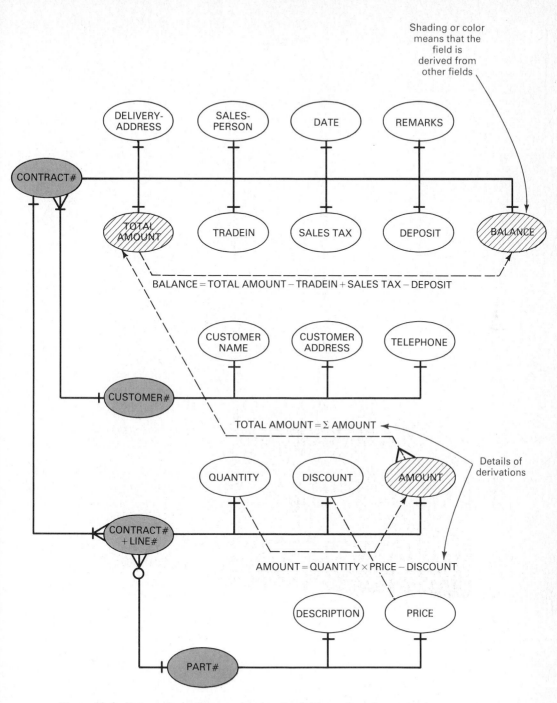

Figure 10.6 Data analysis diagram showing the fields on the sales contract of Fig. 10.5 and the associations among them. The diagram is drawn in a more formal style than the others in the chapter for ease of computer representation.

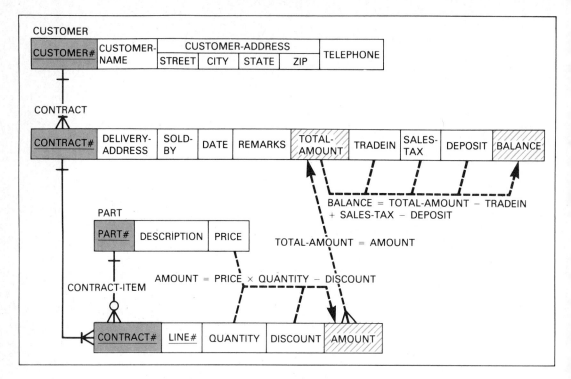

Figure 10.7   Record diagram of the data in Fig. 10.6. The derivation expressions could be recorded separately.

In drawing associations between records, it helps to draw the one-with-one indicators pointing up and the one-with-many indicators pointing down, where possible. Lines with a one-with-one indicator at one end and a crow's-foot at the other are the basic component or hierarchies and can be drawn as follows:

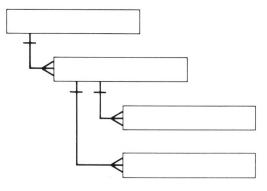

The offsetting to the right in the structure shows the depth in the tree, as discussed in Chapter 3.

The data in Figs. 10.6 or 10.7 are a portion of the data likely to reside in a data base. The data base contains more detail identified by the keys CUS-TOMER# and PART#, for example. An overall data model, drawn something like Fig. 10.7, represents the data in the data base or a conceptual representation of data needed for running data processing that may reside in several data bases. This is discussed in the following chapter.

DATA STRUCTURE DIAGRAMS

Whereas data analysis diagrams are concerned with the inherent properties of the data (functional dependencies and normalization), data structure diagrams are concerned with how the data are represented in a data-base management system or file system. Their format varies with the type of system used.

Some data-base management systems represent data hierarchically, as a data structure diagram is a tree structure of record types (segment types). Some, like IMS, have pointers spanning tree structures. Figure 10.8 shows an IMS data structure diagram. Others, like IDMS or other CODASYL systems, use network structures. Figure 10.9 shows an IDMS data structure diagram.

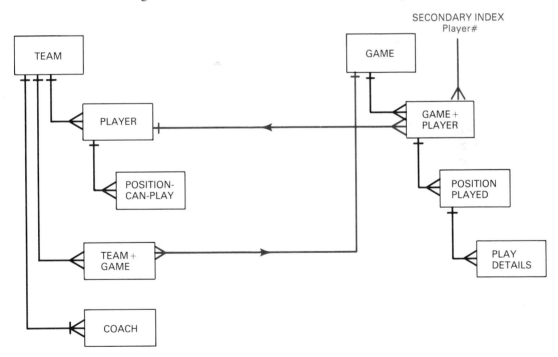

Figure 10.8   Data structure diagram with an IMS data base. The red lines are logical linkages that can be followed in the direction of the arrows. A secondary index is shown with PLAYER# as its source field, and GAME + PLAYER as its target.

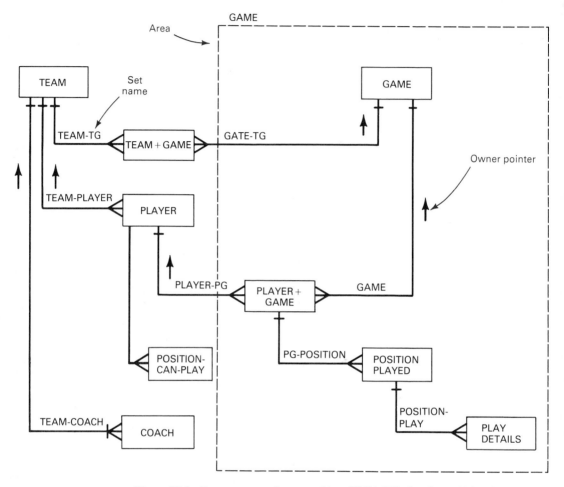

Figure 10.9 Data structure diagram with a CODASYL data base. Using the command SHOW with a box or line shows details of a record or set.

Much information may be recorded about the data, the types of access to them, the frequency of access, and so on. This can be displayed on a workstation screen by pointing to blocks or links on the data structure diagram and using the command SHOW DETAIL.

**BOX 10.1   Notation used on data analysis
(compare with Box 11.2)**

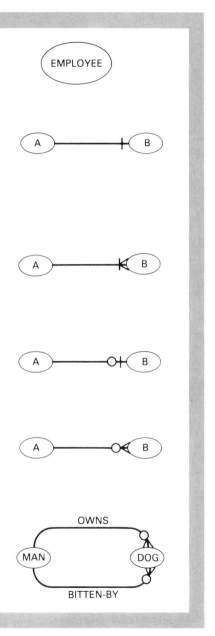

A data-item (field) type is drawn as a named bubble.

One-with-one association
- A identifies B.
- B is functionally dependent on A.
- For one occurrence of A, there is always one and only one occurrence of B.

One-with-many association
For one occurrence of A, there are one or several occurrences of B.

Optional one-with-one association
For one occurrence of A, there is zero or one occurrence of B.

Optional one-with-many association
For one occurrence of A, there are zero, one, or several occurrences of B.

Labeled associations
A label may be written on an association. This is normally done when two associations with different meanings exist between the same two data-item types.

(Continued)

BOX 10.1 *(Continued)*

Composite field
Several data-item types are given
a group name but do not constitute
a record.

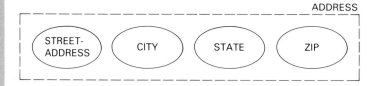

Primary key
A primary key is a
data-item type with a
one-with-one link to
other data-item types;
that is, it *identifies* other
data-item types. The
name of the primary key
data item is underlined.

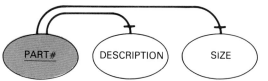

Concatenated keys
When a primary key con-
sists of several data-item
types, these are drawn as
one bubble. Their names
are separated with a +.

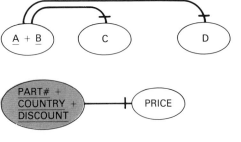

BOX 10.1 *(Continued)*

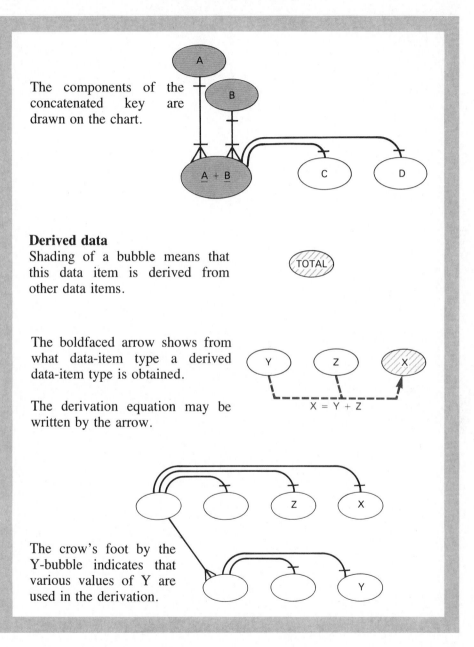

The components of the concatenated key are drawn on the chart.

Derived data

Shading of a bubble means that this data item is derived from other data items.

The boldfaced arrow shows from what data-item type a derived data-item type is obtained.

The derivation equation may be written by the arrow.

$X = Y + Z$

The crow's foot by the Y-bubble indicates that various values of Y are used in the derivation.

REFERENCE

1. J. Martin, *Managing the Data Base Environment*. Englewood Cliffs, N.J.: Prentice-Hall, 1983.

11 ENTITY-RELATIONSHIP DIAGRAMS

Chapter 10 contained detailed low-level diagrams of data. This chapter contains high-level overview diagrams of data that are used at the higher levels of the information-engineering triangle.

Top-down planning of data identifies the entity types involved in running an enterprise and determines the relationships among these entity types. An entity-relationship diagram that can be further decomposed into detailed data models is developed.

To run an enterprise efficiently, certain data are needed regardless of whether computers are used, but computers provide great power in getting the right data to the right people. The data in question need to be planned and described. We need data about these data. Data about data are referred to as *metadata*. A data model contains metadata.

Data analysts need much help from end users and user executives to enable them to understand an organization's data and to design the metadata that will be most useful in managing the organization. They need clear ways of diagramming the data. Diagrams like those in this chapter are an essential part of the overall planning of an organization's information resources.

Box 11.1 summarizes the basic constructs used for describing data.

ENTITIES   An *entity* is something (real or abstract) about which we may store data. Examples of entity types are CUSTOMER, PART, EMPLOYEE, INVOICE, MACHINE TOOL, SALES-PERSON, BRANCH OFFICE, SALES TV AREA, WAREHOUSE, WARE-HOUSE BIN, SHOP ORDER, LEDGER ACCOUNT, JOURNAL POSTING ACCOUNT, PAYMENT, CASH RECEIPT, DEBTOR, CREDITOR.

The name of each entity type should be a noun, sometimes with a modifier word. An entity type may be thought of as having the properties of a noun.

BOX 11.1   Basic constructs used for describing data

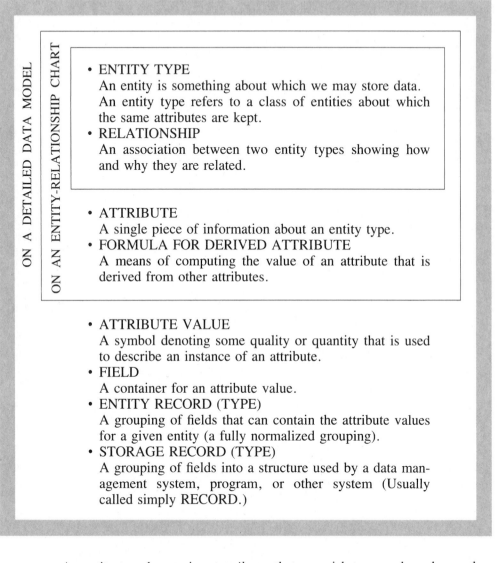

ON A DETAILED DATA MODEL

ON AN ENTITY-RELATIONSHIP CHART

- ENTITY TYPE
  An entity is something about which we may store data.
  An entity type refers to a class of entities about which
  the same attributes are kept.
- RELATIONSHIP
  An association between two entity types showing how
  and why they are related.

- ATTRIBUTE
  A single piece of information about an entity type.
- FORMULA FOR DERIVED ATTRIBUTE
  A means of computing the value of an attribute that is
  derived from other attributes.

- ATTRIBUTE VALUE
  A symbol denoting some quality or quantity that is used
  to describe an instance of an attribute.
- FIELD
  A container for an attribute value.
- ENTITY RECORD (TYPE)
  A grouping of fields that can contain the attribute values
  for a given entity (a fully normalized grouping).
- STORAGE RECORD (TYPE)
  A grouping of fields into a structure used by a data man-
  agement system, program, or other system (Usually
  called simply RECORD.)

An entity type has various *attributes* that we wish to record, such as color, monetary value, percentage utilization, or name.

An *entity type* is a named class of entities that have the same set of attributes; for example, EMPLOYEE is an entity type.

An *entity* is one specific occurrence of an entity type; for example, B. J. WATKINS is an entity of the entity type EMPLOYEE. An entity is described by attribute values.

We describe data in terms of entity types and attributes. An entity-type has several attributes. For example, the entity type PART may have the attributes PART#, NAME, TYPE, COLOR, SIZE, QUANTITY-IN-STOCK, and REORDER-QUANTITY.

A rectangular box is drawn to represent an entity type. For most entities we store records, for example, CUSTOMER records, PART records, EM-PLOYEE records, and so on. The box is sometimes also used to show a record type. However, the intent of our data model is to represent the reality of the data without yet thinking about how we will represent it in computers. We may decide to represent it without a conventional record structure.

Record types consist of *fields*. A field is a container for a data value. A specific record is described by the values of its fields. A flight board at an airport consists of a collection of records of the same type. The board has many fields (which are containers for data values). The data values in the fields change as the passengers watch them.

ENTITY DIAGRAMS

On an *entity-relationship diagram* (often called simply an *entity diagram*), the boxes are interconnected by links that represent relationships between entity types. A *relationship* may be defined as *a business reason why entities may be associated*.

The data in Fig. 10.7 contain four entities: CUSTOMER, PART, CON-TRACT, and CONTRACT-ITEM. An entity-relationship diagram can be drawn as follows:

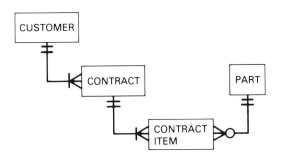

This diagram shows that a customer can have several contracts, a contract is for one customer and can be for one or more contract items. There are zero, one, or many contract items for each part. A contract item relates to one contract and one part.

The "O", "|", and ——< symbols show the minimum and maximum cardinality on each link.

An optional relationship has a circle in the cardinality symbol:

Some analysts have used a crow's-foot alone to mean "zero, one, or many." I advocate that the *zero* or *one* should be explicitly shown because it is often necessary to indicate a "one or many" cardinality where zero is not an option:

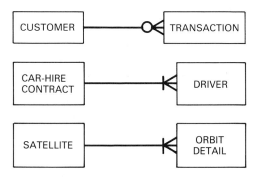

It is thorough to always draw the minimum *and* maximum cardinality. Figure 11.1, for example, uses the ——⫫ convention to mean *one and only one*. Examine Fig. 11.1 to ensure that you understand the meaning of the links.

CONCATENATED ENTITY-TYPE   Some important information does not relate to one entity-type alone but to the conjunction of entity-types. For example, Fig. 11.1 has a product and material. We want to record how much of a given material is used on a given product. This requires a concatenated entity-type PRODUCT + MATERIAL. It is not information about the product alone or the material alone:

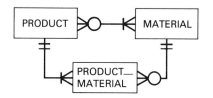

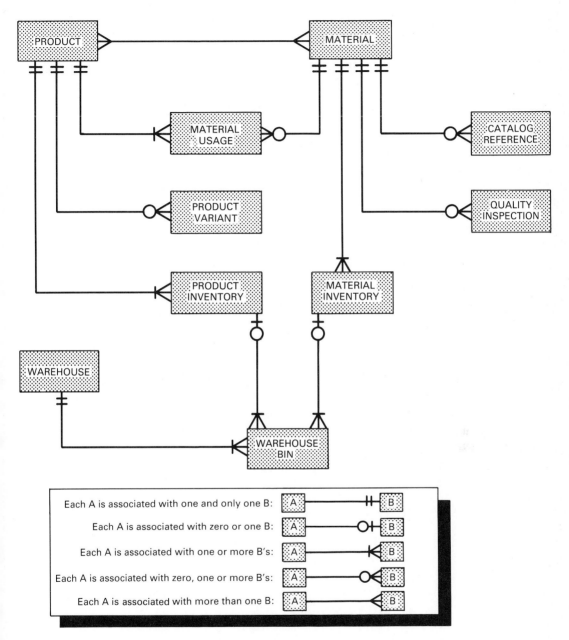

Figure 11.1 An entity-relationship diagram.

Whenever a link has a crow's-foot at both ends, the designer should ask whether there is any information that would need a concatenation of the two entities. Usually there is. A third type of entity is then created, containing intersection data.

MUTUALLY EXCLUSIVE RELATIONSHIPS   Some relationships are mutually exclusive. If A can be associated with either B or C but not with both, we draw the following:

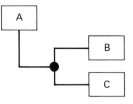

The line branching at a dot is the convention that we have seen on other types of diagrams to show mutual exclusivity.

Suppose, for example, that an aircraft is permittted (for regulatory reasons, say) to carry cargo or passengers but not both, we can draw the following:

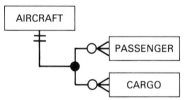

If a driver can be allocated to a truck, car, or motorbike but only to one of these, we can draw:

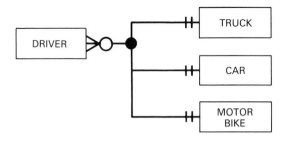

LABELS   Relationships should always be labeled with a verb. If an analyst omits the verb, he may not have thought out the business reason why the entities are associated. Omitting the verb tends to lead to sloppy design.

LABELS AND SENTENCES

The link between entity-types should be thought of as forming a simple sentence. The entity-type at the start of the link is the *subject* of the sentence, and the entity-type to which the link goes is the *object*. For the following link:

the sentence is

AN INVOICE CONTAINS ONE OR MORE LINE-ITEMS.

For the following labeled link connecting a passenger entity-type to a special-catering entity-type:

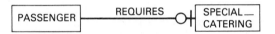

the sentence is

PASSENGER REQUIRES ZERO OR ONE SPECIAL-CATERING ITEM.

For entities with two relationships, there are two sentences:

PASSENGER HAS PURCHASED ZERO, ONE, OR MANY TICKETS.
PASSENGER HAS USED ZERO, ONE, OR MANY TICKETS.

BIDIRECTIONALITY OF RELATIONSHIPS

The relationship between two entity types can be read in both directions. If we labeled both directions, we would have an active and passive form of the same verb. It is therefore unnecessary to write a label for each direction:

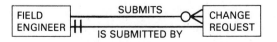

There are two sentences associated with each relationship:

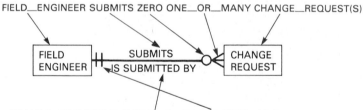

FIELD_ENGINEER SUBMITS ZERO ONE_OR_MANY CHANGE_REQUEST(S)

CHANGE_REQUEST IS SUBMITTED BY ONE FIELD_ENGINEER

If the verbs are different in each direction, there are, in effect, two different relationships. The following is really two relationships and should be drawn as two separate links:

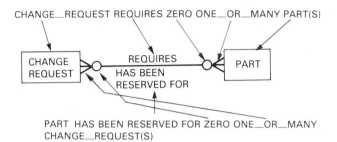

CHANGE_REQUEST REQUIRES ZERO ONE_OR_MANY PART(S)

PART HAS BEEN RESERVED FOR ZERO ONE_OR_MANY CHANGE_REQUEST(S)

Sentence building, as described, should be enforced when links are labeled. A label that does not form a sentence can be vague and consequently should be avoided:

Figure 11.2 shows an entity diagram for a telephone company with labeled links.

SUBJECT AND PREDICATE

The information in an information system can be thought of as consisting of statements—factual assertions on topics of concern to the enterprise; for example:

B. J. Watkins manages the sales department.

K. L. Jones works for the sales department.

March had a net after-tax profit of $150,000.

Order 72193 has a due date of June 17.

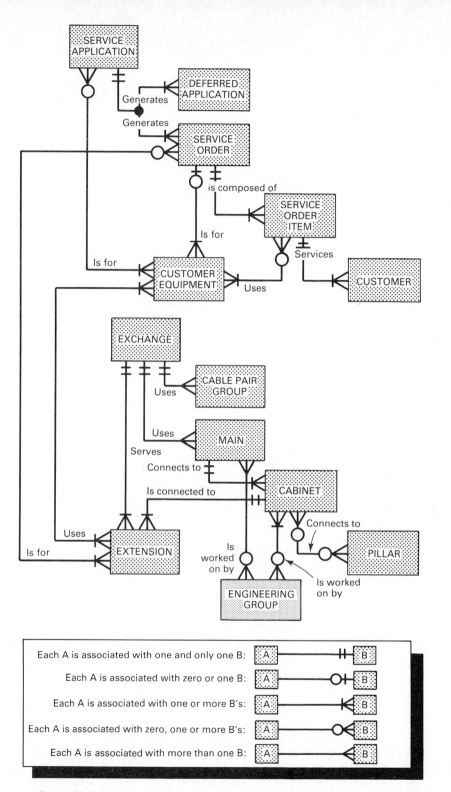

Figure 11.2 Part of an entity-relationship diagram for a telephone company, with the relationships labeled.

Sentences can be parsed into subject and predicate. The predicate can be decomposed into a descriptor and an association that connects the descriptor to the subject:

SUBJECT	PREDICATE	
	ASSOCIATION	DESCRIPTOR
B. J. Watkins	manages	the sales department.
K. L. Jones	works for	the sales department.
March	had a net after-tax profit of	$150,000.
Order 72193	has a due date of	June 17.

The components of these sentences are entity-types, relationships, attributes, or attribute values:

SUBJECT	PREDICATE	
	ASSOCIATION	DESCRIPTOR
B. J. Watkins	manages	the sales department.
(ENTITY)	(RELATIONSHIP)	(ENTITY)
K. L. Jones	works for	the sales department.
(ENTITY)	(RELATIONSHIP)	(ENTITY)
March	had a net after-tax profit of	$150,000.
(ENTITY)	(ATTRIBUTE)	(VALUE)
Order 72193	has a due date of	June 17.
(ENTITY)	(ATTRIBUTE)	(VALUE)

A data model is a framework into which various values can be recorded. The values change while the framework remains the same. The flight-information display at an airport is a framework like a simple data model into which changing values are placed.

We may draw the framework for our sentences showing the entity-types as rectangles. Attributes can be drawn as ellipses (as in Chapter 10). The frameworks or models for the four sentences are as follows:

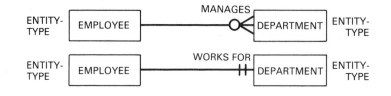

Some research work is in progress on advanced forms of data models in which the *meaning* of the link is encoded so as to be intelligible to computers. This can be used in advanced languages that employ the data base.

LOOPED RELATIONSHIPS

Sometimes an entity of a given type is associated with other entities of the same type. In this case, we draw a loop:

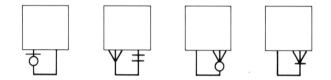

For example, in a zoo data base, we might wish to record which animals are children of other animals and which animal is the mother:

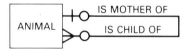

It is important to label looped relationships. Sometimes more than one loop is necessary for the same entity type:

Loops are common in a factory bill of materials. A subassembly is composed of other subassemblies:

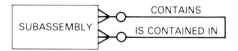

In a personnel data base, some employees manage other employees:

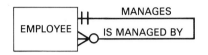

SEMANTIC INDEPENDENCE

The objective of building entity-relationship diagrams and data models is to create a description of the semantics of data that reflects the real enterprise and its informational requirements. The task of the data modeler is to capture reality and communicate about it accurately. The modeler tends to be distracted from this task if he has to think about computer hardware or data-base software or if the line between the semantics and implementation of data becomes blurred.

A well-structured model keeps one fact in one place (a principle of data normalization). Each semantic building block is intended to be as independent as possible from the others. This has a number of practical payoffs [1]:

- Each construct has but one meaning, and each meaning is captured in just one construct. Exceptions and special cases are minimized. Building, reading, learning, and understanding data models is then easier and less error-prone.

- The decisions that a data modeler must make become more distinct and independent, so the analyst can deal with them one at a time. Modeling decisions do not have hidden, unexpected consequences.

- Changes in a logical data model are localized. When some aspect of reality changes, only the constructs that directly represent that aspect need to change. To be stable is the prime virtue for a data model, and in a changing world, the best stability is often the ability to change gracefully.

- Well-defined and decoupled primitives are the best building blocks for creating complex structures to represent complex realities, because they can be freely combined into structures whose meaning is clear.

- The modelers and users are free to attend to what they know best—the reality of their enterprise and the information they need to know about it.

The clean separation of the semantics of data from other considerations is referred to as *semantic independence*.

ENTITY SUBTYPES

It is sometimes necessary to divide entity types into entity subtypes. In a zoo, for example, the entity type ANIMAL might be subdivided into MAMMAL, REPTILE, FISH, and BIRD. We regard these as entity subtypes if they have *different* relationships to other entity-types or have fundamentally different attributes. If, on the other hand, we store essentially the same information about mammals, reptiles, fishes, and birds, we would regard these four categories as merely attribute values of the entity type ANIMAL.

We can draw entity subtypes as divisions of the entity-type box:

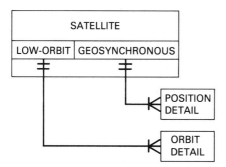

The entity type SATELLITE might be subdivided into LOW-ORBIT and GEOSYNCHRONOUS. LOW-ORBIT SATELLITE has a one-with-many association to the ORBIT DETAIL entity type. GEOSYNCHRONOUS SATELLITE has a one-with-many association with POSITION DETAIL. These two entity types have different attributes. This is drawn as follows:

An *entity subtype* is any subset of entities of a specific entity-type about which we wish to record information special to that subtype.

The values of one or more attributes are used to determine the subtype to which a specific entity belongs. These attributes are called the *classifying attributes*.

**MULTIPLE
SUBTYPE
GROUPINGS**

Our examples so far have had one category of subtyping, drawn as a horizontal band in the entity-type box. There may be more than one independent category of subtyping, in which case we draw several bands in the entity-type box. The horizontal bands represent independent subtype groupings.

For example, SATELLITE may be subtyped into MILITARY and CIVILIAN, independent of whether it is LOW-ORBIT or GEOSYNCHRONOUS. Again, we store different types of information about MILITARY satellites and CIVILIAN satellites.

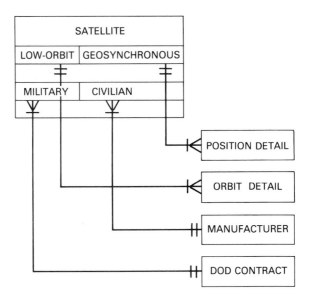

In these illustrations, each horizontal subtype box contains two *mutually exclusive* entity subtypes. Often the entity subtypes are not mutually exclusive. There may be other entities that do not fit into the subtypes shown. This is indicated by leaving blank space in the subtype box:

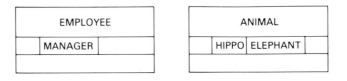

An entity type may contain both mutually exclusive and non–mutually exclusive groupings:

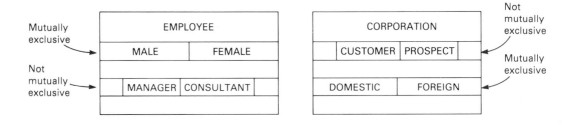

SUBTYPE HIERARCHIES

An entity subtype may itself be subdivided into sub-subtypes:

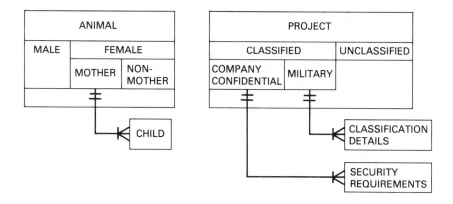

Entity subtypes behave in every way as though they were entity types. They have attributes and relationships with other entity-types.

Palmer stresses that in his experience of data analysis, the newcomer confuses the concepts of entity subtypes and relationships among entity types [2]. He emphasizes the importance of recognizing these to be completely different concepts in spite of the fact that most data-base management systems ignore the concept of entity subtypes.

A simple test can help avoid confusion. We ask, "Is A a B?" and "Is B an A?" The permissible answers are ALWAYS, SOMETIMES, and NEVER. If both answers are NEVER, we are not concerned with subtyping. If both answers are ALWAYS, A and B are synonyms. If the answers are, "Is A a B?" ALWAYS. "Is B an A?" SOMETIMES, A is a subtype of B.

Let's look at a case that might be confusing. A somewhat bureaucratic organization has people with the following titles: OFFICIAL, ADVISER, SUB-AGENT, and REPRESENTATIVE. Should each of these be a separate entity type, or are they subtypes or merely attributes?

The cells in the following table answer the question "Is A a B?"

		B:			
		OFFICIAL	ADVISER	SUBAGENT	REPRESENTATIVE
A:	OFFICIAL		Sometimes	Never	Always
	ADVISOR	Never		Never	Never
	SUBAGENT	Never	Never		Always
	REPRESENTATIVE	Sometimes	Never	Sometimes	

The word *always* appears twice. An OFFICIAL and a SUBAGENT are *always* a REPRESENTATIVE. These can be subtypes of the entity type REPRESENTATIVE. An OFFICIAL is *never* a SUBAGENT and vice versa, so they are mutually exclusive subtypes. Can there be representatives other than OFFICIALS and SUBAGENTS? *No.* Therefore we draw:

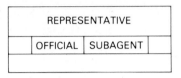

An ADVISER is *never* any of the others, so that is a separate entity type.

Do we really want to regard an OFFICIAL and a SUBAGENT as an entity subtype, or should they be attributes of REPRESENTATIVE? To answer this, we ask, "Do they have associations that are different from those of REPRESENTATIVE that we need to include in the data model?" *Yes,* they do. An OFFICIAL supervises a SUBAGENT. A SUBAGENT is an external employee working for a CORPORATION, about which separate records are kept. An association from OFFICIAL to SUBAGENT is needed. This can be drawn inside the entity-type box:

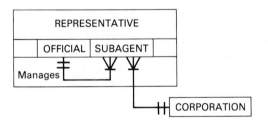

This conveys more information than an attempt at entity analysis without subtyping, which might show the following:

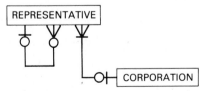

TAXONOMIES

Taxonomies of knowledge are often drawn using entity-types and subtypes. Botanists, for example, draw taxonomies of plants. These are often drawn as tree structures or networks of lines connecting words. No boxes are drawn around the words. For example:

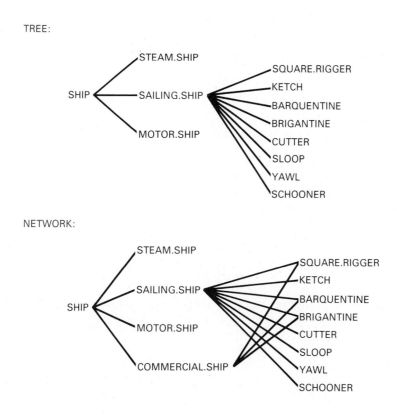

TREE:

NETWORK:

Some taxonomies of knowledge become very complex with many sub-types, sub-subtypes, etc. Entity-types and subtypes in this environment are often called classes and subclasses. Taxonomies are often drawn in the design of artificial intelligence applications such as expert systems. The tools needed for this can display structures such as the preceding. The preceding illustration is taken from the KEE tool from Intellicorp., for example.

Taxonomy trees are useful for displaying alternate approaches to problems:

This, like any tree structure, could be drawn with an action diagram.

In describing knowledge, instances of entity-types are sometimes linked to the entity-type with a dotted line:

This is useful and practical only when there is a small number of instances. It is often useful for taxonomies but not for corporate data bases.

COMPUTER REPRESENTATION OF THE DIAGRAM

Entity diagrams can be drawn in a manageable fashion for a dozen or so entities. With hundreds of entities, the diagram would be difficult to draw and a mess to maintain without computer graphics.

A computerized tool can identify small hierarchies within a more complex structure and assign levels to the structures, as illustrated in Figs. 3.17 through 3.20. Figure 11.3 shows a complex entity diagram simplified by drawing the subhierarchies as in Fig. 3.20. The diagram is split into data subjects.

With computer graphics, the diagram can be constantly edited, added to, and adjusted in the same way that we adjust text with a word processor. A good computer graphics tool makes change easy; hand-drawn diagrams make change difficult. Hand-drawn diagrams of great complexity discourage modification. Often analysts will do anything to avoid redrawing the diagram again. This is a serious concern because on complex projects, the more interaction, discussion, and modification there are at the planning and design stages, the better the results.

A diagram with hundreds of entities is impressive but of little use whether it is computer-drawn or not, except perhaps for the data administrator to impress people by hanging it on a wall. However, with computer graphics, small subset diagrams can be extracted, and these are extremely useful. Subset diagrams relating to specific data subjects are extracted for checking by end users. Subset diagrams are extracted for analysts for specific projects. On these subset diagrams, they can create data access maps and design data-base procedures. Physical data-base designers employ the subset diagrams for designing data bases. Individual data bases normally employ only a portion of the data represented in a large entity diagram.

Figure 11.4 shows an entity diagram of typical complexity drawn with a computerized tool. In this case the tool enables the diagram to be changed and added to easily. It does not level the diagram, producing subhierarchies as in Fig. 11.3. It does not permit subsets to be extracted automatically for users and analysts. Both of these latter properties are desirable. Figure 11.4 is a computerized COW diagram. Computers should be used to clarify the structure and help in employing its information. We regard Fig. 11.4, then, as an example of how computers should *not* be used.

The complete entity diagram should be kept in computerized form, so that it can be conveniently updated and manipulated. From it, small subset diagrams should be creatable graphically when the data administrator, end users, or systems analysts need to study them, argue about them, and overdraw access maps on them. The entity diagram should feed the more detailed data-modeling process that follows.

ALTERNATE NOTATIONS

Three notations are used for drawing entity diagrams: crow's-foot notation, arrow notation, and Bachman notation. This book has used crow's-foot notation.

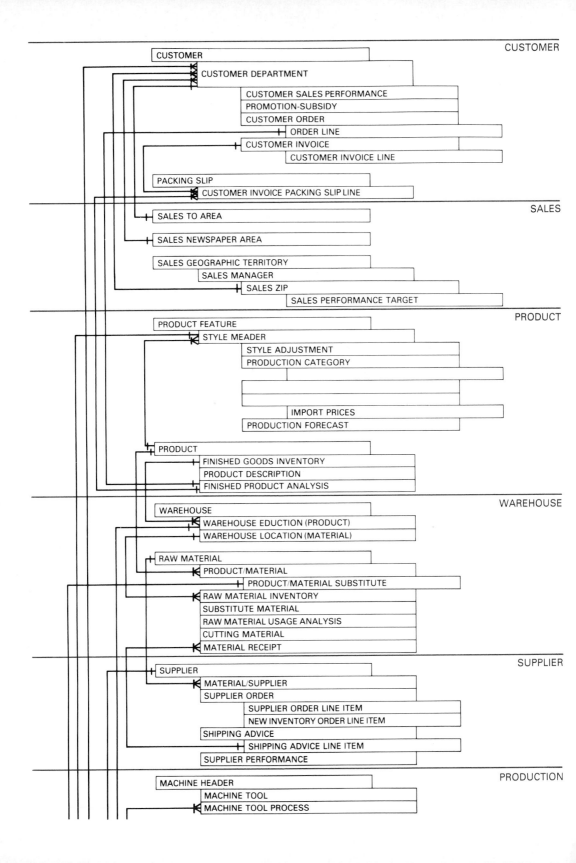

CUSTOMER

CUSTOMER

CUSTOMER DEPARTMENT

CUSTOMER SALES PERFORMANCE

PROMOTION-SUBSIDY

CUSTOMER ORDER

ORDER LINE

CUSTOMER INVOICE

CUSTOMER INVOICE LINE

PACKING SLIP

CUSTOMER INVOICE PACKING SLIP LINE

SALES

SALES TO AREA

SALES NEWSPAPER AREA

SALES GEOGRAPHIC TERRITORY

SALES MANAGER

SALES ZIP

SALES PERFORMANCE TARGET

PRODUCT

PRODUCT FEATURE

STYLE MEADER

STYLE ADJUSTMENT

PRODUCTION CATEGORY

IMPORT PRICES

PRODUCTION FORECAST

PRODUCT

FINISHED GOODS INVENTORY

PRODUCT DESCRIPTION

FINISHED PRODUCT ANALYSIS

WAREHOUSE

WAREHOUSE

WAREHOUSE EDUCTION (PRODUCT)

WAREHOUSE LOCATION (MATERIAL)

RAW MATERIAL

PRODUCT/MATERIAL

PRODUCT/MATERIAL SUBSTITUTE

RAW MATERIAL INVENTORY

SUBSTITUTE MATERIAL

RAW MATERIAL USAGE ANALYSIS

CUTTING MATERIAL

MATERIAL RECEIPT

SUPPLIER

SUPPLIER

MATERIAL/SUPPLIER

SUPPLIER ORDER

SUPPLIER ORDER LINE ITEM

NEW INVENTORY ORDER LINE ITEM

SHIPPING ADVICE

SHIPPING ADVICE LINE ITEM

SUPPLIER PERFORMANCE

PRODUCTION

MACHINE HEADER

MACHINE TOOL

MACHINE TOOL PROCESS

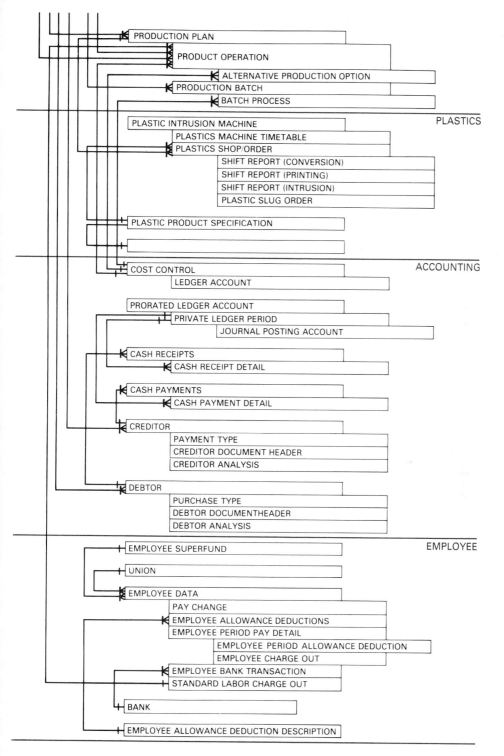

Figure 11.3 Entity chart for a small textile firm.

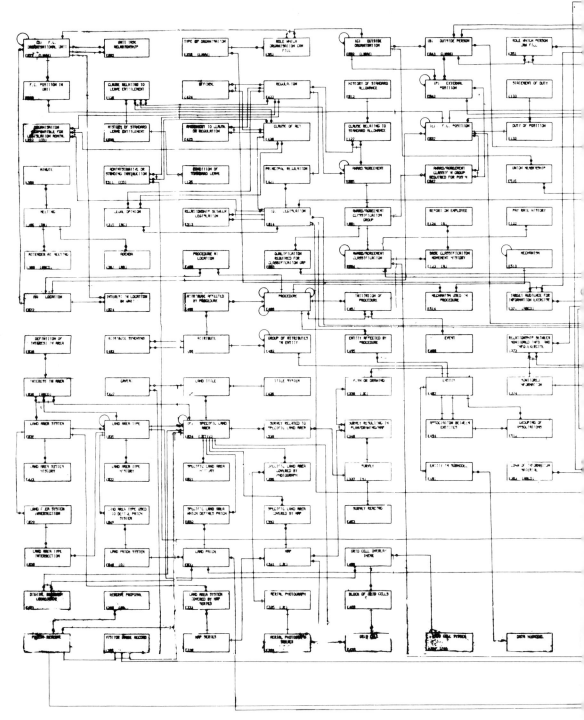

Figure 11.4 Entity chart of typical complexity drawn with a computerized tool. The tool enables the chart to be changed and added to easily. It does not level the chart, producing subhierarchies as in Fig. 11.3. It does not permit

subsets to be extracted automatically for users and analysts. Both of these latter properties are desirable. Therefore, this chart is an example of how computerized graphics should *not* be used.

The following table shows the equivalencies among these notations:

	CROW'S-FOOT NOTATION	ARROW NOTATION	BACHMAN NOTATION
A is always associated with one of B	A ⊢─────╫├ B	A ─────▶ B	A ───── B
A is always associated with one or many of B	A ─────◀├ B	A ├─▶▶ B	A ────▶ B
A is associated with zero or one of B	A ───○├ B	A ───○▶ B	
A is associated with zero, one, or many of B	A ───○◀ B	A ───▶▶ B	

It is generally desirable to use the same notation for data analysis (Chapter 10) as for entity-relationship diagrams.

Bachman notation was an early notation for drawing data-base structures. It deserves a place in the history of systems analysis because it was the first form of data-base diagramming. Bachman notation uses a single-headed arrow for a one-with-many association. It uses an unmarked line for a one-with-one association.

We use an unmarked line to mean that we are uninterested in an association or that we do not know what it is yet. For example, the tail of most links to attributes is unmarked:

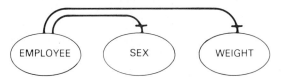

Bachman notation does not distinguish between the uninteresting association and the one-with-one association. It has no specific way to draw functional dependencies—the single most important input to the detailed data-modeling process. It cannot draw many of the situations in Box 11.2.

Crow's-foot notation, as far as we can ascertain, was first used and popularized by Ian Palmer. We have used it instead of arrow notation because arrows tend to suggest flows or time sequence. This notation allows us to achieve consistency among the various diagramming techniques that an analyst needs.

BOX 11.2   Notation used on entity-relationship diagrams

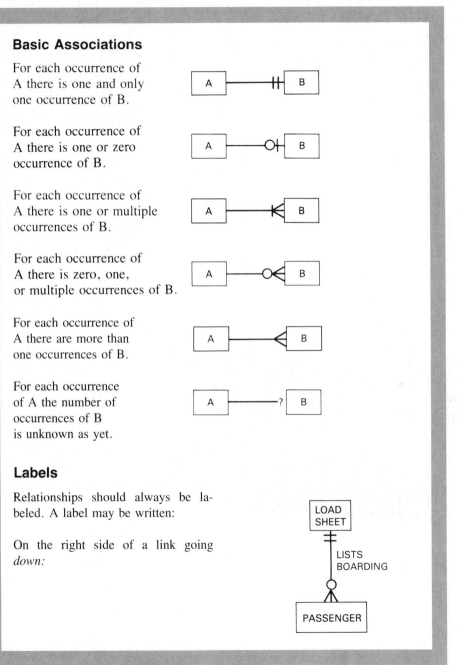

Basic Associations

For each occurrence of
A there is one and only
one occurrence of B.

For each occurrence of
A there is one or zero
occurrence of B.

For each occurrence of
A there is one or multiple
occurrences of B.

For each occurrence of
A there is zero, one,
or multiple occurrences of B.

For each occurrence of
A there are more than
one occurrences of B.

For each occurrence
of A the number of
occurrences of B
is unknown as yet.

Labels

Relationships should always be labeled. A label may be written:

On the right side of a link going *down:*

LOAD
SHEET

LISTS
BOARDING

PASSENGER

(Continued)

BOX 11.2 *(Continued)*

On the left side of a link going *up:*

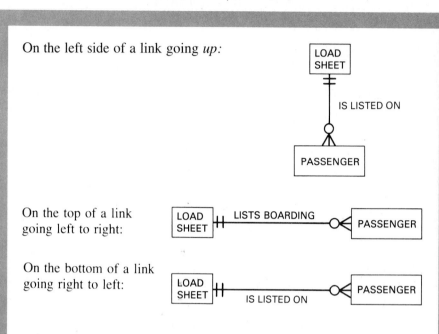

On the top of a link going left to right:

On the bottom of a link going right to left:

The labels should be composed to form a sentence.

Looped Relationships

Any of the relationships may be used in a loop. Here an occurrence of an entity is associated with one or more occurrences of entities *of the same type.*

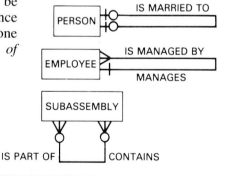

BOX 11.2 *(Continued)*

Mutually Exclusive Relationships

Relationships branching from a dot are mutually exclusive. Only one of them can exist for any one occurrence.

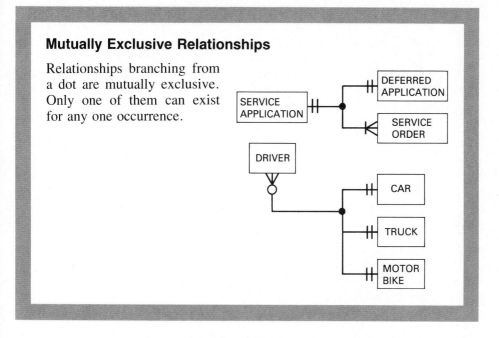

REFERENCES

1. From work done by Ken Winter, Rik Belew, and Bob Walter at Database Design, Inc., Ann Arbor, Michigan.

2. From work done by Ian Palmer at James Martin Associates Ltd., London, England.

12 DATA NAVIGATION DIAGRAMS

Once a thorough, stable, fully normalized data model exists, the task of the systems analyst and application designer is much easier [1]. The designer must determine how he *navigates* through the model. He needs a clear diagramming technique for this. This chapter discusses the diagramming of data navigation.

A *data navigation diagram* is drawn on top of a data model. It can be converted into a program structure as represented in an action diagram.

Data navigation diagrams are also sometimes called *data access maps,* or *logical access maps* when emphasizing that a logical data structure is used. They are sometimes drawn in a file environment as well as in a data-base environment. They are drawn on data structure diagrams (e.g., CODASYL representations) as well as on data models.

DIVIDE AND CONQUER
A basic principle of structured design is *divide and conquer*. Complex, entangled designs need to be reduced to clean, relatively simple modules. The existence of a thoroughly normalized data model enables complex applications to be reduced to relatively simple projects that enter and validate data, update data, perform computations on data, handle queries and generate reports, generate routine documents, conduct audits, and so on. Sometimes these projects use data in complex ways with many cross-references among the data.

Most such projects can be performed by one person, especially when fourth-generation languages are used. The main communication among separate developers is via the data model. Most of the human communication problems of large programming projects can be made to disappear. Figure 12.1 illustrates this.

One-person projects are highly appealing. Management can select the person for the job and motivate him highly for speed and excellence. He is in charge of his own success. He is not a cog in a tangled human machine. He will not be slowed down or have to rewrite his code because of other people.

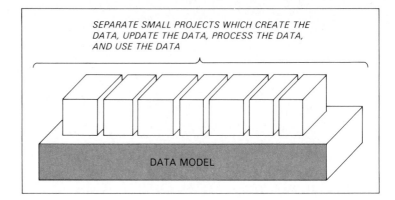

Figure 12.1   A well-designed, stable data model, with appropriate data management facilites, permits application development to be a series of separate,
quick-to-implement projects—mostly one-person projects. Communication
among the projects is via the data model.

When he has finished, management can judge his results and reward him appropriately.

Although one person may be responsible for each of the blocks in Fig.
12.1, a team may sit side by side at terminals so that they can compare notes,
see one another's displays, and help one another to understand the meaning of
the data.

The divide-and conquer strategy resulting in one-person projects is made
stronger by the use of higher-level data-base languages, and fourth-generation
languages in general. With those, one person can often obtain ten times the
results in a given time than he could with COBOL. A one-person team can
replace a ten-person team. Most fourth-generation languages depend heavily on
a data management facility. Nevertheless, with COBOL or PL/I, subdividing
projects into small modules is highly desirable, and good data-base management
assists this greatly.

SEPARATING
DATA FROM
PROCEDURES

The information system needs of some big organizations have grown in complexity as data bases have
become established. It is possible to use the data in
more complex ways. This increase in complexity can
be handled only if there is an easy-to-use set of techniques for charting the way
through the complexity.

A problem with many structured techniques is that they tangle up the structuring of the data with the structuring of the procedures. This complicates the
techniques used. Worse, it results in data that are viewed narrowly and usually
not put into a form suitable for other applications that employ the same data.

This chapter and the next assume that the data are separately designed using sound techniques, preferably automated. Data have properties of their own, independent of procedures that lead to stable structuring. The users or analysts who design procedures employ a data model and consider the program actions that use that data model. Often the data model is designed by a separate data administrator. Sometimes it is designed by the analysts in question.

The data navigation diagram is drawn on top of a portion of the data model and links it to the design of the programs that use that data. In this way it forms a simple, easy-to-use bridge between the data model and the procedure design. Any design of a data-base program should begin by sketching the navigation diagram.

Some fourth-generation languages have enabled data to be used in more complex ways than previously. With some such languages, everything is oriented to the data-base structure. Many users, however, have difficulty learning how to use the full power of the language. They learn to formulate queries and generate reports but not how to handle complex data manipulation. One analyst described it as follows:

> "There is a threshold they cannot get through. It's like flying up through clouds and then all of a sudden the plane breaks out of the clouds and the sun shines. To get through this quickly needs appropriate, ultra-clear diagramming techniques, clearly taught."

DATA SUBMODEL

The first step in creating procedures which use a data model is to identify which entity types will be employed. The designer examines the overall entity-relationship diagram and indicates the entity types he expects to use. A subset diagram is created that shows only these entity types.

To help ensure that the designer has not forgotten any entity-type that is needed, a *neighborhood* may be displayed. The neighborhood of one entity-type is the set of entity types that can be reached from it by traversing one link in the entity-relationship diagram. Sometimes the data model may contain extra information, saying that additional neighbors should be examined. The designer displays a list of such neighbors of the entity-types he is interested in. Occasionally, the neighbor one link away may be a concatenated entity-type (containing intersection data), and the design inspects the other entity-types in the concatenated record.

The designer examines the neighborhood. He sees the entity-types his procedure will use, plus a few more. He eliminates those he does not want. There may be some that he would not have thought about if he had not displayed the neighborhood. There may be some that have *mandatory* links to records he has specified. For example, when a booking record is created, the seat inventory record *must* be updated.

The designer then indicates for each entity-type whether a CREATE, READ, UPDATE, or DELETE will occur. If an entity is to be created, the designer must consider what relationship links must be built to other entities.

These considerations give the designer a subset data model that his procedure will use. Usually this is small enough to draw on one sheet of paper. Where possible, it should be created by a computerized tool.

**ACCESS
SEQUENCE**
The next step is to determine the sequence of accesses through this subset data model. The designer may draw the sequence, perhaps with a colored pen, on the subset data model. He may indicate:

First, READ entity-type A.
Second, READ entity-type B.
Third, CREATE entity-type C.

This might be drawn as follows:

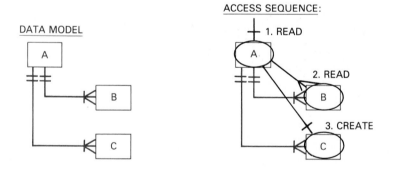

The link between the first READ and the second READ has a crow's foot on it. This means that many entity-type B records may be read in association with one entity-type A record. Only one entity-type C record is created, and it is asociated with the A record. This is shown by the one-with-one link to the creation of the C record.

The three accesses could be drawn on an action diagram as follows:

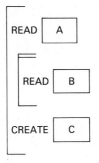

The data navigation diagrams need to be automatically convertible into equivalent action diagrams.

CONDITIONS   Often an access is made only if a certain condition applies. For example, in the processing of an order, the first step may be to check the customer's credit. If the credit is bad, the subsequent accesses are not carried out. This optionality is shown on the data access map using a circle (as on other types of diagrams). You may want to read to circle as *o* for "optional."

In our diagram, the third access, which creates record C, may be optional. We illustrate this as follows:

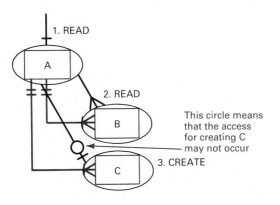

The circle may be given a number, or a condition may be written against it:

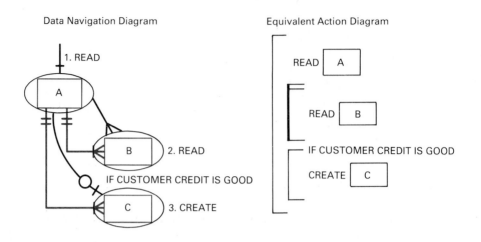

Data Navigation Diagram   Equivalent Action Diagram

MUTUAL
EXCLUSIVITY

As on other types of diagrams, two or more paths may be mutually exclusive. This is represented by a forking line with a filled-in circle at the fork:

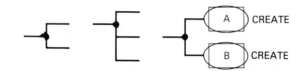

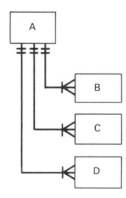

Data Submodel   Data Navigation Diagram

Mutually exclusive access paths translate into a case structure in an action diagram:

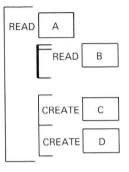

The conditions that control the case structure may be written on the navigation diagram.

LIKE A DEPENDENCY DIAGRAM

A data navigation diagram can be thought of as being like a dependency diagram in which each activity is an access to data. The same constructs are used: optionality, mutual exclusivity, cardinality, conditions, recursion, and concurrency. The navigation diagram has a different shape from a typical dependency diagram because it is drawn on top of a data model. If the data model is removed, the result looks like a dependency diagram. The same algorithm is needed to convert a navigation diagram and a dependency diagram into an action diagram.

Because each activity on a navigation diagram relates to one data access, some precise questions can be asked about it. The answers to these help to enforce thoroughness in design and help with the generation of program code. When the software converts the navigation diagram to an action diagram, the designer can add information about calculations, printouts, or other procedures and can generate an executable program.

The process we describe in this chapter is ideal for a computerized tool that enables the designer to extract a portion of a data model, explore its neighborhood, draw a navigation diagram on it, convert this to an action diagram, add details to and edit the action diagram, and possibly generate executable code from the resulting action diagram.

Figure 12.2 illustrates navigation diagram constructs and their equivalent action diagrams.

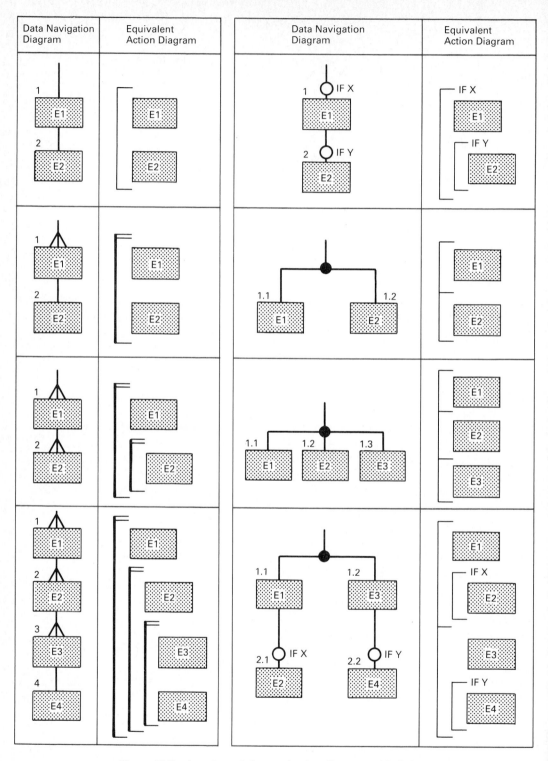

Figure 12.2 A variety of data navigation diagrams with their equivalent action diagrams.

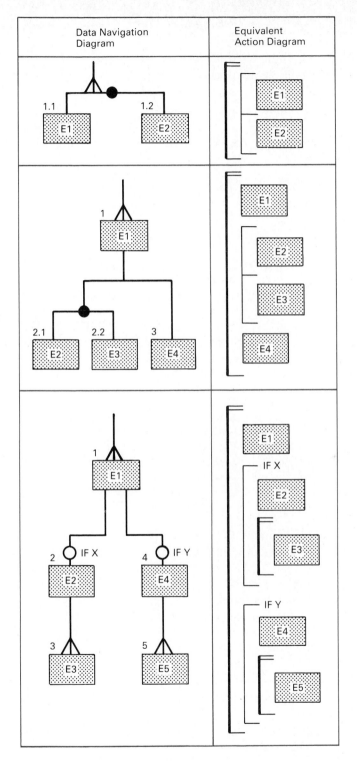

Figure 12.2 (Continued)

Figure 12.3 lists the steps for designing data-base applications in this way. These steps are often applied manually. They also are ideal for the computerization of application building.

COMPUTERIZED
DIAGRAMMING

The navigation diagrams so far in this chapter show hand-drawn rings around the entity types. For computerization, a less casual diagram is needed. Figure 12.4 shows a computer-drawn version of the diagram. It should be noted that the boxes and symbols on the action diagram are as similar as possible to those on the navigation diagrams.

DESIGN OF
AN ORDER
ACCEPTANCE
SYSTEM

We will illustrate this technique with the design of an order acceptance application for a wholesale distributor. A third-normal-form data model exists, as shown in Fig. 12.5. The designer knows that the application requires CUSTOMER-ORDER records and PRODUCT records. The neighborhood of these includes the records:

> CUSTOMER-ORDER
> CUSTOMER
> ORDER-LINE
> BACKORDER
> INVOICE
> PRODUCT
> ORDER-RATE
> QUOTATION
> INVOICE-LINE-ITEM
> PURCHASE-LINE-ITEM

The designer examines the data items in these records. The application does not need any data in the INVOICE, INVOICE-LINE-ITEM, PURCHASE-LINE-ITEM, or QUOTATION records. The ORDER-RATE record *should* be updated. The designer would have neglected the ORDER-RATE record if he had not printed the neighborhood.

The designer decides, then, that he needs six records and creates a submodel containing these records, as shown in Fig. 12.6. His program will access these records in the following sequence:

1. The CUSTOMER record will be inspected to see whether the credit rating is good.

2. If the credit rating is good, an ORDER record is created, linked to the CUSTOMER record.

3. For each product on the order, the PRODUCT record is retrieved to see whether stock of the product is available.

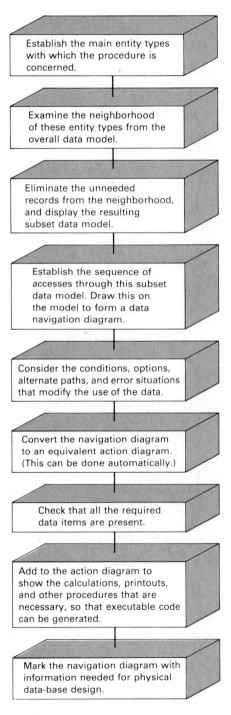

Figure 12.3 Steps for designing data-base applications.

The boxes in the figure contain, from top to bottom:

1. Establish the main entity types with which the procedure is concerned.

2. Examine the neighborhood of these entity types from the overall data model.

3. Eliminate the unneeded records from the neighborhood, and display the resulting subset data model.

4. Establish the sequence of accesses through this subset data model. Draw this on the model to form a data navigation diagram.

5. Consider the conditions, options, alternate paths, and error situations that modify the use of the data.

6. Convert the navigation diagram to an equivalent action diagram. (This can be done automatically.)

7. Check that all the required data items are present.

8. Add to the action diagram to show the calculations, printouts, and other procedures that are necessary, so that executable code can be generated.

9. Mark the navigation diagram with information needed for physical data-base design.

Data Submodel:

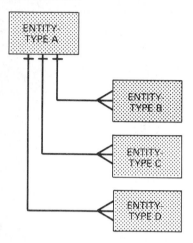

Navigation Diagram Drawn
by Hand on the Data Model:

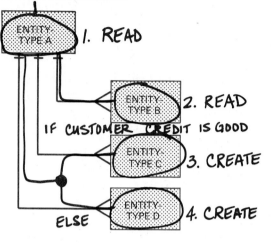

Navigation Diagram Drawn by
Computer on the Data Model:

Corresponding Action Diagram:

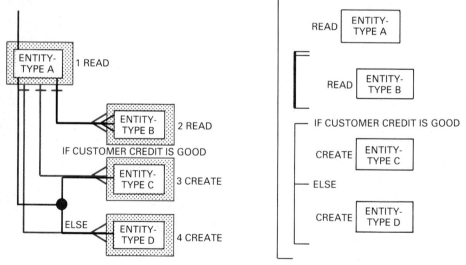

Figure 12.4 A navigation diagram drawn on top of a data submodel and then converted to an action diagram.

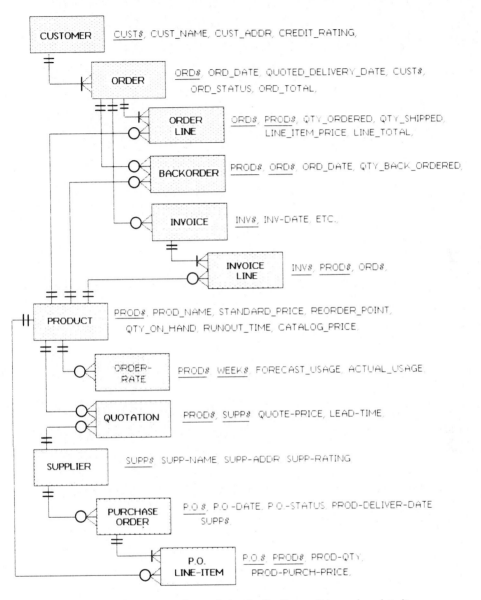

CUSTOMER | CUST#, CUST_NAME, CUST_ADDR, CREDIT_RATING,

ORDER | ORD#, ORD_DATE, QUOTED_DELIVERY_DATE, CUST#, ORD_STATUS, ORD_TOTAL,

ORDER LINE | ORD#, PROD#, QTY_ORDERED, QTY_SHIPPED, LINE_ITEM_PRICE, LINE_TOTAL,

BACKORDER | PROD#, ORD#, ORD_DATE, QTY_BACK_ORDERED,

INVOICE | INV#, INV-DATE, ETC.,

INVOICE LINE | INV#, PROD#, ORD#,

PRODUCT | PROD#, PROD_NAME, STANDARD_PRICE, REORDER_POINT, QTY_ON_HAND, RUNOUT_TIME, CATALOG_PRICE,

ORDER-RATE | PROD#, WEEK#, FORECAST_USAGE, ACTUAL_USAGE,

QUOTATION | PROD#, SUPP#, QUOTE-PRICE, LEAD-TIME,

SUPPLIER | SUPP#, SUPP-NAME, SUPP-ADDR, SUPP-RATING

PURCHASE ORDER | P.O.#, P.O.-DATE, P.O.-STATUS, PROD-DELIVER-DATE, SUPP#

P.O. LINE-ITEM | P.O.#, PROD#, PROD-QTY, PROD-PURCH-PRICE,

Figure 12.5   Data model for a wholesale distributor. Primary-key data items are underlined. This model is not complete, but because it is correctly normalized, it can be grown without pernicious impact to include such things as SALESPERSON, WAREHOUSE, and ALTERNATE-ADDRESSES.

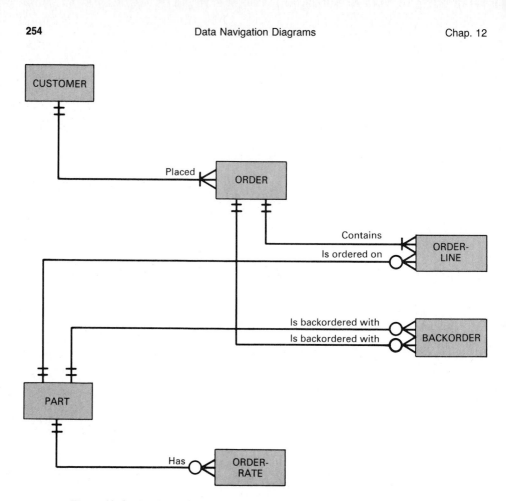

Figure 12.6   A subset of the data model in Fig. 12.5, extracted for the design of the order acceptance procedure. This is printed from a computerized diagramming tool. The positions of the blocks can be changed with the cursor.

4. If stock is available, an ORDER-LINE record is created, linked to the ORDER record and PRODUCT record for that item.

5. If stock is available, a BACKORDER record is created, linked to the ORDER and PRODUCT records.

6. The ORDER-RATE record for that PRODUCT is retrieved, a new order rate is calculated, and the ORDER-RATE record is updated.

7. When all items are processed, an order confirmation is printed and the ORDER record is updated with ORD-STATUS, ORD-TOTAL, and QUOTED-DELIVERY-DATE.

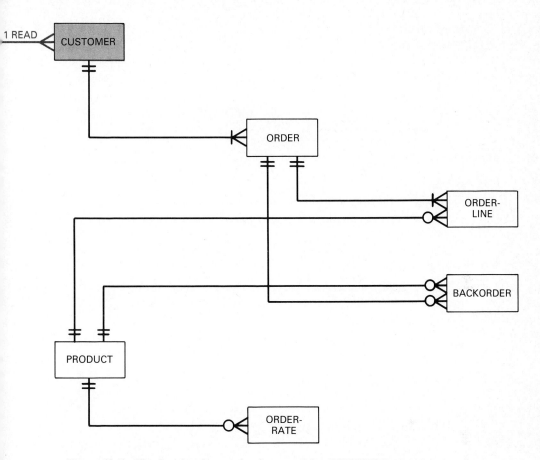

Figure 12.7   The first data-base action is to read the CUSTOMER record as shown here. The crow's foot on this access indicates that many CUSTOMER records are read.

Figures 12.7 through 12.12 show the data navigation diagram growing as the designer describes the seven accesses. The resulting navigation diagram of Fig. 12.12 is converted to an action diagram in Fig. 12.13.

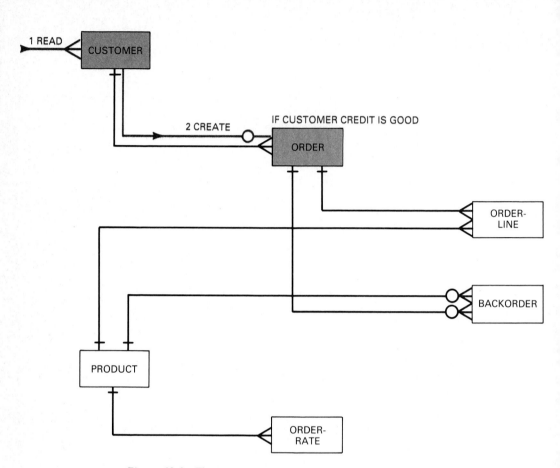

Figure 12.8 The second data-base access is to create an ORDER record. This is done if the condition shown applies.

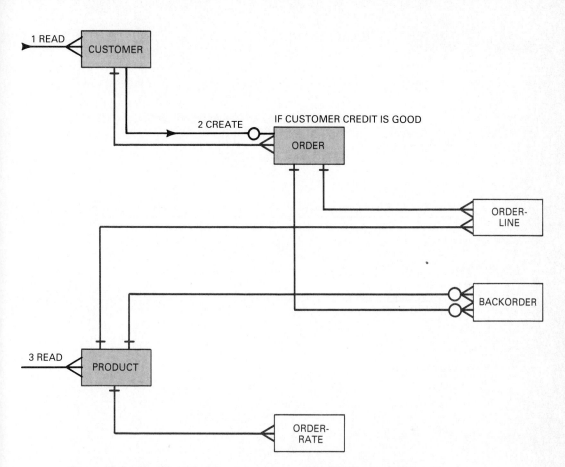

Figure 12.9 The third data-base access is to read the PART record. This will be done for each part on the order, hence the crow's foot. PART is not accessed *via* ORDER. Separate information is needed about how PART is accessed.

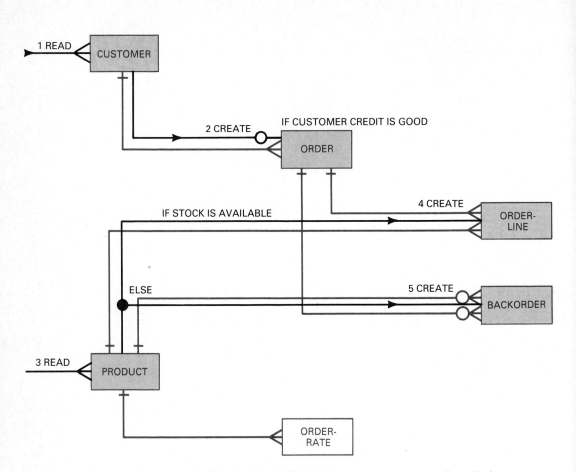

Figure 12.10 The fourth and fifth data-base accesses are mutually exclusive. They result in the creation of either an ORDER-LINE record or a BACKOR-DER. The conditions are written on the diagram.

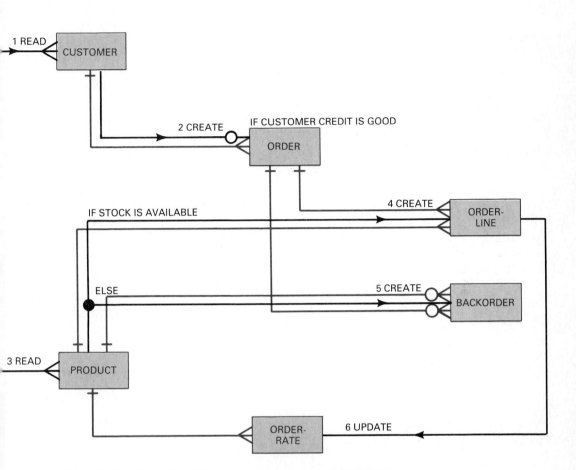

Figure 12.11 The sixth data-base access updates the ORDER-RATE record. This is accessed via its parent PART record. (The dependency line goes from ORDER-LINE to ORDER-RATE, not from PART to ORDER-RATE.)

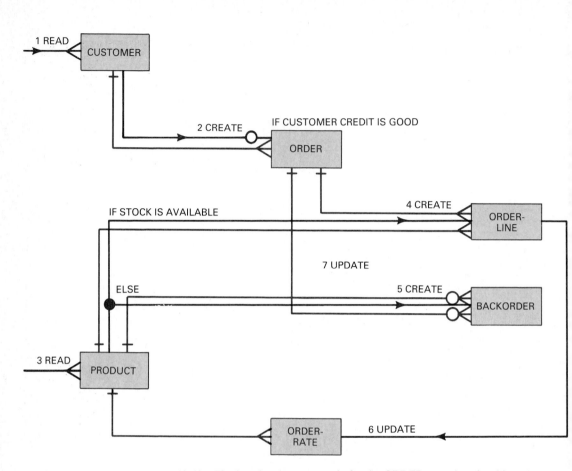

Figure 12.12 The last data-base access is for the ORDER record again, this time to update its ORDER-STATUS, DELIVERY-DATE, and ORDER-TO-TAL fields (all of which depend on accesses made since the ORDER record was created).

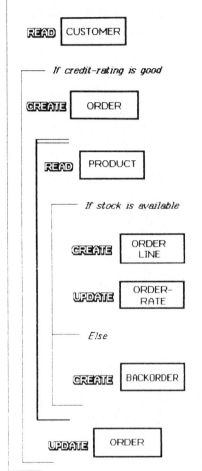

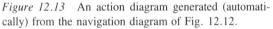

Figure 12.13   An action diagram generated (automatically) from the navigation diagram of Fig. 12.12.

The designer may now add more detail to the action diagram. Fig. 12.14 shows the action diagram with the data items for each entity type displayed. The designer now represents the condition statements so that they use the date items:

IF CREDIT-RATING > 3
IF QTY-ON-HAND > 0

Figure 12.15 shows details of the calculations and printouts added to the action diagram.

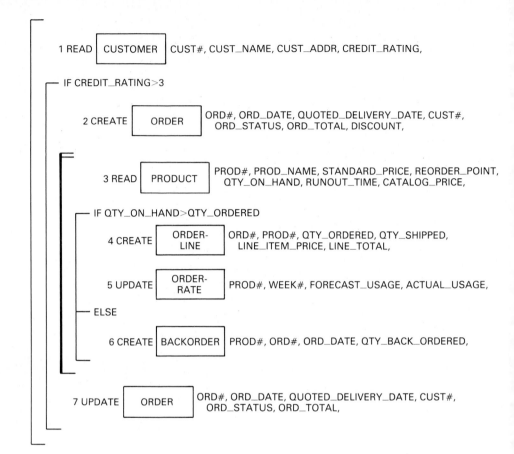

Figure 12.14 The action diagram of Fig. 12.13 annotated with the attributes of each entity type accessed. The condition statements are changed to appropriate attribute names.

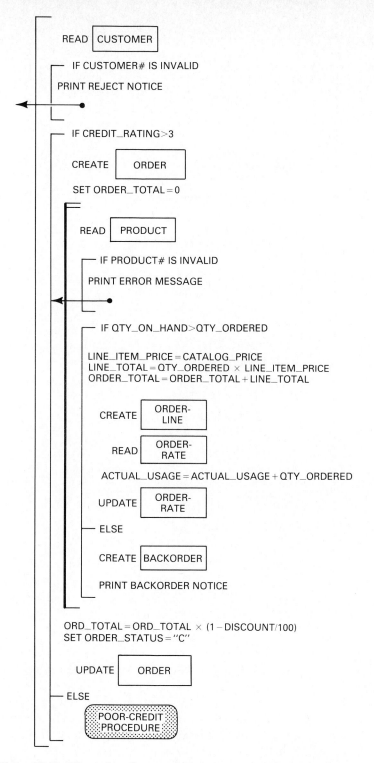

READ | CUSTOMER

IF CUSTOMER# IS INVALID

PRINT REJECT NOTICE

IF CREDIT_RATING>3

CREATE | ORDER

SET ORDER_TOTAL = 0

READ | PRODUCT

IF PRODUCT# IS INVALID

PRINT ERROR MESSAGE

IF QTY_ON_HAND>QTY_ORDERED

LINE_ITEM_PRICE = CATALOG_PRICE
LINE_TOTAL = QTY_ORDERED × LINE_ITEM_PRICE
ORDER_TOTAL = ORDER_TOTAL + LINE_TOTAL

CREATE | ORDER-LINE

READ | ORDER-RATE

ACTUAL_USAGE = ACTUAL_USAGE + QTY_ORDERED

UPDATE | ORDER-RATE

ELSE

CREATE | BACKORDER

PRINT BACKORDER NOTICE

ORD_TOTAL = ORD_TOTAL × (1 − DISCOUNT/100)
SET ORDER_STATUS = "C"

UPDATE | ORDER

ELSE

POOR-CREDIT PROCEDURE

Figure 12.15 The action diagram of Fig. 12.14 expanded to show the calculations, printouts, and so on.

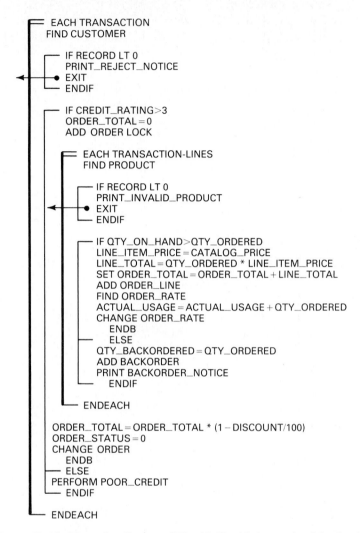

```
    EACH TRANSACTION
    FIND CUSTOMER

        IF RECORD LT 0
        PRINT_REJECT_NOTICE
        EXIT
        ENDIF

        IF CREDIT_RATING>3
        ORDER_TOTAL=0
        ADD ORDER LOCK

            EACH TRANSACTION-LINES
            FIND PRODUCT

                IF RECORD LT 0
                PRINT_INVALID_PRODUCT
                EXIT
                ENDIF

                IF QTY_ON_HAND>QTY_ORDERED
                LINE_ITEM_PRICE=CATALOG_PRICE
                LINE_TOTAL=QTY_ORDERED * LINE_ITEM_PRICE
                SET ORDER_TOTAL=ORDER_TOTAL+LINE_TOTAL
                ADD ORDER_LINE
                FIND ORDER_RATE
                ACTUAL_USAGE=ACTUAL_USAGE+QTY_ORDERED
                CHANGE ORDER_RATE
                    ENDB
                    ELSE
                QTY_BACKORDERED=QTY_ORDERED
                ADD BACKORDER
                PRINT BACKORDER_NOTICE
                    ENDIF

            ENDEACH

        ORDER_TOTAL=ORDER_TOTAL * (1-DISCOUNT/100)
        ORDER_STATUS=0
        CHANGE ORDER
            ENDB
            ELSE
        PERFORM POOR_CREDIT
            ENDIF

    ENDEACH
```

Figure 12.16   The action diagram of Fig. 12.15 with the words of the fourth-generation language APPLICATION FACTORY. This is an executable program written in APPLICATION FACTORY.

FOURTH-GENERATION LANGUAGES

Figure 12.15 is independent of the programming language used. It is, however, designed to be as close as possible to the code representation used in fourth-generation languages and application generators. It can be converted directly into languages such as FOCUS, RAMIS, MANTIS, NOMAD, IDEAL, and CSP.

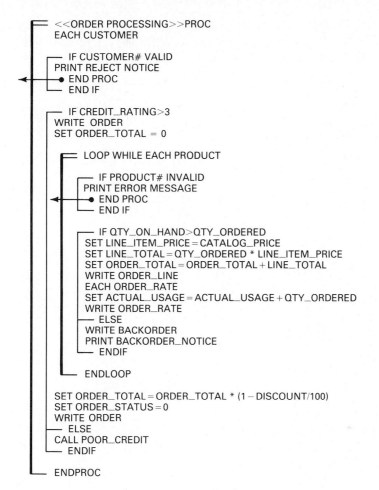

```
 ┌─ <<ORDER PROCESSING>>PROC
 │  EACH CUSTOMER
 │    ┌─ IF CUSTOMER# VALID
 │    │  PRINT REJECT NOTICE
←┼───●  END PROC
 │    └─ END IF
 │    ┌─ IF CREDIT_RATING>3
 │    │  WRITE ORDER
 │    │  SET ORDER_TOTAL = 0
 │    │    ┌─ LOOP WHILE EACH PRODUCT
 │    │    │    ┌─ IF PRODUCT# INVALID
 │    │    │    │  PRINT ERROR MESSAGE
←─────┼────┼──●  END PROC
 │    │    │    └─ END IF
 │    │    │    ┌─ IF QTY_ON_HAND>QTY_ORDERED
 │    │    │    │  SET LINE_ITEM_PRICE = CATALOG_PRICE
 │    │    │    │  SET LINE_TOTAL = QTY_ORDERED * LINE_ITEM_PRICE
 │    │    │    │  SET ORDER_TOTAL = ORDER_TOTAL + LINE_TOTAL
 │    │    │    │  WRITE ORDER_LINE
 │    │    │    │  EACH ORDER_RATE
 │    │    │    │  SET ACTUAL_USAGE = ACTUAL_USAGE + QTY_ORDERED
 │    │    │    │  WRITE ORDER_RATE
 │    │    │    ├─ ELSE
 │    │    │    │  WRITE BACKORDER
 │    │    │    │  PRINT BACKORDER_NOTICE
 │    │    │    └─ ENDIF
 │    │    └─ ENDLOOP
 │    │  SET ORDER_TOTAL = ORDER_TOTAL * (1 − DISCOUNT/100)
 │    │  SET ORDER_STATUS = 0
 │    │  WRITE ORDER
 │    ├─ ELSE
 │    │  CALL POOR_CREDIT
 │    └─ ENDIF
 └─ ENDPROC
```

Figure 12.17 The action diagram of Fig. 12.15 with the words of the fourth-generation language IDEAL. This is an executable program written in IDEAL.

Figure 12.16 shows its coding in APPLICATION FACTORY. Figure 12.17 shows its coding in IDEAL.

It could also be coded in COBOL or PL/I, or it could form the basis for a tool that generates code in these languages.

Fourth-generation languages or application generators of the future ought to assist an analyst or user in creating and manipulating diagrams and then generate efficient executable code directly from the diagram.

CONCURRENCY

With disk storage, it is common to access two or more records concurrently. The semicircular concurrency symbol can be used on navigation diagrams to indicate this:

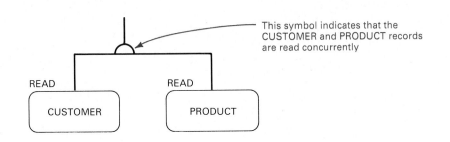

A navigation diagram with concurrency can be translated into an action diagram with concurrency:

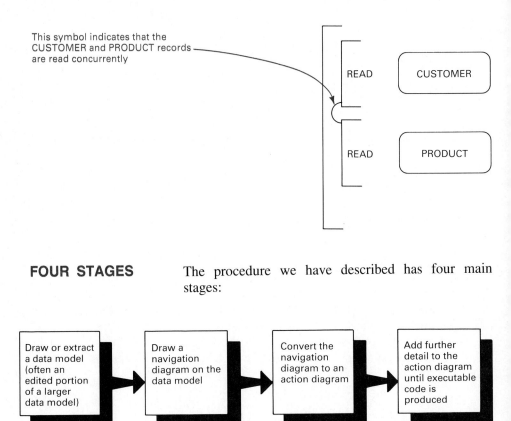

FOUR STAGES

The procedure we have described has four main stages:

| Draw or extract a data model (often an edited portion of a larger data model) | → | Draw a navigation diagram on the data model | → | Convert the navigation diagram to an action diagram | → | Add further detail to the action diagram until executable code is produced |

These steps can be used at two different stages in the design. First, they can be used as illustrated in Figs. 12.3 through 12.13 when *specifying a procedure*. The initial specification may relate to a fully normalized data model and the navigation paths through it. Second, they may relate to *designing a program* that employs storage structures that are not those of a fully normalized model. The navigation may be drawn on a CODASYL data-base schema or an IMS structure, for example.

For data-base management systems that directly represent the fully normalized data models, there is no difference between these. Unfortunately, many data-base management systems employ physical data structures that deviate from the conceptual clarity of the entity-relationship model, and with these, the navigation diagram may be somewhat different from the navigation diagram drawn on the normalized model. Even with a fully relational data base, there can be good reasons, associated with machine performance, for denormalizing the data in certain cases. The navigation diagram then employs a data structure diagram rather than a pure entity-relationship diagram:

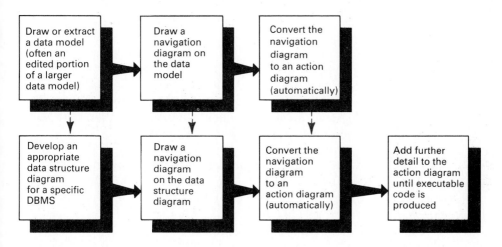

PHYSICAL DESIGN   Initially the physical aspects of accessing the data are ignored. The navigation diagram is drawn as though the data existed in memory for this application alone. Later the physical designer adjusts the navigation diagram as appropriate. To help the physical designer, the navigation diagram should be annotated with details of quantities of accesses.

The accesses on the physical navigation diagram may not be in the same sequence as the accesses on the logical navigation diagram. A logical diagram may have two updates of the same record type. Physically, both these updates would be done at the same time. The first update may be done in computer main memory and not written on the external storage medium until the second update can be completed. Similarly, if a parent record has a child in a physical data base, the two may be updated together. A child record is not created physically until the parent is created, although it could appear first as a logical navigation diagram.

COMPUTERIZED HELP IN DESIGN

As the analyst goes through the steps of application design, there are certain questions he should ask at each stage. This can be made into a formal procedure. If he is using a computerized tool for carrying out the design steps of Fig. 12.3, the machine should make him address the relevant design questions at each stage. This leads to a better-quality design with well-thought-out controls and should go as far as possible to generating automatically the next stage of the design until executable code is reached.

When extracting and editing the data submodel, the computer can show the designer the neighborhood of the entity types in question and display their attributes. It can ask which entity types are to be created, retrieved, updated, or deleted.

The computer asks the designer to select choices from a panel for each access in turn. This establishes the crow's feet, circles, and other symbols that appear on the navigation diagram. Where there is a circle (optional link or mutually exclusive links), the designer is asked to enter a condition. Where there is a crow's foot, the designer might enter loop control information. (He might enter this at the action diagram stage).

There is other information that ought to be collected besides that shown in Figs. 12.7 through 12.12. The computer may take the designer through the accesses a second time, asking questions such as how each record is accessed, what happens if it cannot be found, which fields are changed in an update access, and how the new values are computed.

A panel asking for more details about the first access (in Fig. 12.7) is shown in Fig. 12.18. Panels asking for details about the updating of ORDER-RATE (in Fig. 12.11) are shown in Fig. 12.19.

The objective of such a design dialog is to speed up the design and to ensure that all necessary controls and error conditions are thought about. The system should convert the results to an action diagram from which executable code can be created, as in Figs. 12.16 and 12.17. The dialog should also collect figures that will assist the physical designer who is concerned with performance.

COMPLEXITY

The subset data model that is used for one application usually does not become very big. It can usually be drawn on one page or screen and so can be the associated navigation diagram.

```
┌─────────────────────────────────────────────────────────────────┐
│ PROCEDURE: ACCEPT ORDER                                           │
├─────────────────────────────────────────────────────────────────┤
│ ACCESS 1: READ CUSTOMER                                           │
├─────────────────────────────────────────────────────────────────┤
│                                                                   │
│  Is access via primary key CUSTOMER# ■            Other □         │
│                                                                   │
│  What happens if no CUSTOMER record is found:                     │
│      ● An exception procedure is triggered: □                     │
│          The exception procedure is called: [              ]      │
│          The exception procedure is:                              │
│              An interrupt to ACCEPT-ORDER: □                      │
│              Does not return to ACCEPT-ORDER: □                   │
│      ● ACCEPT–ORDER is terminated: ■                              │
│                                                                   │
│  The message provided to the user is as follows:                  │
│  ┌─────────────────────────────────────────────────────────┐     │
│  │                                                         │     │
│  └─────────────────────────────────────────────────────────┘     │
└─────────────────────────────────────────────────────────────────┘
```

Figure 12.18   A panel asking for more detailed information about the first access in Fig. 12.7. The designer clicks on the entry boxes as shown by the red color here.

```
┌─────────────────────────────────────────────────────────────────┐
│ PROCEDURE: ACCEPT ORDER                                           │
├─────────────────────────────────────────────────────────────────┤
│ ACCESS 6: Update ORDER-RATE                                       │
├─────────────────────────────────────────────────────────────────┤
│                                                                   │
│  Which data-items will be changed in ORDER-RATE?                  │
│                      PRODUCT#          □                          │
│                      WEEK#             □                          │
│                      FORECAST-USAGE    □                          │
│                      ACTUAL-USAGE      ■                          │
│  Are any other data-items needed in ORDER-RATE? Yes: □   No: ■    │
└─────────────────────────────────────────────────────────────────┘

┌─────────────────────────────────────────────────────────────────┐
│ PROCEDURE: ACCEPT ORDER                                           │
├─────────────────────────────────────────────────────────────────┤
│ ACCESS 6: Update ORDER-RATE                                       │
├─────────────────────────────────────────────────────────────────┤
│                                                                   │
│  Enter a formula or procedure for computing ACTUAL-USAGE:         │
│  ┌─────────────────────────────────────────────────┐             │
│  │                                                 │             │
│  └─────────────────────────────────────────────────┘             │
└─────────────────────────────────────────────────────────────────┘
```

Figure 12.19   Panels asking for details about the updating of ORDER-RATE in the access shown in Fig. 12.11.

In some corporations with highly complex data processing, the subset data models have never exceeded a dozen third-normal-form records. Most do not exceed six or so.

STANDARD   It is very simple to *teach* the use of data navigation
PROCEDURE   diagrams. These should be an installation standard
                       rather than a tool of certain individuals. Paper forms
and guidelines are often used, rather than computer-aided design.

One giant aerospace corporation, where more than a thousand navigation diagrams were drawn, found that this approach highlighted the transaction-driven nature of good data-base usage. Transaction-driven design had been surprisingly difficult for many analysts to grasp because they had learned techniques that (like many structured techniques) were batch-oriented.

REFERENCE

1. J. Martin, *Managing the Data Base Environment*. Englewood Cliffs, N.J.: Prentice-Hall, 1983.

13 COMPOUND DATA ACCESSES

Traditional data-base navigation, as described in Chapter 12, uses *simple* data-base accesses: CREATE, READ, UPDATE, and DELETE. These carry out an operation on *one* instance of *one* record type.

Some high-level languages permit the use of statements that relate to not one but many instances of records and sometimes more than one record type. We refer to these as *compound* data-base accesses.

Examples of such statements are:

SEARCH

SORT

SELECT (certain records from a relation or file)

JOIN (two or more relations or files)

PROJECT (a relation or file to obtain a subset of it)

DUPLICATE

CREATE, READ, UPDATE, and DELETE may also be used to refer to several instances of a record type. DELETE, for example, could be used to delete a whole file.

Where a data-base access refers to one instance of a record type, we have used a single box containing the name of the record type:

Where a compound access that refers to more than one instance is used, we use a double box containing the name of the record type or entity type:

Often this double box needs a qualifying statement associated with it to say how it is performed, for example:

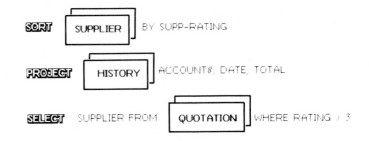

The type of operation is again written in large letters.

RELATIONAL JOINS

A *relational join* merges two relations (logical files or tables) on the basis of a common field [1]. For example, the EMPLOYEE relation and the BRANCH relation might look like this:

BRANCH

BRANCH-ID	LOCATION	BRANCH-STATUS	SALES-YEAR-TO-DATE
007	Paris	17	4789
009	Carnforth	2	816
013	Rio	14	2927

EMPLOYEE

EMPLOYEE#	EMPLOYEE-NAME	SALARY	CODE	MANAGER	CITY
01425	Kleinrock	42000	SE	Epstein	Rio
08301	Ashley	48000	SE	Sauer	Paris
09981	Jenkins	45000	FE	Growler	Rio
12317	Bottle	91000	SE	Minski	Carnforth

These relations are combined in such a way that the CITY field of the EMPLOYEE relation becomes the same as the LOCATION field of the BRANCH relation. We can express this with the statement:

BRANCH.LOCATION = EMPLOYEE.CITY

The result is, in effect, a combined record, as follows:

EMPLOYEE#	EMPLOYEE-NAME	SALARY	CODE	MANAGER	CITY	BRANCH-ID	BRANCH-STATUS	SALES-YEAR-TO-DATE
01425	Kleinrock	42000	SE	Epstein	Rio	013	14	2927
08301	Ashley	48000	SE	Sauer	Paris	007	17	4789
09981	Jenkins	45000	FE	Growler	Rio	013	14	2927
12317	Bottle	91000	SE	Minski	Carnforth	009	2	816

This data-base system may not combine them in reality but may join the appropriate data in response to queries or other operations. For example, if we ask for the MANAGER associated with each BRANCH-ID, the system will look up the BRANCH-LOCATION for each BRANCH-ID, search for an EM-PLOYEE.CITY data item with the same value, and find the MANAGER data item associated with that.

A join is shown on a navigation chart by linking two or more entity-type access boxes together with a double line:

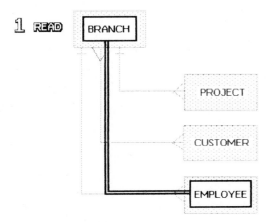

It is shown on an action diagram also by linking the boxes, with an access operation applying the combination:

A statement may be attached to the joined entity types showing how they are joined, like the above BRANCH.LOCATION = EMPLOYEE.CITY. Often this is not necessary because the joined entity records contain one common attribute that is the basis for the join. For example, the EMPLOYEE record probably contains the attribute BRANCH#, in which case we can simply show:

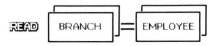

Using this join, we might say SELECT EMPLOYEE-NAME, MAN-AGER, BRANCH-STATUS, CITY. The result is as follows:

EMPLOYEE-NAME	MANAGER	BRANCH-STATUS	CITY
Kleinrock	Epstein	14	Rio
Ashley	Sauer	17	Paris
Jenkins	Growler	14	Rio
Bottle	Minski	2	Carnforth

We might constrain the join operation by asking for employees whose code is SE and whose salary exceeds $40,000. The result would then be:

EMPLOYEE-NAME	MANAGER	BRANCH-STATUS	CITY
Kleinrock	Epstein	14	Rio
Ashley	Sauer	17	Paris
Bottle	Minski	2	Carnforth

With the data-base language SQL from IBM, and others, this operation would be expressed as follows:

```
SELECT EMPLOYEE-NAME, MANAGER, BRANCH-STATUS, CITY
FROM BRANCH, EMPLOYEE
WHERE BRANCH.LOCATION = EMPLOYEE.CITY
AND CODE = SE
AND SALARY > 40000
```

This can be written on an action diagram as follows:

For a simple query such as this, we do not need a diagramming technique. The query language itself is clear enough. For a complex operation, we certainly need to diagram the use of compound data-base actions. Even for queries, if they are complex, diagrams are needed.

AUTOMATIC   A compound data-base action may require *automatic*
NAVIGATION   *navigation* by the data-base management system. Re-
                    lational data bases and a few nonrelational ones have
this capability. For a data base without automatic navigation, a compiler of a
fourth-generation language may generate the required sequence of data accesses.

With a compound data-base action, search parameters or conditions are often an integral part of the action itself. They are written inside a bracket containing the access box.

SIMPLE VERSUS   There are many procedures that can be done with ei-
COMPOUND   ther simple data-base accesses or compound ac-
DATA-BASE   cesses. If a traditional DBMS is used, the program-
ACCESSES   mer navigates through the data base with simple
                    accesses. If the DBMS or language compiler has au-
tomatic navigation, higher-level statements using compound data-base accesses may be employed.

Suppose, for example, that we want to give a $1000 raise in salary to all employees who are engineers in Carnforth. With IBM's data-base language SQL, we would write:

```
UPDATE EMPLOYEE
GET SALARY = SALARY + 1000
WHERE JOB = 'ENGINEER'
AND OFFICE = 'CARNFORTH'
```

We can diagram this with a compound action as follows:

With simple actions (no automatic navigation), we can diagram the same procedure thus:

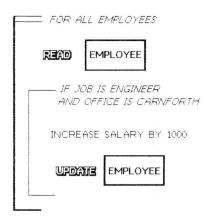

Similarly, a relational join can be represented with either a sequence of single actions or one compound action, as shown in Fig. 13.1. In this example, there are several projects of an EMPLOYEE-PROJECT record showing how employees were rated for their work on each project they were assigned to. They are given a salary raise if their average rating exceeds 6.

It ought to be an objective of nonprocedural languages to enable their user to achieve as much as possible without separate diagramming. The best way to achieve this may be to incorporate the graphics technique into the language itself. In other words, executable code is generated from the diagrams.

**INTERMIXING
SIMPLE AND
COMPOUND
ACTIONS**

Sometimes compound and simple data-base actions are used in the same procedure. Figure 13.2 illustrates this. It uses the data structure shown in Fig. 12.5 and shows the process of reordering stock as it becomes depleted.

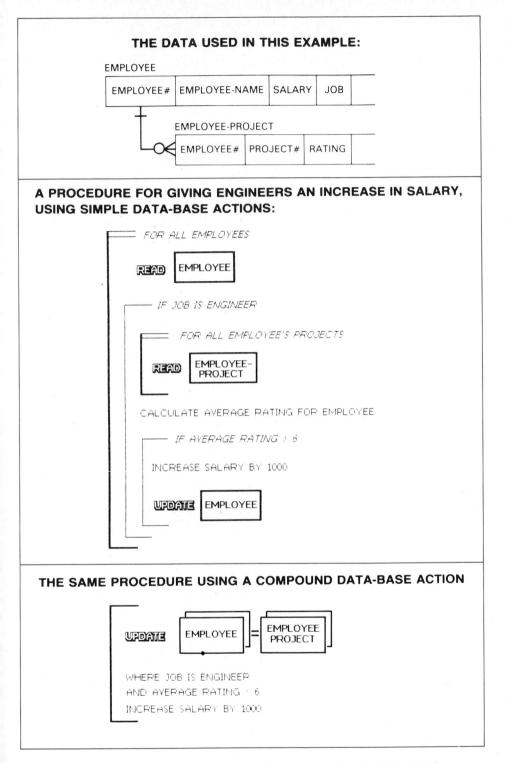

Figure 13.1 Illustration of a procedure that may be done with either several simple data-base access commands or one compound access command action.

As a request for parts is satisfied, the quantity on hand, recorded in the PART record, is depleted. Each time this happens, the program calculates whether to create an order for more parts from their supplier.

The request for parts are handled interactively throughout the day. The person designing the procedure decides to create a temporary file of order requisitions, to accumulate such requisitions as they occur, and then to sort them and place the orders at the end of the day. In this way an order for many parts can be sent to a supplier, rather than creating a separate order each time a part reaches its reorder point.

Figure 13.2 shows the results. In the top part of the figure, the selection of suppliers is done with a compound action. This can be represented with one statement of some fourth-generation languages. For example, in SQL it might be:

```
SELECT SUPPLIER
FROM QUOTATION
WHERE RATING > 3
AND MIN (QUOTE-PRICE)
```

In the bottom part of the figure, the order requisition file is sorted by supplier. This can also be represented by one fourth-generation language statement:

```
ORDER REQUISITION BY SUPPLIER
```

THREE-WAY JOINS   In some cases three-way joins are useful. Suppose an accountant is concerned that accounts receivable are becoming too high. He wants to phone any branch office manager who has six-month-old debt outstanding from a customer.

The following record structures exist:

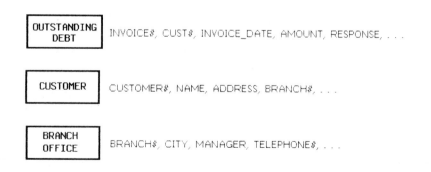

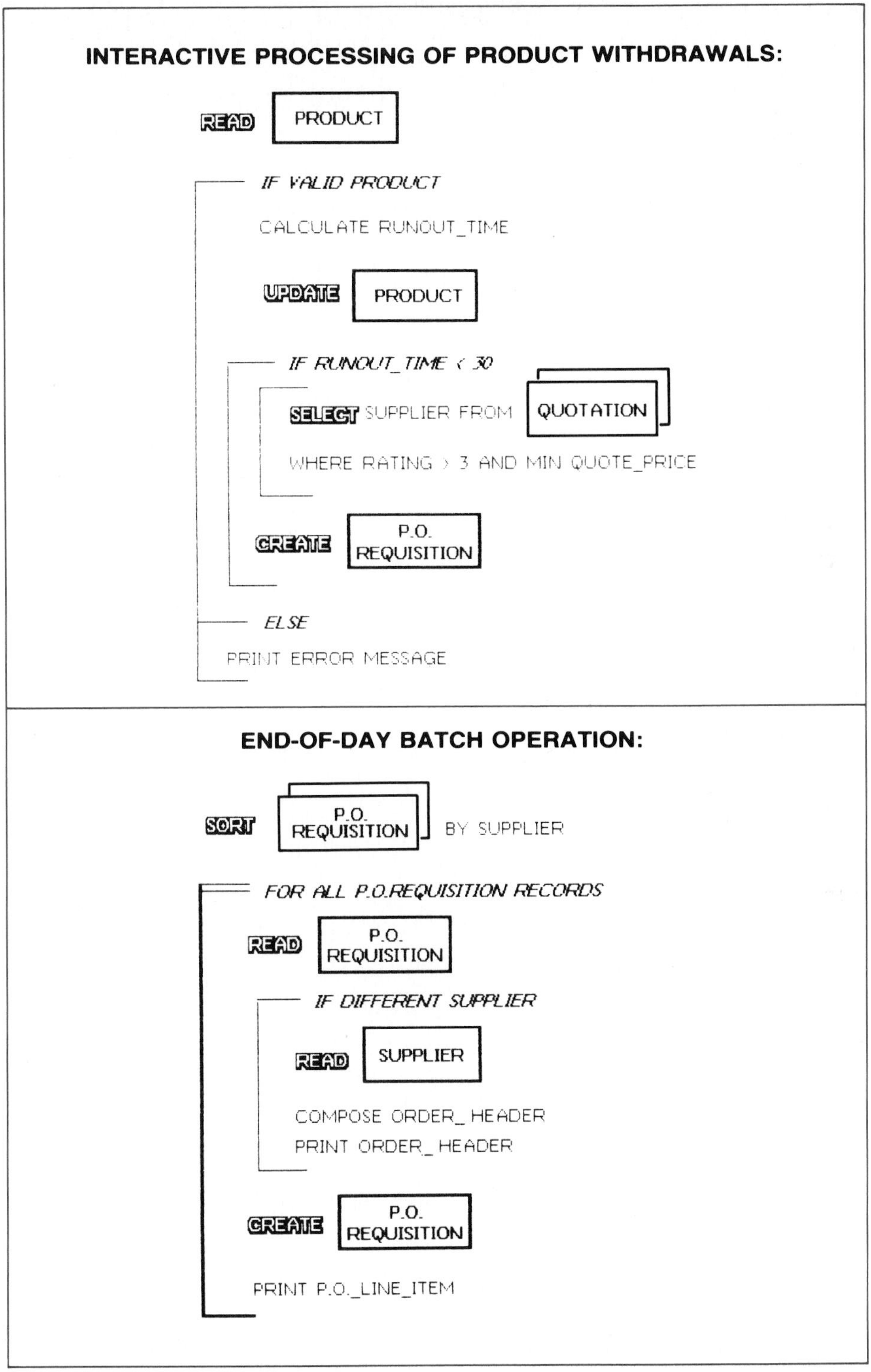

INTERACTIVE PROCESSING OF PRODUCT WITHDRAWALS:

READ | PRODUCT

    IF VALID PRODUCT

        CALCULATE RUNOUT_TIME

        UPDATE | PRODUCT

            IF RUNOUT_TIME < 30

                SELECT SUPPLIER FROM | QUOTATION

                WHERE RATING > 3 AND MIN QUOTE_PRICE

                CREATE | P.O. REQUISITION

    ELSE

        PRINT ERROR MESSAGE

END-OF-DAY BATCH OPERATION:

SORT | P.O. REQUISITION | BY SUPPLIER

    FOR ALL P.O.REQUISITION RECORDS

        READ | P.O. REQUISITION

            IF DIFFERENT SUPPLIER

                READ | SUPPLIER

                COMPOSE ORDER_HEADER
                PRINT ORDER_HEADER

        CREATE | P.O. REQUISITION

        PRINT P.O._LINE_ITEM

Figure 13.2 Procedures for product withdrawal and reordering using the data structure in Fig. 12.5 and a temporary P.O.-REQUISITION file. Two compound accesses are used in these procedures.

The accountant enters the following query:

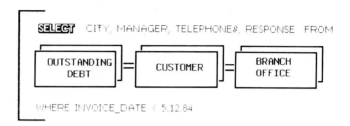

The three-way join is shown in a similar fashion to two-way joins. It could also be drawn on a data model to show a compound access in a navigation chart. Figure 13.3 shows this three-way join expressed with the language SQL.

SEMANTIC DISINTEGRITY

Unfortunately, compound accesses in high-level database languages sometimes give rise to subtle problems. A user may enter a query with an easy-to-use query language; the query looks correct and the results look correct, but the results are in fact wrong.

Our query with triple join is correct because OUTSTANDING-DEBT is associated with *one* CUSTOMER and CUSTOMER is associated with *one* BRANCH. In the data model, these associations are as follows:

Suppose, however, that one CUSTOMER can be served by more than one BRANCH-OFFICE:

Then the use of the join is incorrect; there is *semantic disintegrity* in the query. The accountant might be phoning a branch manager who is not responsible for a customer's debt.

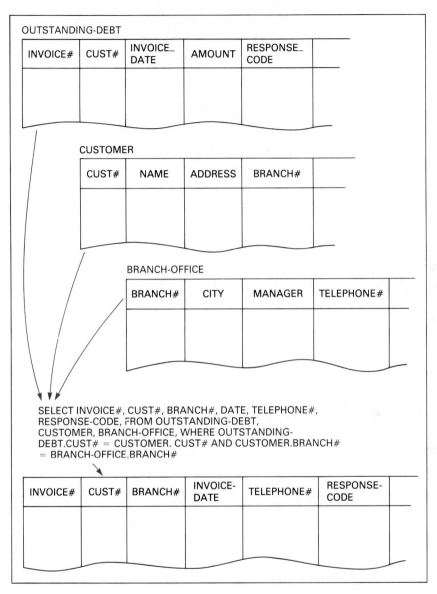

OUTSTANDING-DEBT

INVOICE#	CUST#	INVOICE_DATE	AMOUNT	RESPONSE_CODE	

CUSTOMER

CUST#	NAME	ADDRESS	BRANCH#	

BRANCH-OFFICE

BRANCH#	CITY	MANAGER	TELEPHONE#	

SELECT INVOICE#, CUST#, BRANCH#, DATE, TELEPHONE#,
RESPONSE-CODE, FROM OUTSTANDING-DEBT,
CUSTOMER, BRANCH-OFFICE, WHERE OUTSTANDING-
DEBT.CUST# = CUSTOMER. CUST# AND CUSTOMER.BRANCH#
= BRANCH-OFFICE.BRANCH#

INVOICE#	CUST#	BRANCH#	INVOICE-DATE	TELEPHONE#	RESPONSE-CODE	

Figure 13.3   A join between three relations expressed with SQL.

Again, suppose that two relations were joined as follows:

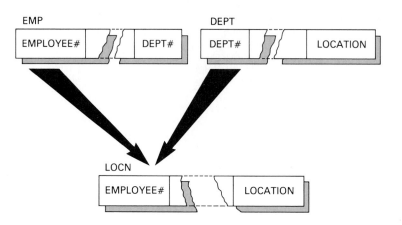

This join is valid if there is a one-with-one association between DEPT# and LOCATION. It is not valid if there is a one-with-many association between DEPT# and LOCATION, because although a department can have more than one location, an employee works in only one location. Drawing data items as ellipses, we have the following associations between data items:

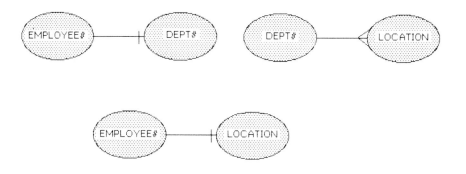

NAVIGATION PATHS   We can understand what a query or relational operation is doing by drawing a navigation path. To perform the join under discussion, we start with EMPLOYEE# and find the associated DEPT#. For that DEPT# we find the associated LOCATION. We can draw this navigation path as follows:

Here we have only one-with-one paths, so there is no problem. If, however, there were a one-with-many path from DEPT# to LOCATION, we would draw:

This is invalid because there is *one* LOCATION, not many, for one employee.

We have the possibility of semantic disintegrity if the navigation path has a one-with-many link that is not the first link, for example:

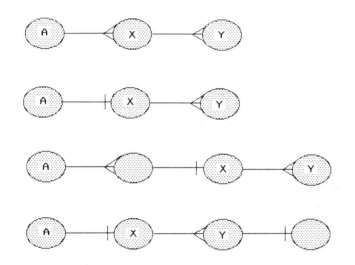

Many values of Y are associated with X, but they might not all be associated with A.

We do not necessarily know whether such a navigation path will be valid or not. Figure 13.4 shows two queries employing a join. Their data and navigation paths are similar in structure. Both use fully normalized data. The one-with-many path makes the bottom one invalid, but not the top one. Because the software cannot tell for sure, it should warn the user that the results might be invalid. The problems in these examples can be controlled if the data are correctly modeled and the software for compound accesses uses the model. In Fig. 13.4 entity-relationship modeling is incomplete in the bottom example. It should show the relationship between employee and project. If the software knew this relationship, it could prevent the invalid join.

To ensure integrity in relational operations, it is essential that the data

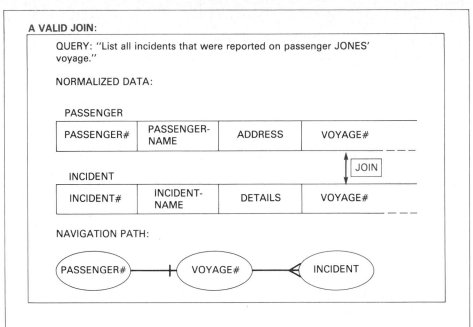

A VALID JOIN:

QUERY: "List all incidents that were reported on passenger JONES' voyage."

NORMALIZED DATA:

PASSENGER

PASSENGER#	PASSENGER-NAME	ADDRESS	VOYAGE#

JOIN

INCIDENT

INCIDENT#	INCIDENT-NAME	DETAILS	VOYAGE#

NAVIGATION PATH:

PASSENGER# ———|— VOYAGE# ——< INCIDENT

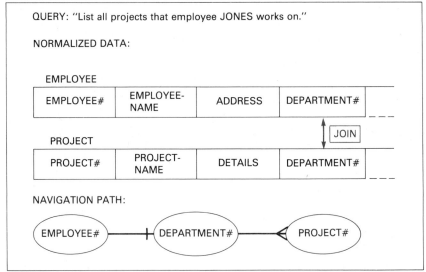

AN INVALID JOIN:

QUERY: "List all projects that employee JONES works on."

NORMALIZED DATA:

EMPLOYEE

EMPLOYEE#	EMPLOYEE-NAME	ADDRESS	DEPARTMENT#

JOIN

PROJECT

PROJECT#	PROJECT-NAME	DETAILS	DEPARTMENT#

NAVIGATION PATH:

EMPLOYEE# ———|— DEPARTMENT# ——< PROJECT#

The top join is valid because every incident on passenger JONES' voyage is needed.

The bottom join is *not* valid because employee JONES does not work on *every* project in his department.

The entity-relationship modeling is incomplete in the bottom example. It should show the relationship between employee and project. Compound relational accesses are only safe when thorough data modeling has been done. The software should warn the user about potentially invalid JOINS and PROJECTS.

Figure 13.4   Two queries with similar data structures using a join.

be correctly and completely modeled. The designer can understand the effect of compound navigation by drawing appropriate diagrams. Diagrams showing details of the navigation path can warn of the danger of semantic disintegrity [2].

FOURTH-GENERATION LANGUAGES

Different fourth-generation languages or high-level data-base languages have different dialects [3]. It would be useful if vendors of such languages would draw illustrations of the set of control structures and compound data-base accesses that their languages employ.

A compound data-base access is rather like a macroinstruction that is decomposed into primitive instructions by a compiler or interpreter before it is executed.

To clarify how a compound data-base access in a language operates, the vendor might draw a diagram decomposing it into simple accesses. This is not always useful because some compound accesses are easy to understand but difficult to draw in a decomposed form (e.g., SORT).

Compound accesses, like simple accesses, need to be converted directly into the code of very high level languages. Often the wording inside the bracket should resemble the resulting code. The dialect of the language is thus incorporated into the diagram. Converting the action diagrams to code can be computer-assisted and ought to form part of an interactive design tool.

The software designer creating a fourth-generation language would do well to start with navigation diagrams and action diagrams, design an easy-to-use technique for charting procedures, and then create an interpreter or compiler with which code can be generated from the diagrams.

The systems analyst needs a computer screen that enables him to edit diagrams rapidly and add more detail until working code is created.

REFERENCES

1. J. Martin, *Managing the Data Base Environment*. Englewood Cliffs, N.J.: Prentice-Hall, 1983.

2. For a more detailed discussion of semantic disintegrity, see *System Design from Provably Correct Constructs*. Englewood Cliffs, N.J.: Prentice-Hall, 1985.

3. J. Martin, *Fourth-Generation Languages*. Englewood Cliffs, N.J.: Prentice-Hall, 1985.

14 DECISION TREES AND DECISION TABLES

A BROADLY USED DIAGRAMMING TECHNIQUE   Decision trees and decision tables did not originate as computer diagramming techniques. They have much broader applicability. Decision trees and decision tables are used in biology, computer science, information theory and switching theory. There are four main fields of application [1]:

1. Taxonomy, diagnosis, and pattern recognition

2. Circuit (logic) design and reliability testing

3. Analysis of algorithms

4. Decision-table programming and data bases

DECISION TREE   A *decision tree* consists of a hierarchy of decision points. At each decision point, an action, based on the value of a variable, is taken. The output of the decision point is either a value or the choice of another decision point. Thus each action taken depends on the current value of the variable being tested and the previous actions that have been taken. In a formally defined decision tree, a variable is tested only once on any path through the tree. This restriction is to prevent redundant testing.

Decision trees are normally constructed from a problem description. They give a graphic view of the decision making that is needed. They specify the variables tested, the actions to be taken, and the order in which decision making is performed. Each time a decision tree is "executed," one path, beginning with the root of the tree and ending with a leaf on the tree, will be followed, depending on the current value of the variable or variables tested.

Consider the following description:

In the subscription system, subscription transactions are processed. First, each transaction is validated. Invalid transactions are rejected with an appropriate error message. Valid transactions are processed according to type: new subscription, renewal, or cancellation. For new subscriptions, a customer record is built and a bill is generated for the balance due. For renewals, the expiration date is updated and a bill is generated for the balance due. For cancellations, the record is flagged for deletion and a refund is issued.

A decision tree for the subscription system is shown in Fig. 14.1. The root of the tree is the condition test VALID TRANSACTION? which is answered YES or NO. If a transaction is valid and it is a new subscription, the path with YES in response to VALID TRANSACTION? and NEW SUBSCRIPTION for TRANSACTION TYPE will be followed. This path ends with processing a new subscription by building a customer record and generating a bill.

Figure 14.2 shows a more complex (and more useful) decision tree. It relates to complex rules for determining how much discount a customer receives. At the top of the diagram are the names of data attributes. CUSTOMER.ANNUAL-PURCHASES, for example, refers to the data item ANNUAL-PURCHASES in the CUSTOMER record. If this has a value greater than one million, the bottom part of the tree is used. The values of four attributes are used to determine ORDER.DISCOUNT.

Mutual Exclusivity

The paths on a decision tree are normally mutually exclusive. The circle on the branch, which we employed earlier to represent mutual exclusivity, is shown on our drawings of decision trees.

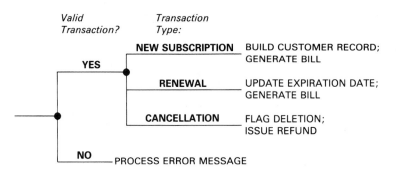

Figure 14.1 A decision tree is a graphic view of the decision logic in a program module.

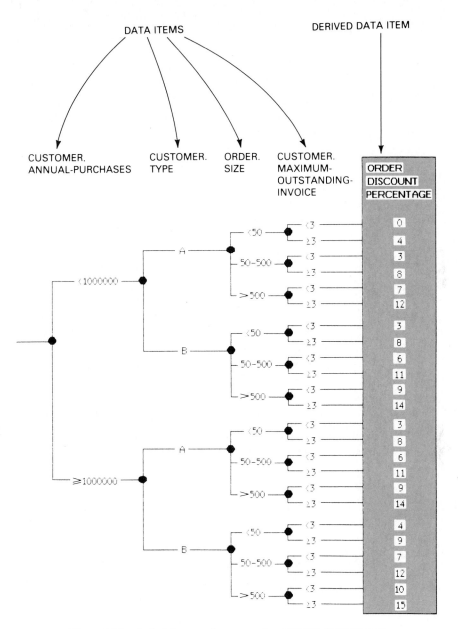

Figure 14.2 A decision tree for computing ORDER.DISCOUNT.

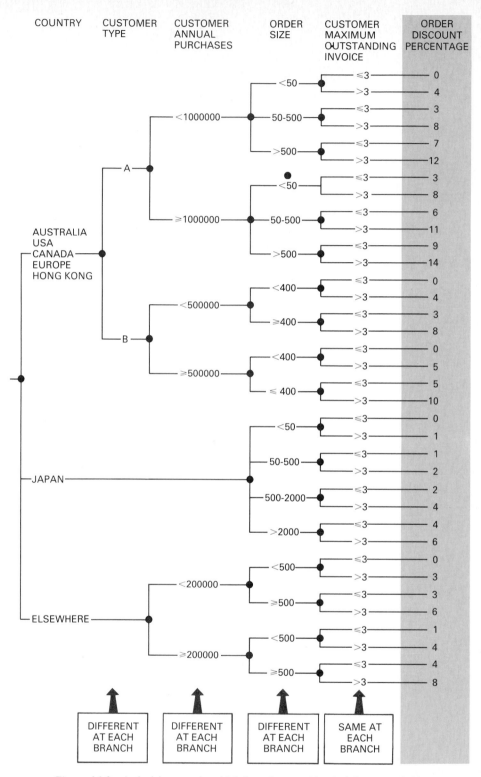

Figure 14.3 A decision tree in which branches are identical for some fields and different for others.

Identical Versus Different Branches

In Fig. 14.2, in any one column each branch is identical. Such is not always the case. Figure 14.3 shows a decision tree in which only one column has the property that all its branches are identical. In some positions there is no branch.

When a column has the property that all branches are identical, it is useful for the computer to know that. Then if a value is changed for one branch in the column, the computer will change it for all branches in that column. If more branches are added (by increasing the number of values in a column to the left), the computer can add the new branches in the identical-branch columns automatically.

Each column may therefore be marked "Different at each branch" or "Same at each branch" by using a menu when the decision tree is built.

Translation into Action Diagrams

The shape of a case structure bracket on an action diagram is similar to the shape of a branching line in the decision tree:

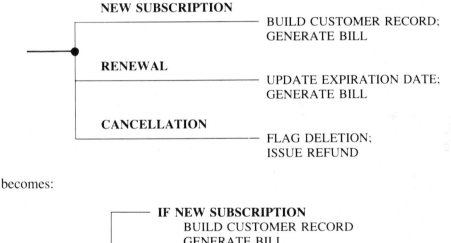

NEW SUBSCRIPTION
BUILD CUSTOMER RECORD;
GENERATE BILL

RENEWAL
UPDATE EXPIRATION DATE;
GENERATE BILL

CANCELLATION
FLAG DELETION;
ISSUE REFUND

becomes:

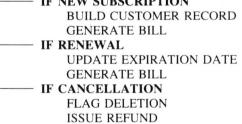

IF NEW SUBSCRIPTION
   BUILD CUSTOMER RECORD
   GENERATE BILL
IF RENEWAL
   UPDATE EXPIRATION DATE
   GENERATE BILL
IF CANCELLATION
   FLAG DELETION
   ISSUE REFUND

Decision trees or tables can be automatically converted into action diagrams. They often form part of an action diagram that contains other constructs as well. Figure 14.4 shows an action diagram equivalent to the decision tree in Fig. 14.2.

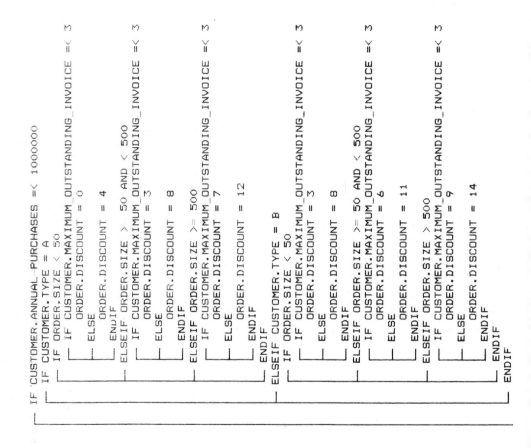

```
IF CUSTOMER.ANNUAL_PURCHASES =< 1000000
┌─ IF CUSTOMER.TYPE = A
│  ┌─ IF ORDER.SIZE < 50
│  │  ┌─ IF CUSTOMER.MAXIMUM_OUTSTANDING_INVOICE =< 3
│  │  │     ORDER.DISCOUNT = 0
│  │  │  ELSE
│  │  │     ORDER.DISCOUNT = 4
│  │  └─ ENDIF
│  ┌─ ELSEIF ORDER.SIZE > 50 AND < 500
│  │  ┌─ IF CUSTOMER.MAXIMUM_OUTSTANDING_INVOICE =< 3
│  │  │     ORDER.DISCOUNT = 3
│  │  │  ELSE
│  │  │     ORDER.DISCOUNT = 8
│  │  └─ ENDIF
│  ┌─ ELSEIF ORDER.SIZE >= 500
│  │  ┌─ IF CUSTOMER.MAXIMUM_OUTSTANDING_INVOICE =< 3
│  │  │     ORDER.DISCOUNT = 7
│  │  │  ELSE
│  │  │     ORDER.DISCOUNT = 12
│  │  └─ ENDIF
│  └─ ENDIF
┌─ ELSEIF CUSTOMER.TYPE = B
│  ┌─ IF ORDER.SIZE < 50
│  │  ┌─ IF CUSTOMER.MAXIMUM_OUTSTANDING_INVOICE =< 3
│  │  │     ORDER.DISCOUNT = 3
│  │  │  ELSE
│  │  │     ORDER.DISCOUNT = 8
│  │  └─ ENDIF
│  ┌─ ELSEIF ORDER.SIZE >= 50 AND < 500
│  │  ┌─ IF CUSTOMER.MAXIMUM_OUTSTANDING_INVOICE =< 3
│  │  │     ORDER.DISCOUNT = 6
│  │  │  ELSE
│  │  │     ORDER.DISCOUNT = 11
│  │  └─ ENDIF
│  ┌─ ELSEIF ORDER.SIZE > 500
│  │  ┌─ IF CUSTOMER.MAXIMUM_OUTSTANDING_INVOICE =< 3
│  │  │     ORDER.DISCOUNT = 9
│  │  │  ELSE
│  │  │     ORDER.DISCOUNT = 14
│  │  └─ ENDIF
│  └─ ENDIF
└─ ENDIF
```

```
─ ELSE
│   ─ IF CUSTOMER.TYPE = A
│   │   ─ IF ORDER.SIZE < 50
│   │   │   ─ IF CUSTOMER.MAXIMUM_OUTSTANDING_INVOICE =< 3
│   │   │   │     ORDER.DISCOUNT = 3
│   │   │   ─ ELSE
│   │   │   │     ORDER.DISCOUNT = 8
│   │   │   ─ ENDIF
│   │   ─ ELSEIF ORDER.SIZE >= 50 AND < 500
│   │   │   ─ IF CUSTOMER.MAXIMUM_OUTSTANDING_INVOICE =< 3
│   │   │   │     ORDER.DISCOUNT = 6
│   │   │   ─ ELSE
│   │   │   │     ORDER.DISCOUNT = 11
│   │   │   ─ ENDIF
│   │   ─ ELSEIF ORDER.SIZE > 500
│   │   │   ─ IF CUSTOMER.MAXIMUM_OUTSTANDING_INVOICE =< 3
│   │   │   │     ORDER.DISCOUNT = 9
│   │   │   ─ ELSE
│   │   │   │     ORDER.DISCOUNT = 14
│   │   │   ─ ENDIF
│   │   ─ ENDIF
│   ─ ELSEIF CUSTOMER.TYPE = B
│   │   ─ IF ORDER.SIZE < 50
│   │   │   ─ IF CUSTOMER.MAXIMUM_OUTSTANDING_INVOICE =< 3
│   │   │   │     ORDER.DISCOUNT = 4
│   │   │   ─ ELSE
│   │   │   │     ORDER.DISCOUNT = 9
│   │   │   ─ ENDIF
│   │   ─ ELSEIF ORDER.SIZE >= 50 AND < 500
│   │   │   ─ IF CUSTOMER.MAXIMUM_OUTSTANDING_INVOICE =< 3
│   │   │   │     ORDER.DISCOUNT = 7
│   │   │   ─ ELSE
│   │   │   │     ORDER.DISCOUNT = 12
│   │   │   ─ ENDIF
│   │   ─ ELSEIF ORDER.SIZE > 500
│   │   │   ─ IF CUSTOMER.MAXIMUM_OUTSTANDING_INVOICE =< 3
│   │   │   │     ORDER.DISCOUNT = 10
│   │   │   ─ ELSE
│   │   │   │     ORDER.DISCOUNT = 15
│   │   │   ─ ENDIF
│   │   ─ ENDIF
│   ─ ENDIF
```

Figure 14.4   An action diagram equivalent to the decision tree of Fig. 14.2.

293

If good program efficiency is to be obtained, the condition tests that are most likely to be successful ought to be placed first on decision trees that are automatically translated to programs.

DECISION TABLE

A *decision table* is an alternative representation of a procedure. It shows the procedure in a tabular or matrix form in which the upper rows of the table specify the *variables* or *conditions* to be evaluated and the lower rows specify the *corresponding action* to be taken when an evaluation test is satisfied. A column in the table is called a *rule*. Each rule defines a procedure of the type "If condition is true, execute the corresponding action."

Figure 14.5 shows a decision table for the subscription system. The rule for processing a new subscription (the second column) tells us that if the transaction is valid, the actions to take are to build a customer record and generate a bill.

A dash in the condition row means "do not care." In the first column of Fig. 14.5, the dashes mean that nothing else matters if the transaction is invalid.

The decision table in Fig. 14.5 relates to relatively simple decisions. They are sufficiently simple that other forms of diagram are probably better and relate more directly to program structure—for example, the action diagram shown in Fig. 14.3.

However, if the decisions relate to complex combinations of conditions, a decision table is a major help in clear thinking. Figure 14.6 shows a decision table where this is the case. Some software exists that can convert decision tables like this one into program code.

An attempt to draw the logic of Fig. 14.6 with flowcharts, Nassi-Shneiderman charts, Warnier-Orr charts, or other such methods would be clumsy, time-consuming, and prone to errors.

CONDITIONS				
Valid transaction	NO	YES	YES	YES
New subscription	—	YES	NO	NO
Renewal	—	NO	YES	NO
Cancellation	—	NO	NO	YES
ACTIONS				
Process error message	x			
Build customer record		x		
Generate bill		x	x	
Update expiration date			x	
Flag deletion				x
Issue refund				x

A column is referred to as a "rule"

Figure 14.5 A decision table can give a tabular view of the decision logic in a program. This table is equivalent to the decision tree in Fig. 14.1

CONDITIONS:

	P1						P2						P3						P4						P5						P6						P7					
STATE OF THE INTERFACE																																											
TYPE OF MESSAGE RECEIVED	CALL REQUEST	CALL ACCEPTED	CLEAR REQUEST	CLEAR CONFIRM	DATA	RESET	CALL REQUEST	CALL ACCEPTED	CLEAR REQUEST	CLEAR CONFIRM	DATA	RESET	CALL REQUEST	CALL ACCEPTED	CLEAR REQUEST	CLEAR CONFIRM	DATA	RESET	CALL REQUEST	CALL ACCEPTED	CLEAR REQUEST	CLEAR CONFIRM	DATA	RESET	CALL REQUEST	CALL ACCEPTED	CLEAR REQUEST	CLEAR CONFIRM	DATA	RESET	CALL REQUEST	CALL ACCEPTED	CLEAR REQUEST	CLEAR CONFIRM	DATA	RESET	CALL REQUEST	CALL ACCEPTED	CLEAR REQUEST	CLEAR CONFIRM	DATA	RESET

ACTIONS:

	P1 CR	P1 CA	P1 CLR	P1 CC	P1 D	P1 R	P2 CR	P2 CA	P2 CLR	P2 CC	P2 D	P2 R	P3 CR	P3 CA	P3 CLR	P3 CC	P3 D	P3 R	P4 CR	P4 CA	P4 CLR	P4 CC	P4 D	P4 R	P5 CR	P5 CA	P5 CLR	P5 CC	P5 D	P5 R	P6 CR	P6 CA	P6 CLR	P6 CC	P6 D	P6 R	P7 CR	P7 CA	P7 CLR	P7 CC	P7 D	P7 R
PROCEDURE 1	X																																									
PROCEDURE 2								X																																		
PROCEDURE 3																																										
PROCEDURE 4																			X	X																						
PROCEDURE 5													X																													
ERROR MESSAGE A	X													X																												
ERROR MESSAGE B			X						X						X						X						X						X						X			
ERROR MESSAGE C				X						X						X						X						X						X						X		
ERROR MESSAGE D					X						X						X						X						X						X						X	
ERROR MESSAGE E						X						X						X						X						X						X						X
PRINT INSTUCTION K							X																														X					
ERROR PROCEDURE 1	X		X	X		X			X	X	X	X	X	X	X	X		X	X	X	X	X	X	X	X	X	X	X		X	X	X	X			X	X	X	X			X
ERROR PROCEDURE 2															X	X		X																								
LOG OPERATION					X						X						X						X						X						X						X	
SECURITY PROCEDURE																																										
SEE DECISION TABLE 13																														X												
SEE DECISION TABLE 14																														X												
SEE DECISION TABLE 15																																				X						
SEE DECISION TABLE 16																																				X						

Figure 14.6 Whereas simple decisions like those in Fig. 14.5 can be handled by other methods, complex decisions like those illustrated here require a decision table. Program code can be generated automatically from decision tables.

TREE OR TABLE?   When should you use decision trees and when decision tables? Decision trees are easier to read and understand when the number of conditions is small. Most persons would grasp the meaning of Fig. 14.1 without special training, for example. They might be more bewildered by Fig. 14.5.

If there are a substantial number of conditions and actions, a decision tree becomes too big and clumsy. A decision tree for the situation in Fig. 14.6 would be too large. The patterns in a table like Fig. 14.6 give a clearer idea of what is required and encourage visual checking.

A decision table, like Fig. 14.6, causes the designer to look at every possible combination. Without such a technique, he would probably miss certain combinations. The decision tree does not provide a matrix for every condition and action. It is thus easier to omit important combinations when using a decision tree.

USING DECISION   Because a decision table (tree) maps inputs (con-
TREES AND TABLES   ditions) to outputs (actions) without necessarily specifying how the mapping is to be done, it has been used as a system analysis and system design tool. It has been used to describe the decision-making logic in procedure specifications and the program control structure in a program design.

Traditionally, flowcharts have been used for graphic representations of detailed and complex logic. However, decision tables or trees are preferable because they offer a more compact view of the logic.

Not only can decision tables (trees) model program control logic, but they can also model an entire program. Theoretically, they can represent any computable function and therefore replace any program flowchart [2]. The control constructs of sequence, selection, and repetition can be represented by a decision table or tree.

Decision tables and decision trees are used as detail design tools for complex program logic. They are seldom used at a high level to show program control structure. In general, they should not be used as a stand-alone design tool. They should be used to supplement other design tools such as dependency diagrams, navigation diagrams, and action diagrams.

REFERENCES

1. B. Moret, "Decision Trees and Diagrams," *Computing Surveys*, 14, no. 4 (Dec. 1982), 593–623.

2. A. Lew, "In the Emulation of Flowcharts by Decision Tables," *CACM*, 25, no. 12 (Dec. 1982), 895–905.

15 STATE TRANSITION DIAGRAMS

Decision trees and tables provide a valuable means of designing certain types of logic. This chapter describes another tool for designing certain categories of logic: finite-state machine notation. It is useful where entity types, switches, or variables can be thought of as being in a given number of states and where complex logic governs the transitions among these states. It has been used in the design of control program mechanisms, systems software, and computer network protocols. It has much wider applicability but is generally not understood by many systems analysts.

FINITE-STATE
MACHINE
NOTATION

A finite-state machine is a hypothetical mechanism that can be in one of a discrete number of conditions or states. Certain events can cause it to change its state.

A procedure can be represented as a collection of finite-state machines. This gives a precise way to draw and conceptualize complex procedures and to check that all possible state transitions have been thought about.

DISCRETE POINTS
IN TIME

In this view of the world, events occur at discrete points in time. There is no slow, continuous change. Events cause an instantaneous change in the state of a finite-state machine. The events can occur asynchronously, that is, at any point in time, or synchronously, at clock intervals.

State transition diagrams are drawn to represent the behavior of finite-state machines. In the common way of drawing these, the possible states are drawn in circles.

To illustrate a state transition diagram, Fig. 15.1 shows a dismal view of the life of a man. The man is regarded as a finite-state machine that can be in one of four states: active, sleeping, and two intermediate states. Various events

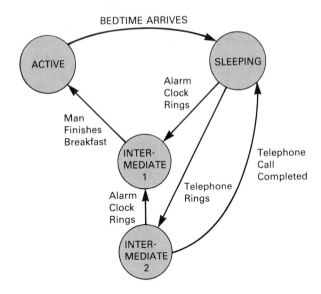

Figure 15.1   An illustration of a state transition diagram for a man who can be in one of four states.

cause transitions between the states, as shown by the arrows. Two intermediate states are needed because the period in those states terminates in different ways.

State transition diagrams are commonly employed for representing the complex protocols that are needed in computer networks. Fig. 15.2 shows a diagram with five states that is used to define a standard interface to packet-switching networks [1]. The diagram refers to the interface between a data processing machine or terminal and the network transport subsystem. The former is referred to as the DTE (data terminal equipment) and the latter as the DCE (data communications equipment). The diagram relates to the initiation of a call and the consequent change of the interface state from READY to DATA TRANSFER. The call may be initiated by the DTE, or it may be an incoming call, in which case the DCE initiates the process.

In complex system design, we have to consider the errors, failures, and exception conditions that can occur. In Fig. 15.1, an error condition might be that the alarm clock fails. The man then appears to be permanently in the SLEEPING state. On the other hand, he might go to bed and find a beautiful woman there. Such exception conditions greatly complicate the protocols.

MACHINES AND SUBMACHINES   A highly complex system, such as a packet-switching network or IBM's Systems Network Architecture, could be described as being an extremely elaborate finite-state machine with many states. This would not be a useful description because it would be too complex for human comprehension. Therefore, such

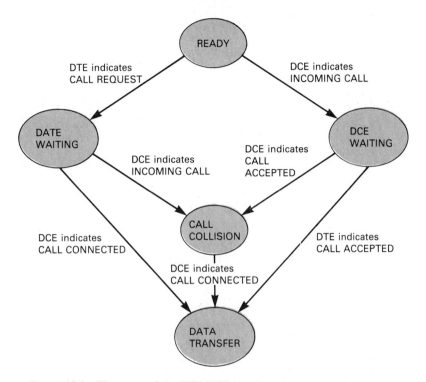

Figure 15.2   The states of the DTE/DCE interface during the setup phase of a call with CCITT Recommendation X.25 [1]. (*DTE* stands for *data terminal equipment,* terminal or host computer; *DCE* stands for *data communications equipment,* network interface minicomputer.)

systems are decomposed into submachines—interconnected or nested finite-state machines. The submachines can be further decomposed until we arrive at finite-state machines that are easy to comprehend, usually with not more than ten or so states.

This is a form of decomposition like that described earlier. Complex processes are decomposed into subprocesses. Subprocesses are decomposed into sub-subprocesses. On a state transition diagram, a circle may be the boundary of another finite-state machine. ACTIVE, for example, in Fig. 15.1, is a highly complex state decomposable into many substates.

The state transition diagrams used to describe the logic of distributed processing software are highly complex, and appropriate fragmentation into separate modules is important. Figure 15.3 illustrates how this is done for computer-networking software. A session between machines is divided into layers as shown, with a finite-state machine for each layer defining the interlayer protocols. These finite-state machines are themselves subdivided into several smaller machines.

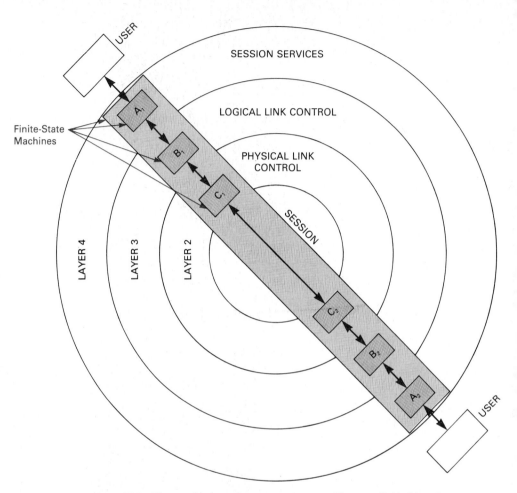

Figure 15.3 The mechanisms for computer networking are divided into layers. A finite-state machine is defined for each layer as shown here. These machines defined the interlayer protocols and are themselves subdivided into several smaller finite-state machines.

FINITE-STATE MACHINES

A finite-state machine is thought of as a black box that can be in one of a number of states (Fig. 15.4).

A finite set of input types can reach it. Inputs reach it one at a time, hence time is regarded as a set of discrete points. Two inputs cannot arrive at the same instant, although they could be infinitesimally close. It is possible that two inputs on different communication lines could arrive at exactly the same time, but the machine will be scanning its sources of input and so will receive one before the other. Queuing mechanisms permit the inputs to be handled one at a time.

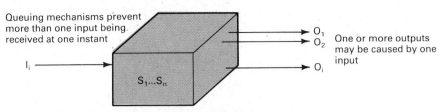

Queuing mechanisms prevent
more than one input being
received at one instant

I_i

$S_1...S_n$

O_1
O_2

O_i

One or more outputs
may be caused by one
input

The mechanism exists in one of several states.

Figure 15.4   A finite-state machine has (1) a finite set of *states, S;* (2) a finite
set of *input* types, *I;* (3) a finite set of *output* types, *O;* (4) a mapping of *input*
and *present state* into *next state;* and (5) a mapping of *input* and *present state*
into *output.*

In addition to causing state changes, as in Figs. 15.1 and 15.2, input can
also cause outputs to be sent. The input and its resulting state change and output
are thought of as occurring at the same instant.

An input or output can be thought of as a *pulsed* variable that exists only
at an instant in time. The state of the machine is a static discrete variable that
can change only at the instant when an input is received.

Suppose an input is received at time t_i. The state of the machine at time
t_{i+1} is a function of the state $S(t_i)$ at time t_i and the input $I(t_i)$ at time t_i. We
refer to this as the *next-state function,* FNS.

The output $O(t_i)$ at time t_i is also a function *f* the state $S(t_i)$ and input $I(t_i)$
at that time. We refer to this as the *output function,* FOUT.

$$S(t_{i+1}) = FNS (S(t_i), I(t_i))$$
$$O(t_i) = FOUT (S(t_i), I(t_i))$$

To define a finite-state machine, we must define these two functions.

If circles are drawn to represent the states, the arrows between them should
show the inputs that cause the change of state and also the outputs that accompany it. Figure 15.5 shows this type of diagram. The arrows between circles,
showing the state transitions, are labeled with the input that causes the transition
and with the resulting output(s).

In some cases, an input causes no change of state but does cause an output, as when input I_1 is received when the machine is in state 3. Sometimes
more than one input can cause the same state transition as between states 3 and
4. Sometimes one input causes several outputs, as when state 4 received I_4.

The type of drawing shown in Fig. 15.5 is useful for human perception of
protocol mechanisms. It does, however, leave a number of questions unan-
swered. For example, what would the machine do in state 2 if it received input
I_4? This and many similar possibilities are not shown on the diagram. To force
complete thinking about a protocol, a *state transition matrix* may be drawn
instead of a diagram like Fig. 15.5.

Figure 15.6 gives a state transition matrix which contains the same infor-

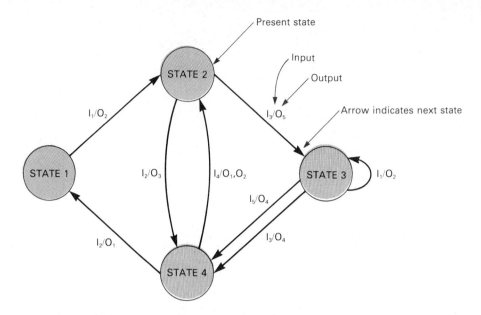

Figure 15.5 A finite-state machine transition diagram, showing outputs as well as state changes.

mation as Fig. 15.5. The matrix shows the blanks in the protocol thinking. The designer should fill in all the blanks in the table. He may simply put a line through the blank spaces to indicate that certain inputs are ignored. Often, however, some form of error indication is needed if a useless input is received.

FENCE DIAGRAMS   Although state transition diagrams are normally drawn with the states represented as circles, as in Figs. 15.2 and 15.5, a neater way to draw them is to use fence diagrams, with states represented as horizontal bars. Figure 15.7 shows Fig. 15.1 with the man's four states shown as horizontal bars.

		STATE			
		1	2	3	4
INPUT	I_1	$2/O_2$		$3/O_2$	
	I_2		$4/O_3$		$1/O_1$
	I_3		$3/O_5$	$4/O_4$	
	I_4				$2/O_1,O_2$
	I_5			$4/O_4$	

NEXT STATE/ OUTPUT

Figure 15.6 A state transition matrix that contains the same information as Fig. 15.5. It is desirable, however, to fill in the blank entries.

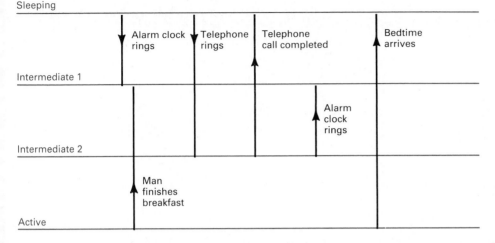

Figure 15.7 Figures 15.1 redrawn as a fence diagram. The states are shown
as horizontal bars. State transitions are vertical lines linking the states.

With complex mechanisms (like those in network architectures), there may
be many transitions among a relatively small number of states. Bubble diagrams
for showing state transitions become cluttered and confusing. Fence diagrams
are much neater. Figure 15.8 shows a typical state transition diagram in IBM's
SNA. This illustrates the need for clean, formal, computer-printable state transition diagrams. (In this example the states are drawn vertically, not horizontally.)

Another reason for avoiding bubble-chart state transition diagrams is that
they look like data flow diagrams, and this sometimes causes confusion about
their true meaning. The circles show states and must not be confused with processes.

The vertical lines in Figs. 15.7 and 15.8 show the input that causes the
transition between states. The output that results when the state transition occurs
can be written after in input (separated by a slash, as in Figs. 15.5 and 15.6).
Figure 15.9 shows Fig. 15.4 redrawn in this way. If input I_1 occurs when the
system is in state 3, output O_2 occurs with no change of state. This is shown by
the loop on state 3.

In some cases, the input is complex; several input conditions have to apply
in order for a change of state to occur. In Fig. 15.8, for example, most of the
vertical lines indicate compound inputs that cause changes of state.

**CONVERSION TO
ACTION DIAGRAMS**
State transition diagrams and tables can be converted
automatically to action diagrams to help speed up the
programming work. Figure 15.10 shows an action
diagram equivalent to the state transition diagram of Fig. 15.2.

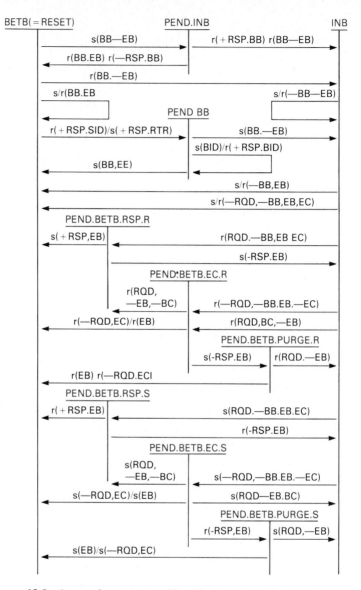

Figure 15.8 A complex state transition diagram, one of many finite-state machines that define the protocols of IBM's SNA (Systems Network Architecture) [2, 3]. Such diagrams are much clearer if drawn as fence diagrams rather than bubble charts.

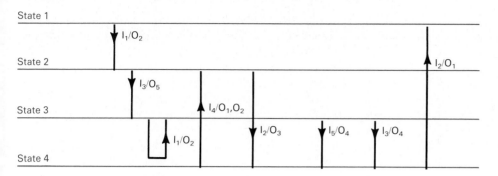

State 1

I_1/O_2

State 2

I_2/O_1

I_3/O_5

State 3

$I_4/O_1,O_2$

I_2/O_3 I_5/O_4 I_3/O_4

I_1/O_2

State 4

Figure 15.9 Figure 15.4 redrawn as a fence diagram. The inputs that cause a state change are written by the vertical lines; the outputs corresponding to the state change are written after the inputs.

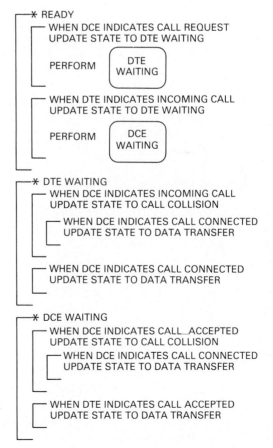

```
─✳ READY
    ┌─ WHEN DCE INDICATES CALL REQUEST
    │  UPDATE STATE TO DTE WAITING
    │
    │  PERFORM      ╭─────────╮
    │               │  DTE    │
    │               │ WAITING │
    └               ╰─────────╯
    ┌─ WHEN DTE INDICATES INCOMING CALL
    │  UPDATE STATE TO DTE WAITING
    │
    │  PERFORM      ╭─────────╮
    │               │  DCE    │
    │               │ WAITING │
    └               ╰─────────╯

─✳ DTE WAITING
    ┌─ WHEN DCE INDICATES INCOMING CALL
    │  UPDATE STATE TO CALL COLLISION
    │     ┌─ WHEN DCE INDICATES CALL CONNECTED
    │     │  UPDATE STATE TO DATA TRANSFER
    │     └
    └
    ┌─ WHEN DCE INDICATES CALL CONNECTED
    │  UPDATE STATE TO DATA TRANSFER
    └

─✳ DCE WAITING
    ┌─ WHEN DCE INDICATES CALL ACCEPTED
    │  UPDATE STATE TO CALL COLLISION
    │     ┌─ WHEN DCE INDICATES CALL CONNECTED
    │     │  UPDATE STATE TO DATA TRANSFER
    │     └
    └
    ┌─ WHEN DTE INDICATES CALL ACCEPTED
    │  UPDATE STATE TO DATA TRANSFER
    └
```

Figure 15.10 An action diagram generated from the state transition diagram in Fig. 15.2.

305

ENTITY LIFE CYCLES

State transition diagrams are most commonly employed for systems that have complex state transition logic like that found often in software for telephone switching. They can, however, be useful in commercial systems to clarify the representation of changes in state of entity types.

An entity type may exist in a variety of states. Business processes change these states. A state transition diagram may show the states and the processes that change the states.

Often in business systems, an entity type has a life cycle. It is created, various processes are applied to it, and eventually it is deleted. A state transition diagram can help clarify the states that comprise the life cycle. This analysis tool can help give a completeness and consistency check on the analyst's representation of processes and their dependencies.

Consider the recording of student bookings in an organization giving seminars. The booking can be in one of the following possible states: BOOKED, NOT-BOOKED, NOT-ACCEPTABLE, FOLLOWED-UP, CANCELED, REGISTERED, REJECTED, NO-SHOW, COMPLETED, and ARCHIVED. The analyst needs to clarify his understanding of these states and of what processes take place when a student books, arrives, arrives without paying, and so on. Figure 5.11 shows these states and the processes that cause state transitions. The *process* is drawn on the state transition diagram with its usual representation, a round-cornered box.

Figure 15.11 shows six events that trigger the execution of processes. The information in Fig. 15.11 can be drawn in a table like Fig. 15.6 to help ensure complete representation of possible state transitions.

MUTUAL EXCLUSIVITY

It would be redundant to draw mutual-exclusivity symbols on a state transition diagram. The states *must* be mutually exclusive because an entity can be in only one state at a time. In Fig. 15.11, where three arrows leave the PROCESS NEW APPLICATION box, these state transitions *must* be mutually exclusive.

There can, however, be different types of states applying to the same entity type. For example, when students register for and attend seminars, we are interested not only in their registration state but also in whether they have paid. A state transition diagram different from Fig. 15.11 applies to the states of payment. This is shown in Fig. 15.12. In this figure, the state transitions are mutually exclusive.

RELATIONSHIP BETWEEN DIAGRAMS

There is a connection between whether students pay and whether they book or are registered in seminars. There may be processes that appear on both state transition diagrams; for example, REGISTER UNBOOKED STU-

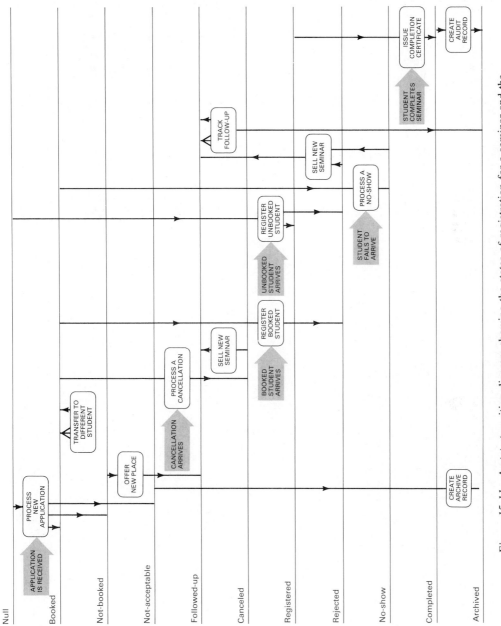

Figure 15.11 A state transition diagram showing the states of registration for a seminar and the processes that cause transitions among these states.

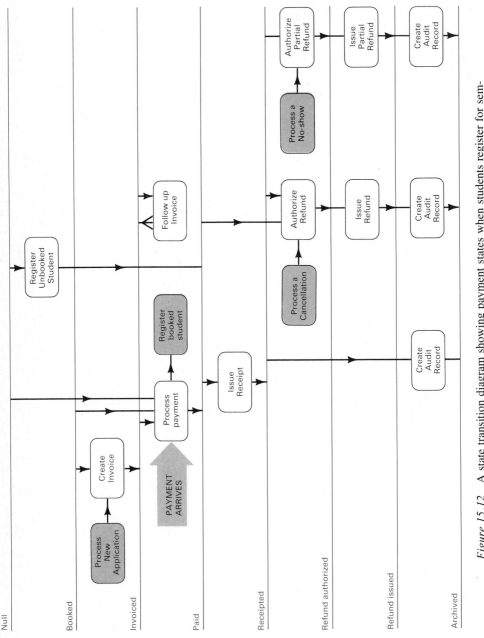

Figure 15.12 A state transition diagram showing payment states when students register for seminars. The processes colored red do not themselves cause state transitions. They have a dependency-diagram relation with the states shown in black, which do cause state transitions. All four red processes are also shown on Fig. 15.11 and demonstrate the relationship between these diagrams.

DENT appears on both Figs. 15.11 and 15.12. Some of the processes on one state transition diagram are related to those on another by a dependency diagram. The processes colored red in Fig. 15.12 show this. They illustrate a dependency relationship between the processes in Fig. 15.11 and those in Fig. 15.12.

Crow's Feet

When a transition from one state to another occurs, the process that causes this is executed once. There are no one-to-many cardinalities and hence no crow's feet on the transition line.

However, when a process results in a transition from a state to itself, this may occur several times. For example, in Fig. 15.11, TRANSFER TO DIFFERENT STUDENT may occur several times. In this case a crow's foot, meaning *one or more* executions of the process, is used as shown.

USES

State transition diagrams are a useful tool in the systems analyst's kit. They are easy to draw and help to clarify situations where various changes of state occur. Like decision tables, they are not needed in the design of every type of system, but for certain types of systems, they are invaluable.

They are useful in showing the several states possible for entity types in data-base systems. They are useful for diagramming the behavior of systems with several message types and complex processing and synchronization requirements. Fence diagrams of state transitions are particularly useful for systems with many transitions among a relatively small number of states. The table of state transitions (like Fig. 15.6) encourages the analyst to examine all possible state transitions. He is less likely to forget one that might be critical.

REFERENCES

1. *Recommendation X.25: Interface Between Data Terminal Equipment and Data Circuit-Termination Equipment for Terminals Operated in the Packet Mode on Public Data Networks.* Geneva: CCITT, 1977.

2. T. Pietkowski introduced this form of diagram and finite-state techniques to specify IBM's Systems Network Architecture.

3. *IBM Systems Network Architecture. Format and Protocol Reference Manual: Architecture Logic.* Manual No. SC 30.3112, White Plains, N.Y.: IBM, 1977.

16 DIALOG DESIGN DIAGRAMS

A diagram similar to a state transition diagram is useful for designing dialogs. The states (horizontal lines) become screens (panels, maps) of a dialog. The transitions among states (vertical lines) represent operator actions. Figure 16.1 illustrates this.

Every transition line needs a statement saying what causes the transition. Usually it is caused by the operator making an entry or selecting a menu item. When the operator selects one of a set of choices, as with menu selection, a mutually exclusive circle will show this, as in Fig. 16.1. Often conditions are needed to show the choice of the next screen. For example, if the operator enters invalid data, an error screen will appear.

A dialog diagram like Fig. 16.1 can be converted directly into an action diagram, as shown in Fig. 16.2. Like action diagrams generated from other forms of design diagrams, the result is far from a complete program, and the designer needs the ability to cut and paste and edit action diagrams as the design evolves into executable code.

A dialog design tool is best used in conjunction with a screen painter, a component of many fourth-generation languages. The screen painter enables the programmer to design screens quickly and generate the code for displaying those screens. The screens then reside in a library.

COMBINING DEPENDENCY AND DIALOG DIAGRAMS

As with state transition diagrams (Figs. 15.11 and 15.12), the procedures or program modules that generate screens can be shown on the diagram. These activities may themselves be interlinked into a data flow diagram. A data flow diagram and a dialog diagram may thus be combined.

Figure 16.3 shows the same dialog as Fig. 16.1 but shows the program

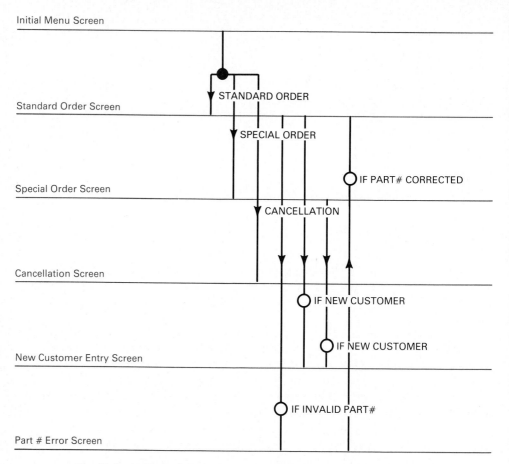

Fig. 16.1   A simple dialog structure showing transitions among screens. With a computerized tool, the black part of the diagram may be slid horizontally along the fence lines to examine dialogs with a large number of transitions. The fence lines representing screens may be scrolled and nested. By pointing at any fence line and commanding SHOW, the screen it represents may be examined.

modules that create and interact via the dialog screens. The black part of Fig. 16.3 is a dependency diagram. The red part shows how it relates to dialog screens.

ICONS FOR DIALOG SCREENS   When a computer-aided design tool is used for dialog design, icons may be used to show what types of screens are employed in the dialog. Such icons may be connected to the left of the lines representing screens.

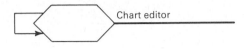

Box 16.1 shows a number of categories of screen. Some are unchanging displays. Others are displays that change and hence have some form of computation associated with them. These are shown as follows:

An unchanging display   A display that changes

Some displays involve operator interaction that causes the display to change. This is shown with a looped arrow:

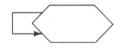

It is useful to associate several screens with one horizontal line on a dialog diagram. Multiple screens are indicated by two overlapping boxes:

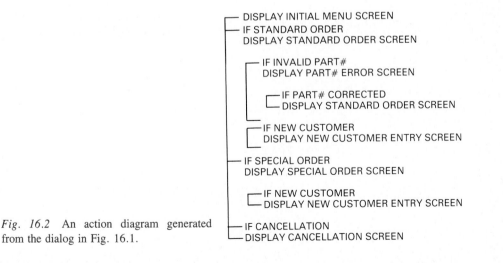

Fig. 16.2 An action diagram generated from the dialog in Fig. 16.1.

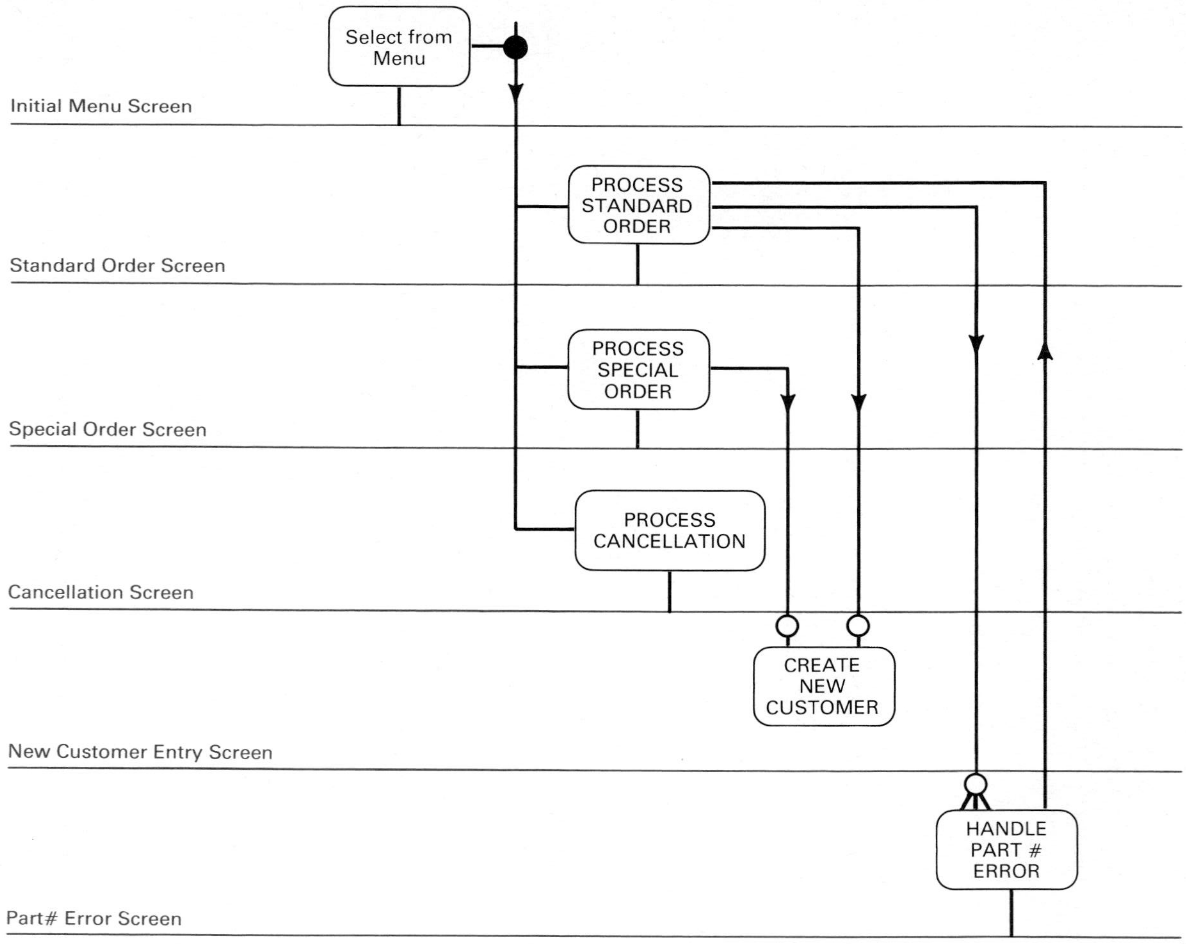

Fig. 16.3 A dependency diagram and dialog diagram combined. The dependency diagram shows the processes, procedures, or program modules that create and interact via the dialog screens.

314

BOX 16.1 Icons representing types of screens employed in a dialog design

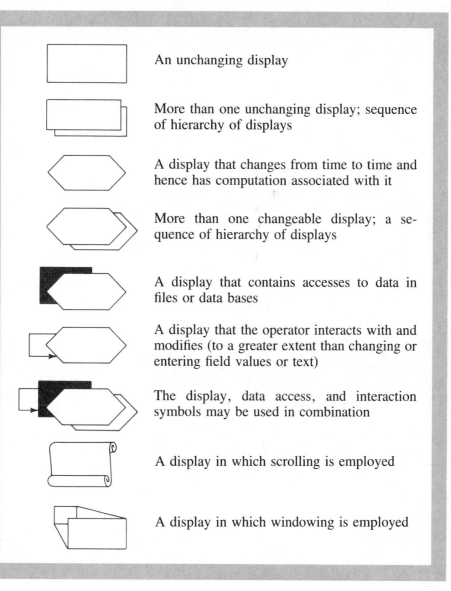

An unchanging display

More than one unchanging display; sequence of hierarchy of displays

A display that changes from time to time and hence has computation associated with it

More than one changeable display; a sequence of hierarchy of displays

A display that contains accesses to data in files or data bases

A display that the operator interacts with and modifies (to a greater extent than changing or entering field values or text)

The display, data access, and interaction symbols may be used in combination

A display in which scrolling is employed

A display in which windowing is employed

The multiple screens may be a sequence of screens that the operator steps through, a hierarchy of screens, or a dialog, the details of which are shown elsewhere.

A dialog screen is often associated with stored records. It may display data that are read from a file or data base. The association with stored data is shown by a black data box behind the screen symbol:

Using an encyclopedia-based design tool, the dialog designer can display details of the data in question and how they are used.

The blank icons of Box 16.1 can be filled in with words indicating a category of usage of that type of screen—for example, MENU, DIRECTORY, SEQUENCE, and so on. A DATA ENTRY screen is a particularly important type of screen. A MAIN MENU screen has the property that it may be returned to from any point in the dialog. A HIERARCHY is a set of screens with its own tree-structured linkage.

Box 16.2 shows words for category of usage of screens. Figure 16.4 shows a dialog design diagram with the icons on the left.

CROW'S FEET   A crow's-foot (one-to-many) indicator is placed by a screen type in a dialog diagram when there can be many such screens following one screen, for example:

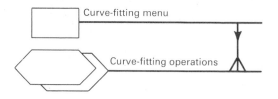

CONTRACT   Sometimes dialog diagrams become large and, as
AND EXPAND   with other large diagrams, need to be nested with CONTRACT and EXPAND commands. Three dots, as elsewhere, show that a portion of the design has been CONTRACTed and may be EXPANDed using the EXPAND command:

BOX 16.2 Words used in the screen icons to show category of usage

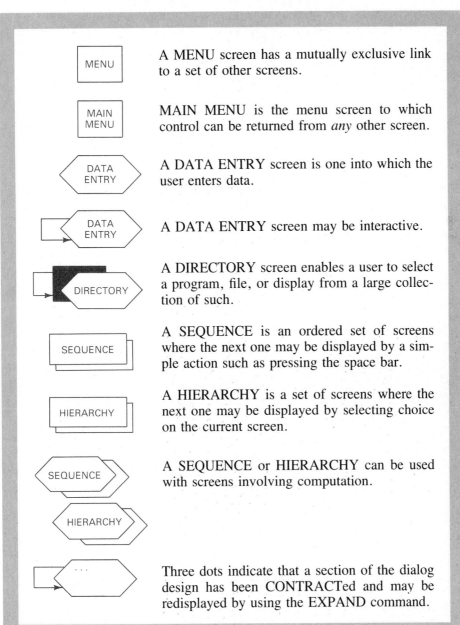

MENU — A MENU screen has a mutually exclusive link to a set of other screens.

MAIN MENU — MAIN MENU is the menu screen to which control can be returned from *any* other screen.

DATA ENTRY — A DATA ENTRY screen is one into which the user enters data.

DATA ENTRY — A DATA ENTRY screen may be interactive.

DIRECTORY — A DIRECTORY screen enables a user to select a program, file, or display from a large collection of such.

SEQUENCE — A SEQUENCE is an ordered set of screens where the next one may be displayed by a simple action such as pressing the space bar.

HIERARCHY — A HIERARCHY is a set of screens where the next one may be displayed by selecting choice on the current screen.

SEQUENCE / HIERARCHY — A SEQUENCE or HIERARCHY can be used with screens involving computation.

. . . — Three dots indicate that a section of the dialog design has been CONTRACTed and may be redisplayed by using the EXPAND command.

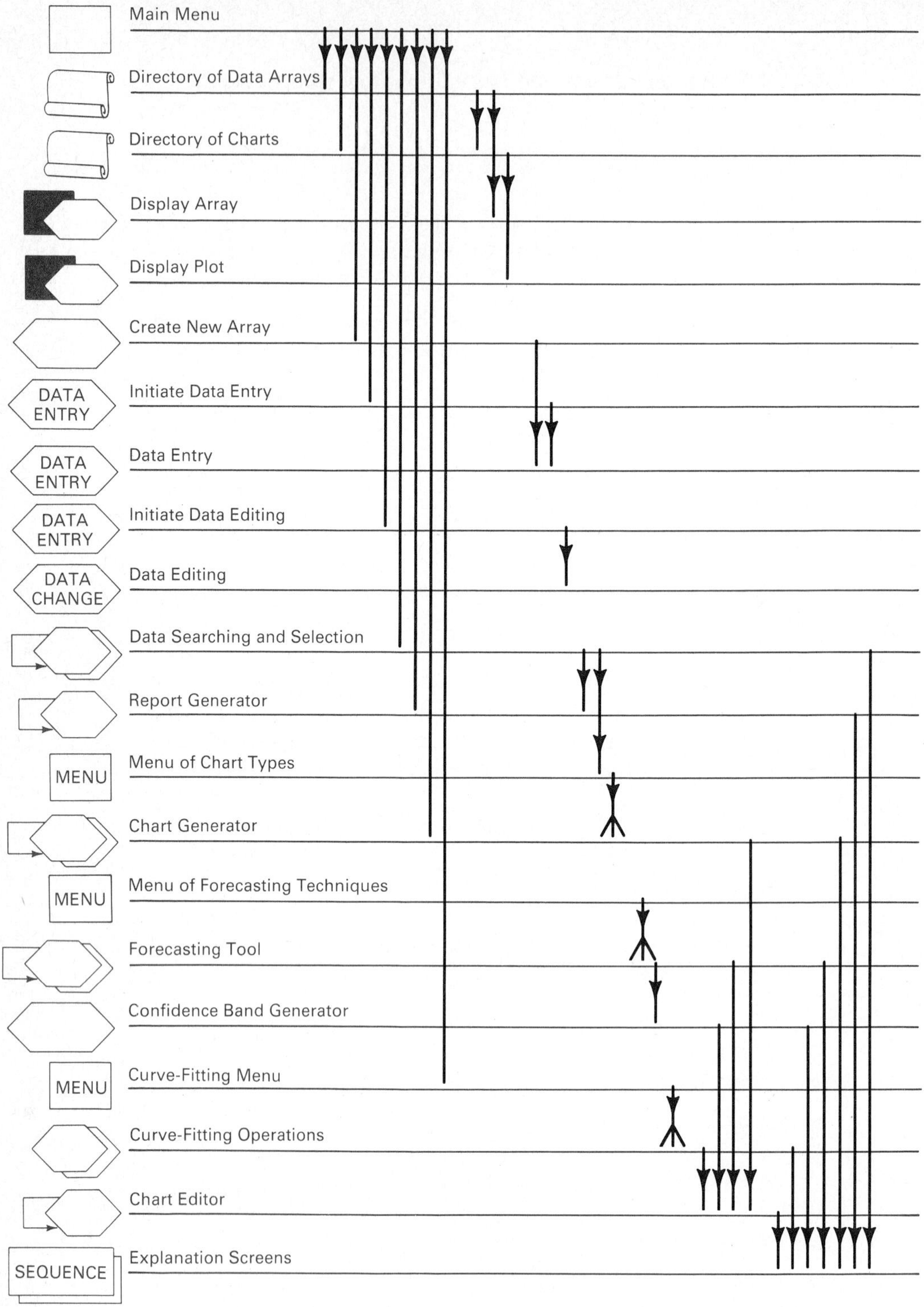

Main Menu

Directory of Data Arrays

Directory of Charts

Display Array

Display Plot

Create New Array

DATA ENTRY — Initiate Data Entry

DATA ENTRY — Data Entry

DATA ENTRY — Initiate Data Editing

DATA CHANGE — Data Editing

Data Searching and Selection

Report Generator

MENU — Menu of Chart Types

Chart Generator

MENU — Menu of Forecasting Techniques

Forecasting Tool

Confidence Band Generator

MENU — Curve-Fitting Menu

Curve-Fitting Operations

Chart Editor

SEQUENCE — Explanation Screens

Fig. 16.4 Structure of a dialog for displaying data and carrying out graphics operations on data.

INDEX